CONTENTS

TABLES AND FIGURES

Tables

innovation

MAIN RESULTS OF THE SOUTH AFRICAN INNOVATION SURVEY 2005

WILLIAM BLANKLEY
AND CHERYL MOSES

Produced by the Centre for Science, Technology and Innovation Indicators (CeSTII) of the Human Sciences Research Council (HSRC) on behalf of the Department of Science and Technology (DST)

Published by HSRC Press
Private Bag X9182, Cape Town, 8000, South Africa
www.hsrcpress.ac.za

First published 2009

ISBN (soft cover) 978-0-7969-2240-3
ISBN (pdf) 978-0-7969-2257-1

Copy-edited by Gudrun Elliott
Typeset by Robin Taylor
Cover by Fuel Design
Printed by Logo Print, Maitland, Cape Town

Distributed in Africa by Blue Weaver
Tel: +27 (0) 21 701 4477; Fax: +27 (0) 21 701 7302
www.oneworldbooks.com

Distributed in Europe and the United Kingdom by Eurospan Distribution Services (EDS)
Tel: +44 (0) 20 7240 0856; Fax: +44 (0) 20 7379 0609
www.eurospanbookstore.com

Distributed in North America by Independent Publishers Group (IPG)
Call toll-free: (800) 888 4741; Fax: +1 (312) 337 5985
www.ipgbook.com

Appendices

Appendix 1

Appendix 2

Figures

ACKNOWLEDGEMENTS

We would like to thank the Department of Science and Technology for their support and encouragement at the time that the survey was conducted. Statistics South Africa supplied the sample for the survey and we would like to thank them for their sound advice and excellent documentation. We would like to acknowledge the contributions made by Monique Ritter (Survey Manager) and the Centre for Science Technology and Innovation Indicators (CeSTII) Research Assistants: Prudence Sotashe, Maalikah van der Schyff, Karen Heath, Mtembukazi Sibindlana and Ikageng Moduka. We would also like to thank Anthony Burns, Steven Davis and Professor Tim Dunne for assisting with extracting data and compiling statistics. We benefited greatly from the advice and input from Professor Norbert Janz from Aachen University (previously manager of the German Innovation Survey conducted by the Centre for European Economic Research (ZEW)) who spent his sabbatical at CeSTII through a National Research Foundation (NRF) grant. We especially wish to thank August Goetzfried, Paul Crowley and Sergiu-Valentin Parvan of Eurostat for their assistance and support, and Professor Michael Kahn (Executive Director of CeSTII) for his contributions, encouragement and support. Last, but not least, we thank all the respondents who participated in the survey.

EXECUTIVE SUMMARY

Background

The Centre for Science, Technology and Innovation Indicators (CeSTII) was commissioned by the Department of Science and Technology (DST) to undertake a national innovation survey based on international best practice. This report presents the main findings of the South African Innovation Survey 2005, covering the period 2002–2004. Where available, comparisons are made with the results of the Fourth Round of the Community Innovation Survey (CIS4) for European Union (EU) countries, as provided by Eurostat.

Methodology

The design of the Innovation Survey 2005 was informed by Eurostat guidelines and the structure of the Statistics South Africa business register. The survey design thus comprises:

- a random stratified sample (by sector and size of enterprise) drawn from the business registry database of Statistics South Africa in conformity with the Small Business Amendment Act (No. 26 of 2003);
- a postal survey with at least two telephonic and two written correspondences;
- provision for a non-response survey if the response rate is below 70%;
- extrapolation of results to the target population based on the weighted sample.

After cleaning the final returned questionnaires and data, an overall response rate of 37.3% from a sample size of 2 627 enterprises was obtained. This was a relatively high response rate in comparison with two previous unofficial innovation surveys undertaken in South Africa in which the response rates were less than 10%. The results of the survey were extrapolated to the target business population of 31 456 enterprises based on the weights of 120 strata.

Results

The results of the Innovation Survey 2005 indicate that 51.7% of South African enterprises were engaged in innovation activities between 2002 and 2004. This compares favourably with the European Union (EU) average of 40%. The proportion of EU enterprises engaged in innovation activities ranged from 16% in Bulgaria to 65% in Germany.

Total turnover of the enterprises was recorded as R1 144.4 billion. About 75.5% of this turnover is accounted for by enterprises with innovation activities. Innovative enterprises also employed more staff than non-innovative enterprises and accounted for 78% of total employees. Another feature of innovative enterprises is that they are more export-oriented than non-innovative enterprises.

Enterprises that had product innovations (comprising innovation in either goods or services) accounted for the majority of innovators in the survey. Approximately 10% of the turnover of product innovators in 2004 was generated by innovations that were new to the market, representing turnover of about R67.8 billion. A further 11.8% was generated by the sale of products that were new to the enterprise concerned but not new to the market. About 80% of innovative South African enterprises introduced new or improved products to the market, which is higher than what has been recorded for any European countries. In comparison, about 78% of innovative enterprises in Iceland introduced new or improved products to the market.

South Africa performs relatively well in terms of the percentage share of turnover generated by the sale of new or significantly improved products (new to the market and not just new to the enterprise) compared with other countries. In South Africa, this share is 10.1%, compared to the 8.6% average for EU countries.

Product innovations by innovative enterprises in South Africa were developed mainly by the enterprises themselves (51.3%). About 23% of enterprises collaborated with other enterprises or institutions to develop product innovations, while a further 6.4% relied on other enterprises or institutions to develop their innovations.

About a quarter of all enterprises (24.8%) introduced process innovations involving new or significantly improved methods of manufacturing or producing new goods and services. Some 21.3% developed new delivery or distribution methods, and 22% produced new or significantly improved supporting processes for their operations.

Of the 16 264 innovative enterprises, 54.9% reported that their innovations originated in South Africa, and 25.4% reported that their innovations were developed mainly abroad.

Innovative enterprises spent approximately R27.8 billion on innovation activities, which represents about 3.2% of the turnover of these enterprises. In both the industrial and services sector, the bulk of innovation expenditure was devoted to the acquisition of new machinery, equipment and software, and was equivalent to about 2.1% of the turnover of innovative enterprises. Intramural and outsourced research and experimental development (R&D) accounted for 0.69% of the turnover of all enterprises and 1% of the turnover of innovative enterprises. South Africa's profile of expenditure on innovation activities is very similar to the EU average profile of expenditure.

Altogether, about 11.8% of innovative industrial enterprises and 6.5% of all innovative enterprises received public funding for their innovation activities between 2002 and 2004. This does not compare particularly well with European countries, where only Bulgaria reported less public funding for innovation than South Africa. In 10 out of 24 European countries, more than 25% of innovative enterprises receive public funding for innovation.

Almost half of all innovative enterprises rated sources of information within the enterprise as highly important for innovation activities. Clients and customers, as external market sources, were rated as highly important by 35% of innovative enterprises, followed by suppliers (24%) and competitors (13%). Universities and technikons were rated as highly important by only 5% of enterprises, and government and public research institutes by only 3% of enterprises. In terms of highly important sources of information for innovation, South Africa's profile appears to be much the same as that of the average profile for the expanded European Union (EU-27).

Private sector enterprises in South Africa are sometimes criticised for lacking cooperative civilities and partnerships with other organisations. However, in terms of cooperative partnerships related to innovation activities, South African enterprises appear to have a relatively high intensity of cooperative linkages, with 39.9% of innovating enterprises having innovation activities with other enterprises and institutions. By comparison, an average of 26% of innovative enterprises in the EU have collaborative partnerships. As in Europe, the percentage of cooperation partnerships among innovative South African enterprises for innovation with consultants, universities and public research institutes is higher than the corresponding scores for these potential partners as sources of information for innovation.

Improved quality of goods and services was cited as a highly important effect of innovation by about 46% of innovative enterprises. Increasing the range of goods and services was an important outcome for 34.3% of enterprises. Increased capacity of production or service provision was cited as the most important effect of process innovation by 19.1% of innovative enterprises, followed by improved flexibility of production or service provision (15.1%). Other highly important effects of innovation were meeting government regulatory requirements (21.4% of innovators) and reducing environmental impacts or improving health and safety (12.8%).

Innovative industrial enterprises appear to be most hampered in their innovation activities by the lack of funds within their enterprise or group, while non-innovative industrial enterprises cited the domination of the market by established enterprises as the major factor hampering their innovation activities. Both innovative and non-innovative enterprises in the services sector also tended to cite the domination of established enterprises in their market as hampering their innovation activities.

Compared with EU countries, relatively few innovative South African enterprises applied for patents or registered industrial designs, but they were on a par with EU enterprises in terms of registering trademarks and claiming copyright.

Conclusions and recommendations

The Innovation Survey 2005 is South Africa's first official innovation survey based on a proper random stratified sample from the official business register. It is thus difficult to make precise comparisons with previous innovation surveys undertaken in the country. Care must be exercised in reaching policy conclusions based on a single innovation survey.

With this proviso in mind, there are still some obvious conclusions that may be drawn. Despite a relatively low response rate compared with European countries, the survey should be regarded as a success for a developing country. Subsequent

South African innovation surveys will benefit from the learning experience and the database resource that was built in the course of the survey, and will become a more robust source of data for analysis. Much richness in the analysis comes from having undertaken an innovation survey based on international best practice. This means that the results can be readily compared with the results from innovation surveys in numerous other countries, which used the same CIS4 methodology and core questionnaire. The next stage of analysis will be an examination of the micro data.

Despite governments' intentions of stimulating innovation through funding, it is apparent that public funds do not have much penetration into the activities of innovative enterprises in most countries. The reason could be that successful, competitive enterprises are not keen to seek public funds, as this would disclose strategic information to other enterprises about their business activities. Enterprises appear to be more open about engaging in publicly funded R&D where the application of activities is possibly less obvious to those outside the business. Current public funding programmes for innovation in South Africa could perhaps be intensified, better publicised and aimed at establishing more trusting relationships between funders and performers of innovation activities.

Expenditure on innovation activities results in sales of new and improved products by enterprises. Enterprises invested some R27.8 billion in innovation activities in 2004. Previous investment in innovation activities resulted in R67.8 billion sales of products that were new to the market and R147 billion if we include products that are new to the enterprise. These returns on innovation activities do not include the benefits to the enterprise of innovative processes or organisational innovations. Businesses and government need to be made aware of these tangible benefits of innovation in order to further encourage innovation. The closeness of the estimate of expenditure on intramural R&D obtained in the Innovation Survey 2005 (R5.7 billion) compared to the R5.9 billion recorded for the equivalent business sectors in the 2004/05 R&D Survey is encouraging.

The results of the Innovation Survey 2005 clearly show that South African enterprises have much in common with enterprises in many EU countries. For example, the results of the South African survey closely resemble those of the EU-27 profile on questions such as the factors hampering innovation and the most important outcomes of innovation for enterprises. These similarities indicate that South Africa can potentially learn much from the experiences related to policies and instruments for supporting innovation in the EU. In a follow-up exercise, the results will also be compared to those available from other developing countries.

The results of the Innovation Survey 2005 clearly show that South Africa is not a 'technology colony', depending exclusively on foreign technology. Most innovations are developed by enterprises in South Africa, and the influence of foreign partners is comparable to the experience of other countries. South African enterprises are clearly very active in both R&D and innovation, and this bodes well for their future competitiveness.

ACRONYMS AND ABBREVIATIONS

AIDS	Acquired immune deficiency syndrome
BEE	Black economic empowerment
CEO	Chief executive officer
CeSTII	Centre for Science, Technology and Innovation Indicators
CIS	Community Innovation Survey
CIS4	Fourth Round of the Community Innovation Survey (also CIS1, CIS2 and CIS3 – first three rounds of CIS)
DST	Department of Science and Technology
EU	European Union
EU-27	Expanded European Union (27 countries)
FRD	Foundation for Research Development
HIV	Human immunodeficiency virus
HSRC	Human Sciences Research Council
IPR	Intellectual property rights
ISP	Industrial Strategy Project
NACI	National Advisory Council on Innovation
NESTI	National Experts on Science and Technology Indicators
NRF	National Research Foundation
NSI	National System of Innovation
OECD	Organisation for Economic Cooperation and Development
R&D	Research and experimental development
S&T	Science and technology
SACOB	South African Chamber of Business
SAIS	South African Innovation Survey
SIC	Standard Industrial Classification
SPII	Support Programme for Industrial Innovation
TDM	Total Design Method
THRIP	Technology and Human Resources for Industry Programme

Country codes

AT	Austria
BE	Belgium
BG	Bulgaria
CY	Cyprus
CZ	Czech Republic
DE	Germany
DK	Denmark
EE	Estonia

EL	Greece
ES	Spain
EU-27	European Union average (27 countries)
FI	Finland
FR	France
HU	Hungary
IE	Ireland
IS	Iceland
IT	Italy
LT	Lithuania
LU	Luxembourg
LV	Latvia
MT	Malta
NL	Netherlands
NO	Norway
PL	Poland
PT	Portugal
RO	Romania
SA	South Africa
SE	Sweden
SI	Slovenia
SK	Slovakia
UK	United Kingdom

CHAPTER 1

Background

The Centre for Science, Technology and Innovation Indicators (CeSTII) was commissioned by the Department of Science and Technology (DST) to conduct the first of an official series of South African Innovation Surveys as part of DST's effort to establish a baseline set of science and technology (S&T) indicators for monitoring, reporting on and fine-tuning the national system of innovation (NSI) in support of South Africa's National Research and Development Strategy. The broader objectives of the South African Innovation Survey are to:

- collect information on the sources and resources for innovation in enterprises;
- provide an indication of the extent to which public funding for innovation activities is taken up by enterprises;
- uncover the main obstacles preventing enterprises from engaging in innovation activities;
- draw national and international comparisons of innovation intensity;
- obtain an understanding of the importance of research and experimental development (R&D) and non-R&D based innovation in different sectors;
- keep abreast of the European Union (EU) Community Innovation Survey (CIS) developments;
- produce a set of internationally comparable data and indicators for providing insights into the patterns of innovation in the mining, manufacturing and services sectors in South Africa;
- provide special insights into innovation processes in South Africa and inform the development of innovation policy.

In March 2001, Eurostat (the central statistical office of the European Communities) circulated an open invitation to non-EU member states to use the core CIS questionnaire and survey methodology for national innovation surveys in order to improve the comparability of innovation indicators between regions and economies worldwide. The letter and the CIS3 questionnaire and methodology were circulated to the Organisation for Economic Cooperation and Development's (OECD) National Experts on Science Technology and Innovation Indicators (NESTI) group through its website in March 2001 (see Appendices 3 and 4). The current survey was thus aligned with the Fourth Round of the European Community Innovation Survey (CIS4), and CeSTII has worked closely with DST, the OECD, Eurostat and Statistics South Africa in this regard.

CHAPTER 2

Introduction

This report presents the main findings of the South African Innovation Survey 2005, covering the period 2002–2004. Where available, comparisons are made with the results of CIS4 for EU countries, as provided by Eurostat.

Innovation in the private sector is a critical factor in boosting growth in the economy and contributing to the quality of life. While some innovation is based directly on the results of research and experimental development (R&D), much innovation by enterprises is based on non-R&D activities, such as the acquisition of external knowledge or new equipment and machinery. Unlike earlier innovation surveys (CIS1 and CIS2), which tended to be confined to technological innovations, the CIS4-based surveys consider product innovations (both goods and services), process innovations, organisational innovations and marketing innovations.

As in other countries, there are several public programmes and support programmes for R&D and innovation in place in South Africa. These programmes are aimed at stimulating the development of high-level human resources, research outputs and innovations, which will in turn stimulate growth and diversity in the economy. Among other issues, the Innovation Survey looks at how many firms benefit from these public programmes of support for R&D and innovation, and measures innovation activities in small firms and industry sectors that do not usually access such funds.

This report focuses on benchmarking the results of the South African Innovation Survey with the results of CIS4 undertaken in the various EU countries (as well as Norway and Iceland). The results of innovation surveys are also available for several non-EU and non-OECD countries such as Brazil, Malaysia and Argentina. Some of the methodologies employed and the basic results for these other countries are discussed by Mani (2007). However, it is not the intention of this report to analyse the results of these developing countries and other countries in any detail, because the methodologies and timeframes employed in these surveys differ from CIS4. Some of the main results of these surveys are provided for comparative purposes only, mostly with respect to the percentage of innovating enterprises. However, we intend to provide comparisons of the results from these countries and from South Africa in a subsequent report or paper.

Box 1: Definitions of innovation, based on the core CIS4 questionnaire

A *product innovation* is the introduction to the market of a new good or service or a significantly improved good or service with respect to its capabilities, such as improved user-friendliness, components or sub-systems.

A *process innovation* is the use of new or significantly improved methods for the production or supply of goods and services.

The innovation (new or improved) must be new to the enterprise, but it does not need to be new to the industry sector or market.

A distinction is made between product innovations that are new only to the firm and those that are new to the market of the enterprise.

Box 2: Previous innovation surveys in South Africa

There have been two previous innovation surveys in South Africa. The first survey was carried out by the Foundation for Research Development (FRD) and the Industrial Strategy Project (ISP) for the years 1992–1994 and was published in October 1997 (Blankley & Kaplan 1997). This survey covered only the manufacturing sector and was based on the first Community Innovation Survey (now referred to as CIS1). A total of 2 732 questionnaires were distributed, and 244 completed questionnaires were received, giving a response rate of 8.9%. This survey was aimed at covering innovating enterprises (to link up with the R&D survey) and was a pilot project on a very limited budget.

The second survey was undertaken by the University of Pretoria and the Eindhoven University of Technology (in the Netherlands) for the period 1998–2000 and covered the manufacturing and services sectors (Oerlemans et al. 2004). Questionnaires were distributed to 7 039 enterprises, and of these 617, or 8.4%, were returned.

Both these surveys relied on commercially available databases of addresses for their samples.

CHAPTER 3

Methodology

The South African Innovation Survey 2005 was based on the guidelines of OECD's *Oslo manual* (OECD 2005), and more specifically, on the methodological recommendations and core questionnaire for CIS4 provided by Eurostat, the central statistical office of the European Communities (see Appendix 4). The CIS4 core questionnaire was modified slightly for South Africa through piloting exercises with businesses and a national stakeholder workshop organised by the National Advisory Council on Innovation (NACI) and the DST. The main differences between the CIS4 core questionnaire and the South African Innovation Survey 2005 questionnaire were the replacement of EU sources of funds with local ones, the change of EU-specific regions to ones that were relevant to South Africa and the replacement of typical EU terminology with South African terminology. The final South African Innovation Survey 2005 questionnaire was directly comparable with the CIS4 instrument except for these specific differences (see Appendix 5 and Appendix 6).

One of Eurostat's strongest recommendations is that, where possible, countries should make use of the most up-to-date version of their national business register for the innovation survey in order to promote international comparability. Through the Memorandum of Agreement between Statistics South Africa and the DST on official science and technology (S&T) statistics (which includes CeSTII by virtue of its survey agency role for DST), Statistics South Africa agreed to provide a suitable random sample as well as advice on conducting the survey, as requested in the Innovation Survey Sampling Specifications document prepared by CeSTII.

The survey design was informed by Eurostat guidelines and the structure of the Statistics South Africa business register, and comprised:

- a random stratified sample (by sector and size of enterprise) drawn from the business registry database of Statistics South Africa;
- a postal survey with at least two telephonic and two written correspondences;
- a non-response survey if the response rate was below 70%;
- the extrapolation of results to the target population based on the weighted sample.

Innovation surveys require a very high response rate (usually 70% or more) in order to ensure accurate results. Drawing a very large sample from the business register could therefore be counter-productive in that regard. Based on the CeSTII resources available for the survey and on the advice of Statistics South Africa, a random stratified sample of 3 087 enterprises with appropriate strata weights for the mining, manufacturing and services sectors was obtained from the September 2004 business register of Statistics South Africa. Statistics South Africa provided comprehensive documentation to accompany the sample (Statistics South Africa 2004).

The first part of 2005 was dedicated to confirming the accuracy of details in the address list and identifying a contact person (ideally the CEO) in each of the 3 087 enterprises. Through this checking and cleaning process, all non-valid enterprises (in other words, those that were not identifiable or traceable through several methods, as well as duplicates and inactive entities) were removed from the database. The remaining entries in the database totalled 2 627 valid enterprises. The CIS methodological guidelines do not recommend replacing these enterprises.

The postal survey was dispatched in August 2005, and the survey remained in the field until April 2006. During this time, enterprises that did not respond promptly received at least two written correspondences (postal and email) and two telephonic reminders to participate in the survey. The work was carried out by a survey manager and six research assistants operating in a dedicated survey call centre. Completed returned questionnaires were checked, and any incomplete information was supplemented, where possible, by telephoning respondents and asking for the required information. By April 2006, the research assistants were encountering defensiveness from enterprises that had not yet responded, and it was decided to close the fieldwork.

After cleaning the final data, a realised sample total of 979 completed questionnaires was obtained, yielding an overall return rate of 37.3% from a sample size of 2 627. This is a better return rate than in previous surveys (see Box 2) but far short of the Eurostat recommended return rate of at least 70%. Accordingly, a non-response survey became necessary in order to check whether there were any significant differences between respondents and non-respondents regarding their propensity to innovate.

In order to follow up on enterprises that had not responded to the survey, a non-response telephonic survey of a simple random sample of 15% of non-respondents was undertaken (following Eurostat best practice recommendations). Non-respondents were assured that by just answering the three simple questions asked about their innovation activities, they would not be contacted again regarding their obligation to complete the survey questionnaire. An acceptable response rate of 89% was obtained from the non-response survey. An electronic logging system was used throughout the main survey and the non-response survey, and completed questionnaires were recorded and verified on a custom-designed database.

The purpose of the non-response survey was to determine the extent to which non-respondents are less or more innovative than respondents (in other words it was a check for bias). On the whole, non-respondents were found to be slightly less innovative than respondents, and the weights for the proportion of non-respondent innovators were accordingly adjusted at strata level to reflect this difference.

A combination of factors presented challenges to conducting the South African Innovation Survey. Through the efforts of a dedicated survey team and support from the DST and the Human Sciences Research Council (HSRC), these challenges were successfully managed. The South African business sector generally resists participating in surveys, and potential respondents complain of being overburdened by numerous official and unofficial surveys. Large enterprises tend to be fairly cooperative, but small and medium-sized firms are more reluctant to complete questionnaires. Many of the smaller firms did not see the relevance of the Innovation Survey to their businesses. Because of the relatively low response rate to the survey, some of the smaller sub-strata did not obtain any responses, and the sub-sector total had to be compiled on the basis of the available strata data for the sub-sector. This was less of a problem with the larger firms, where the survey tended to be undertaken on a census basis, with corresponding low weights for the strata.

An important aspect of the South African Innovation Survey is that enterprise size classes are officially determined by turnover. Turnover is currently used as an official proxy for the number of personnel in the four size classes of enterprise of the

Statistics South Africa business register. Statistics South Africa plans to update the business register with the numbers of personnel per enterprise in the future. The relationship between turnover and the number of full-time employees is prescribed by a schedule contained in the Small Business Amendment Act (Act No. 26 of 2003). The returned questionnaires indicated that a number of the firms in the smaller size classes (2–4) actually had far higher numbers of staff and greater turnovers than prescribed for the size class to which they had been assigned in the register according to their recorded turnovers for 2002. To overcome this problem, the most obvious outliers were moved upwards to size classes 1 or 2, and the weights were adjusted accordingly.

While Eurostat recommends that the CIS4 should target enterprises with 10 or more employees only, this cut-off point also has to be treated differently in the South African case. The level of turnover of enterprises in the Statistics South Africa business register is used to determine a cut-off point for enterprises with fewer than 10 personnel. Enterprises in size class 4 (firms with a turnover of less than R3–6 million per year, depending on the SIC sector), scheduled by the Small Business Amendment Act as enterprises that employ fewer than 20 personnel, were cut off at the 30.5 percentile. Only enterprises above this percentile were included in the sample frame.

Two senior statisticians at the University of Cape Town were consulted on these statistical and analytical issues. Through a cautious and consultative process, we arrived at a final set of weightings. The final results were thus calculated for a smaller number of enterprises than the population listed in the Statistics South Africa business register, but the results of the mostly qualitative questions are representative of the relevant business sectors. For the quantitative questions on turnover, expenditure and number of personnel, the relatively low response rate and the cut-off percentiles in the sampling of size class 1 and 4 enterprises in the database means that the totals calculated will be less than national totals measured in other specific labour force or industry surveys. However, the relative proportions of these quantitative measures, such as the percentage of employees working for innovative enterprises, are more important than the actual numbers. It should be noted that innovation surveys are generally regarded as a good source of qualitative data on innovation activities rather than a reliable source of quantitative data (such as national R&D surveys).

Although an analysis of the preliminary survey data had shown that there was a significant correlation between turnover and the number of employees of enterprises, this relationship proved to be rather weak for the survey as a whole. The size classes are thus far more representative of the turnovers of enterprises than of the number of employees. Officially, the Small Business Amendment Act prescribes the use of turnover for delineating size classes of enterprises, and the size classes used in this report therefore reflect official South African policy. The results will thus differ from those collected in the EU, where only the number of personnel is used to establish the size classes of enterprises. Furthermore, the size classes prescribed in the Small Business Amendment Act differ from those used in the EU. Comparisons with countries that base their size classes on employee numbers, as recommended by CIS4 methodology, will have to be viewed in the light of these differences.

CHAPTER 4

Results

Rate of innovation

Innovation activities include the acquisition of machinery, equipment, software and licences; engineering and development work; training; marketing and R&D. Only when these activities are specifically undertaken to develop and/or implement a product or process innovation can they be counted as innovation activities. The innovation survey results represent the activities of a total of 31 456 enterprises, 51.7% of which reported undertaking innovation activities. The innovation rate was defined as the proportion of enterprises that undertook any innovation activities during the last three financial years (2002–2004). Table 4.1 shows that 54.8% of industrial enterprises were innovative, compared with 49.3% of service enterprises. Almost 30% of all enterprises had both product and process innovations, while 12% had only product innovations. A total of 4.4% of innovative enterprises reported only ongoing or abandoned innovation activities during 2002–2004 (in other words, the innovation end product was not produced during the period that the survey was undertaken).

Table 4.1: Innovation rate: percentages of innovative and non-innovative enterprises in South Africa, 2002–2004

	Total	Industry[a]	Services[b]
Enterprises with innovation activity	**51.7**	**54.8**	**49.3**
Product only innovators	11.9	10.9	12.7
Process only innovators	5.7	3.8	7.3
Product and process innovators	29.7	38.1	22.9
Enterprises with only ongoing or abandoned activities	4.4	2.0	6.3
Enterprises without innovation activity	**48.3**	**45.2**	**50.7**

Note:

a. Industry comprises mining and quarrying, manufacturing, electricity, gas and water supply.

b. Services comprise wholesale and retail, transport, storage and communication, financial intermediation, computer and related services, R&D services, architectural and engineering, and technical testing.

The EU average for enterprises with innovation activity is 42.0% in total, 41.5% for industry and 37.0% for the services sector.

Source: Appendix Table A1.1

In the case of South Africa, where the size class of enterprises in the national business register is calculated by turnover rather than number of employees, there does not appear to be a strong relationship between the size of enterprises and the rate of innovation. In other countries, and in previous innovation surveys undertaken in South Africa, where the size class of enterprises was determined by the number of personnel, there is a clear trend of increasing innovation activity with increasing size classes of enterprise. Figure 4.1 shows that size class 2 has the highest innovation rate at almost 64%, which is slightly higher than the 60% rate of innovation in size class 1. As expected, however, the innovation rates are lowest (41%) in size class 4, which comprises the smallest enterprises.

Figure 4.1: Innovation rate: enterprises with innovation activities and with only ongoing and/or abandoned innovation activities, 2002–2004

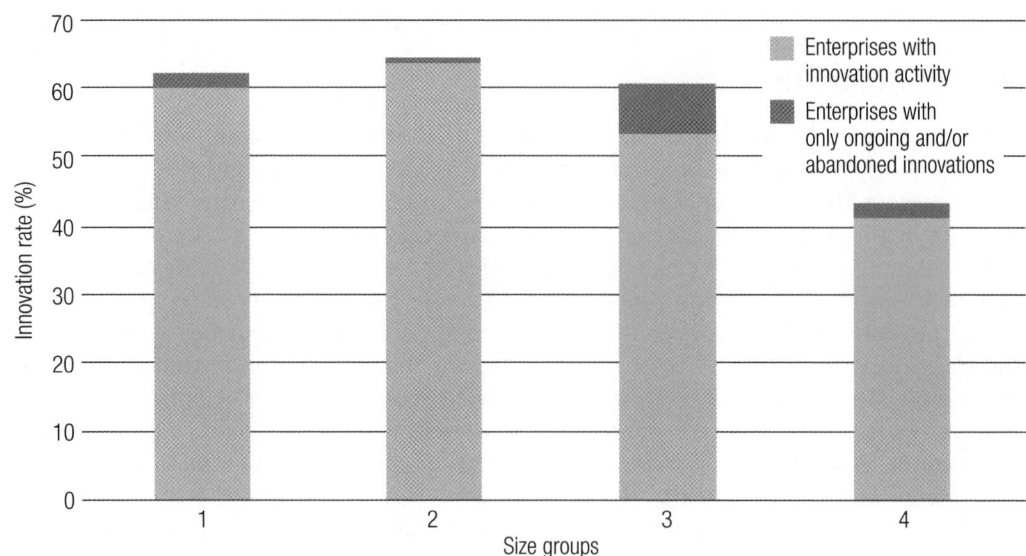

Source: Appendix Table A2.1

The overall innovation rate of 51.7% shown in Figure 4.2 compares favourably with the innovation rates recorded for Iceland and Denmark (52%), Belgium (51%), Sweden (50%), Estonia (49%), Cyprus (46%) and the UK (43%). The figure for South Africa seems fairly high, but in the 1998–2000 survey by Oerlemans et al. (2004), a total of 57% of firms reported innovations in products and services, which is about 5% more than what has been reported in the current survey.

Mani (2007) reports from the Industrial Survey of 2000 in Brazil that approximately 31.5% of enterprises introduced innovations between 1998 and 2000. He also reports that about 35% of Malaysian enterprises reported innovation activities for the period 2000–2001. In Argentina, 59% of manufacturing firms reported innovation activities between 1998 and 2001 (Chudnovsky et al. 2006). However, in order to discuss the results of the surveys in these non-EU and non-OECD countries, the methodologies employed, the sectors surveyed and the years in which the surveys were conducted, as well as prevailing economic conditions, need to be carefully compared, and this should be the topic of a more detailed subsequent report or paper.

Figure 4.2: Share of innovative enterprises as a percentage of all enterprises, 2002–2004 (EU member states and selected countries, including South Africa)

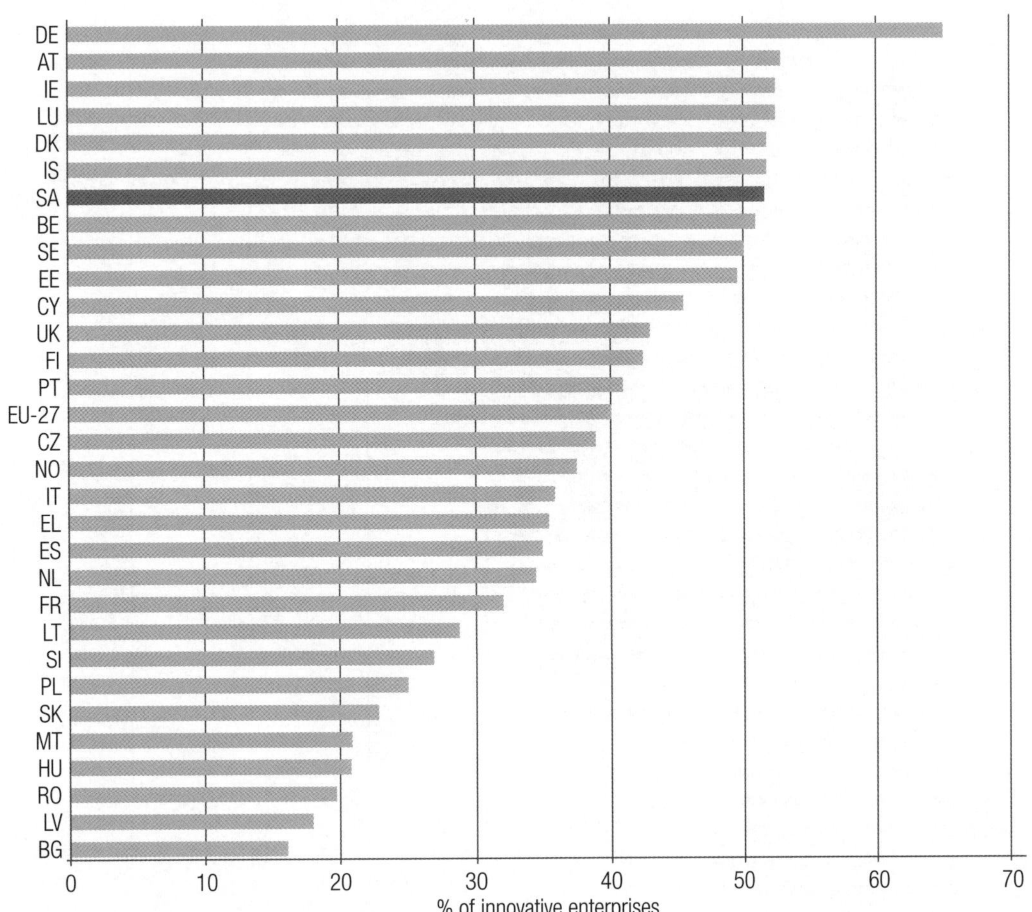

Note:
In this figure and elsewhere, the following country acronyms are used: AT Austria; BE Belgium; BG Bulgaria; CY Cyprus; CZ Czech Republic; DE Germany; DK Denmark; EE Estonia; EL Greece; ES Spain; EU-27 European Union average (27 countries); FI Finland; FR France; HU Hungary; IE Ireland; IS Iceland; IT Italy; LT Lithuania; LU Luxembourg; LV Latvia; MT Malta; NL Netherlands; NO Norway; PL Poland; PT Portugal; RO Romania; SA South Africa; SE Sweden; SI Slovenia; SK Slovakia; UK United Kingdom.

In this figure and elsewhere, the EU-27 average does not include Norway and Iceland, which are not European Union member states.

Source: All data, except for data pertaining to South Africa, are estimates from European Communities (2007b); South African data are from Appendix Table A1.1

In most European countries, industrial enterprises are more innovative than service enterprises, but in a few countries such as Luxembourg, Estonia, Portugal, Greece and Latvia, the services sector rates of innovation are higher than those in industry (see Figure 4.3). The proportion of enterprises engaged in innovation activities ranged from 72.8% in German industry to 12.7% in Bulgarian services. In South Africa, 54.8% of industrial enterprises were innovative, compared with 49.3% of enterprises in the services sector. This compares favourably with the EU-27 averages of 41.5% for industry and 37.0% for services.

Figure 4.3: Enterprises engaged in innovation activity as a percentage of all enterprises in industry and services, 2002–2004

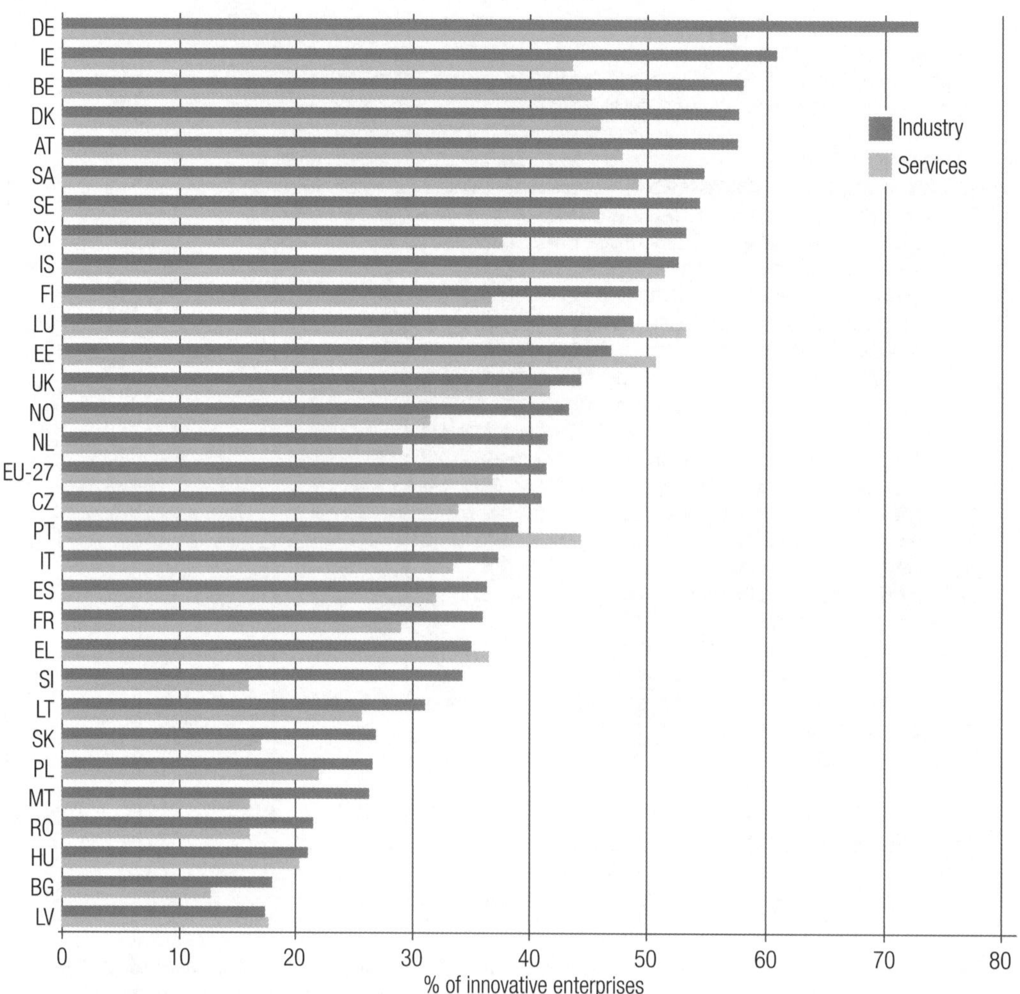

Source: All data, except for data pertaining to South Africa are estimates from European Communities (2007a); South African data are from Appendix Table A1.1

The characteristics of enterprises covered by the survey

The 31 456 enterprises of the survey population employ about 1.77 million employees, of whom some 78% work in enterprises with innovation activities (see Table 4.2).

Table 4.2: Total enterprises, employees and turnovers: comparison of enterprises with innovation activities, 2002–2004

	Total	Industry %	Services %	Total %
Total enterprises	31 456	44.3	55.7	100.0
Enterprises with innovation activities	16 264	47.0	53.0	51.7
Total employees	1 770 745	57.1	42.9	100.0
Total employees in enterprises with innovation activities	1 381 976	78.3	77.6	78.0
Turnover (R million)	1 144 445	45.1	54.9	100.0
Turnover of enterprises with innovation activities	863 632	84.7	67.9	75.5

Source: Appendix Tables A1.1, A1.2, A1.3 and A1.4

The total turnover of the enterprises was recorded as R1 144.4 billion. About 75.5% of this turnover is accounted for by enterprises with innovation activities (see Table 4.2). The industrial sector is more innovation intensive, with 84.7% of turnover accounted for by industrial enterprises with innovation activities, compared with the 67.9% of turnover generated by innovative service enterprises.

The majority of enterprises in the population were independent enterprises and not part of a larger group (see Table 4.3). Only 13.6% of enterprises were part of a larger group, and most of these were medium-sized enterprises in size classes 2 and 3.

Table 4.3: Enterprises stating that they were part of a larger group

	Total				
Size class	1	2	3	4	Total
Number of enterprises					
Part of a larger group	790	1 512	1 465	523	4 289
Not part of a larger group	836	3 848	13 055	8 789	26 527
No response	6	0	634	0	640
Percentage of enterprises					
Part of a larger group	2.5	4.8	4.7	1.7	13.6
Not part of a larger group	2.7	12.2	41.5	27.9	84.3
No response	0.0	0.0	2.0	0.0	2.0

Source: Appendix Table A2.44

Table 4.4: Number and percentage of enterprises with and without innovation activity by size class and turnover, 2004

Size class		1	2	3	4	Total
All enterprises: turnover (R million)		899 169	120 860	104 764	19 651	1 144 444
Enterprises with innovation activity	Turnover (R million) %	708 875 **78.8%**	72 982 **60.4%**	72 422 **69.1%**	9 353 **47.6%**	863 632 **75.5%**
Enterprises without innovation activity	Turnover (R million) %	190 294 **21.2%**	47 878 **39.6%**	32 342 **30.9%**	10 298 **52.4%**	280 812 **24.5%**

Note:
Numbers do not always total exactly because of rounding.

Source: Appendix Table A2.24

Table 4.4 shows that the innovative enterprises of size class 1 were responsible for the greatest turnover contribution through innovation activities (78.8%) and accounted for 82% of all turnover produced by innovative enterprises. Although non-innovative firms comprised 48.3% of all enterprises covered in the survey (Appendix Table A1.1), they accounted for only 24.5% of the total turnover recorded.

Innovative enterprises employed more staff than non-innovative enterprises and accounted for 78% of total employees. Innovative enterprises in size class 1 employed 87.2% of staff in the size class (see Table 4.5).

Table 4.5: Enterprises with and without innovation activity by size class and number of employees, 2002–2004

Size class	1	2	3	4	Total
All enterprises: number of employees (thousands)	1 060	312	298	100	1 771
Enterprises with innovation activity (% employees)	87.2%	68.4	68.1%	70.7%	78.0%
Enterprises without innovation activity (% employees)	12.8%	41.4	31.9%	29.3%	22.0%

Note:
Numbers do not always total exactly because of rounding.

Source: Appendix Table A2.3

Innovative enterprises employed 1 381 976 staff, of whom 179 072 employees, or 13% of the total, had a tertiary education qualification (diploma or degree). In the industrial sector, the manufacturing sector had the highest percentage of employees with a tertiary qualification (16%). The services sector with the highest percentage of employees with a tertiary qualification (48.2%) was R&D, architectural and engineering, and technical testing (see Figure 4.4).

Figure 4.4: Percentage of employees in innovative enterprises with a degree or diploma, 2004

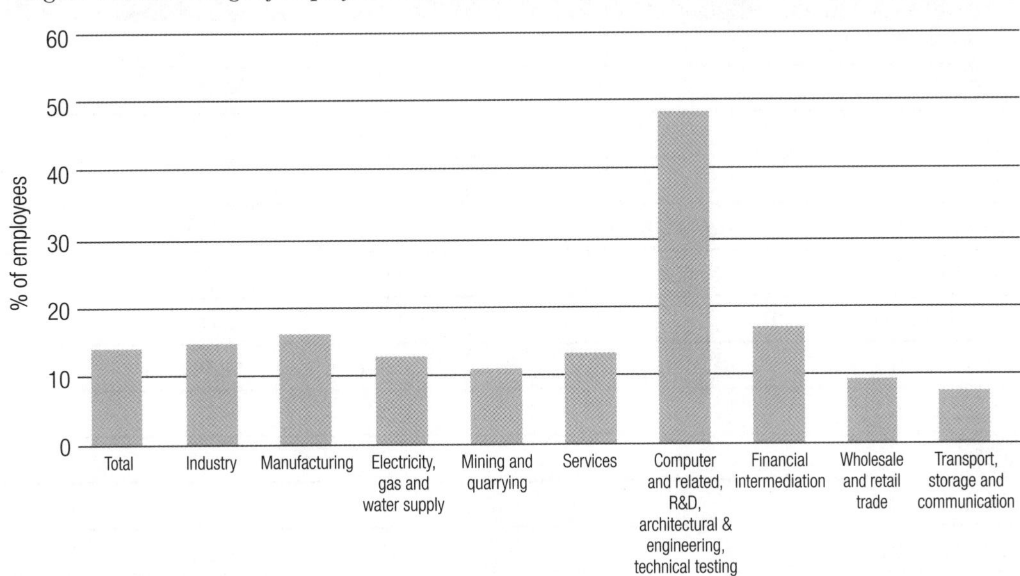

Source: Appendix Table A1.34

Innovative enterprises appear to be more export-oriented than non-innovative enterprises (see Table 4.6). About 67% of non-innovative enterprises sold goods and services in only some provinces of South Africa, compared with 54% of innovative enterprises. Other countries in Africa are an important destination for goods and services produced by innovative South African enterprises (19.3%), followed by Asia (5.4%) and Europe (5.1%).

Table 4.6: Geographic distribution of goods and services sold by innovative and non-innovative enterprises (%), 2002–2004

Proportion of enterprises	Total	Industry	Services
All enterprises			
South Africa (only some provinces)	60.2	60.9	59.7
South Africa (national)	31.3	34.5	28.7
Rest of Africa	14.0	16.2	12.3
Europe	4.2	5.2	3.4
USA	3.0	4.0	2.1
Asia	4.1	2.6	5.4
Other countries	5.4	8.4	3.0
Enterprises with innovation activity			
South Africa (only some provinces)	54.4	50.8	57.5
South Africa (national)	37.5	41.0	34.4
Rest of Africa	19.3	20.1	18.5
Europe	5.1	7.5	3.0

Proportion of enterprises	Total	Industry	Services
Enterprises with innovation activity			
USA	3.9	6.2	1.9
Asia	5.4	3.6	7.0
Other countries	5.4	7.9	3.3
Enterprises without innovation activity			
South Africa (only some provinces)	66.5	73.2	61.8
South Africa (national)	24.5	26.6	23.1
Rest of Africa	8.4	11.5	6.2
Europe	3.2	2.5	3.7
USA	2.0	1.4	2.4
Asia	2.7	1.2	3.8
Other countries	5.4	9.1	2.8

Source: Appendix Table A1.31

Types of innovations

The survey was based on enterprises answering questions concerning their innovation activities in each of the four types of innovation, namely: product, process, organisational and marketing. The rates of innovation for each type of innovation are illustrated in Figure 4.5. Relatively few enterprises had only process innovations (5.7%) or only product innovations (11.9%). About 46% of enterprises had organisational innovations, and almost 28% had marketing innovations.

Figure 4.5: Innovation rate by type of innovation, 2002–2004

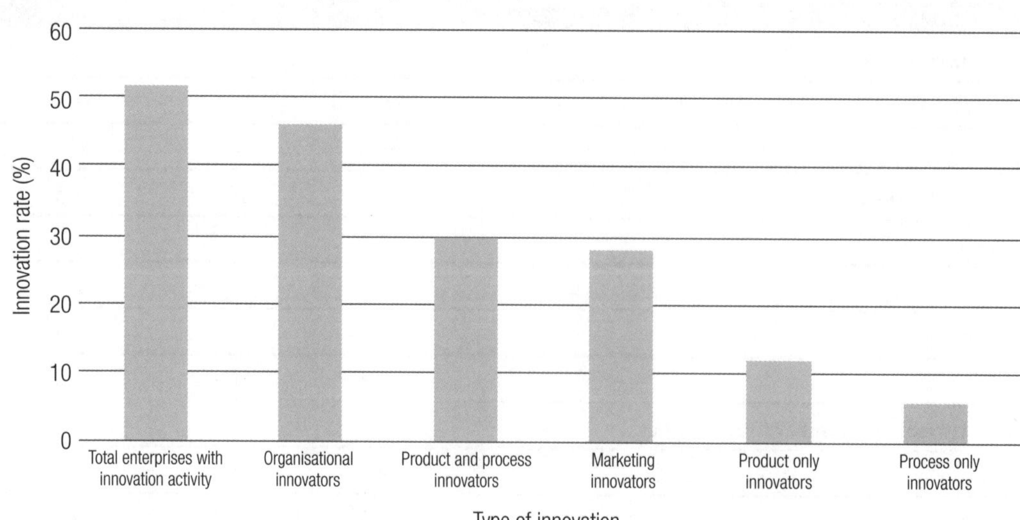

Source: Appendix Tables A1.1 and A1.35

Figure 4.6.1: Percentage of innovative enterprises that undertook new or significantly different organisational or marketing changes, 2002–2004

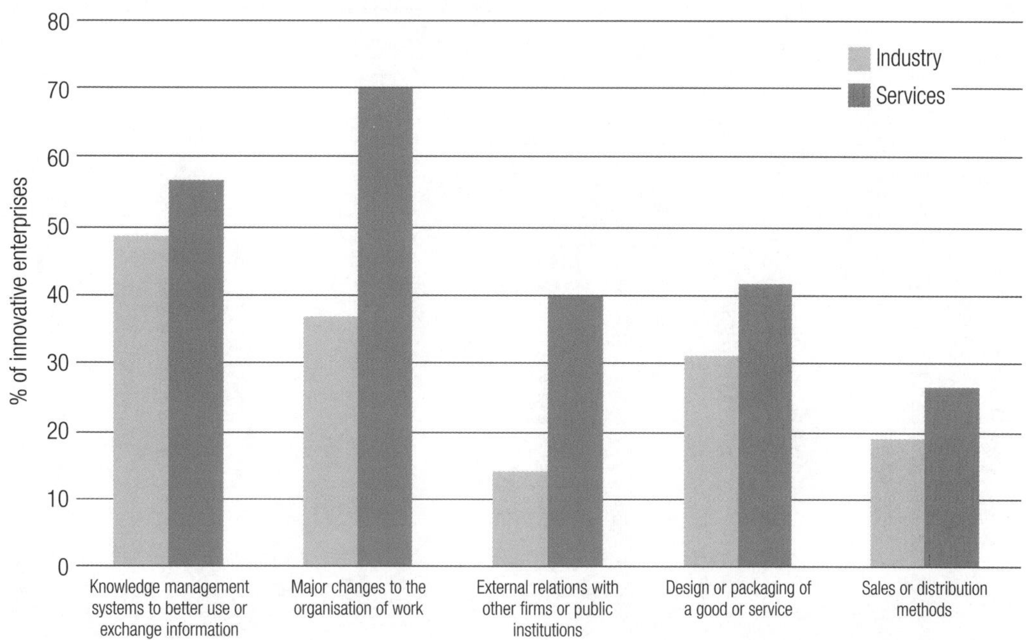

Source: Appendix Table A1.24

Figure 4.6.1 provides more detail on the organisational and marketing innovations undertaken by South African enterprises. Enterprises in the services sector have a greater proportion of organisational and marketing innovations than industrial enterprises (Figure 4.6.1). In terms of organisational innovations, the majority of enterprises (54.1%) introduced major changes to the organisation of work (see Appendix Table A1.24), while 52.6% implemented knowledge management systems to better use or exchange information.

Figure 4.6.2 shows the percentage of international innovative enterprises that introduced innovations in organisation and/or marketing. Innovative South African enterprises were more active in this regard than their European counterparts, with 82.6% of South African enterprises with innovation activity recording some form of organisational or marketing innovations, compared with 67.3% for the EU-27. Luxembourg (81.6%) and Denmark (80.9%) were the only two European countries in which more than 80% of all innovating enterprises introduced this kind of innovation. However, levels of organisational and/or marketing innovations are generally high in all countries, and over 50% of innovative enterprises in all countries surveyed reported innovation activities of this nature. The high score in South Africa could partly reflect the changes many enterprises have had to make in response to national policies such as employment equity and black economic empowerment (BEE) as well as other business regulations. The high rates of organisational innovation in the services sector in South Africa, particularly regarding major changes in the organisation of work, reflect the recent strong growth and consequent competition in this sector.

Figure 4.6.2: Percentage of innovatve enterprises that introduced organisational and/or marketing innovations, 2002–2004

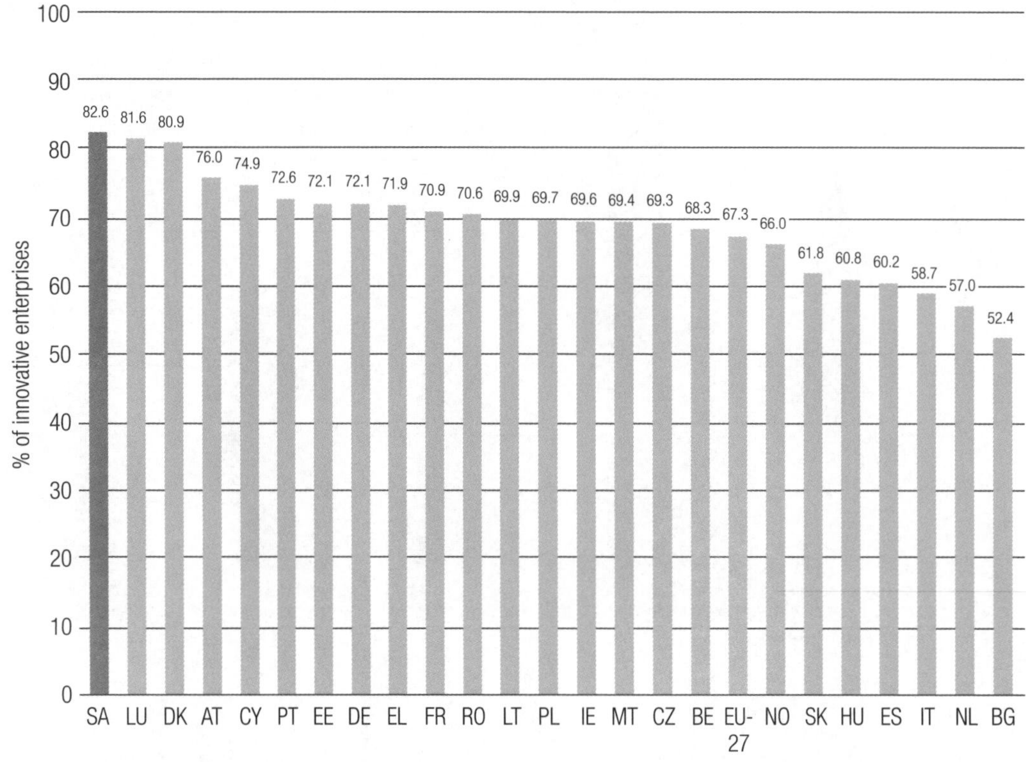

Source: All data, except for data pertaining to South Africa, are from European Communities 2007a; South African data are from Appendix Table A1.35

Product (goods or services) innovation

Enterprises that had product innovations (comprising innovation in either goods or services produced) accounted for the majority of innovators in the survey. Approximately 10% of the turnover of product innovators in 2004 was generated by innovations that were new to the market, representing turnover of about R67.8 billion (see Table 4.7.1). Table 4.7.2 shows that enterprises in size class 4 generated the highest proportion of turnover based on product innovations that were new to the market (13.2%), while size class 3 enterprises generated the highest proportion of turnover from product innovations that were new to the firm (23.6%). Enterprises in size class 1 generated the highest proportion of total turnover for all innovative enterprises from product innovations (82%).

Table 4.7.1: Product innovators: proportion of turnover in 2004 attributed to the different types of product

All product innovators	Turnover generated (R million)	Percentage turnover generated
Product innovations new to the market	67 848	10.1
Product innovations new to the firm	79 194	11.8
Products unchanged or only marginally modified	526 705	78.2
Total	673 747	100

Source: Appendix Table A1.7

Table 4.7.2: Product innovators: proportion of turnover in 2004 attributed to the types of product by size of enterprise (%)

Size class	1	2	3	4	Total
Product innovations new to the market	10.1	12.0	7.1	13.2	10.1
Product innovations new to the firm	9.8	17.8	23.6	19.2	11.8
Products unchanged or only marginally modified	80.1	70.2	69.2	67.6	78.2
Total (% of turnover produced by product innovators per size class)	**82.0**	**8.6**	**8.2**	1.4	**100**

Source: Appendix Table A2.7

Table 4.8 provides an international comparison of the percentage of enterprises that introduced new or improved products to the market as a percentage of innovative enterprises. South Africa appears to have the highest rate of innovation in this regard, but the reasons for South Africa's high performance are not clear. A possible explanation is that there is a fairly low threshold to this question in that the goods or services introduced need only to be new to the enterprise, and not new to the market, and this could have been achieved between 2002 and 2004. Given the relatively positive developments and changes in the economy over these years, this could be a result of businesses expanding and exploring new markets with new or improved goods or services. In Europe, particularly in larger countries, business thresholds related to what constitutes a new or improved product could also be higher than in South Africa, resulting in a lower record of innovation in EU countries. In general, it is easier to introduce new or improved products in less mature economies where there are more opportunities or gaps in the market than it is in more established economies.

In the EU, it was only in three countries (Bulgaria, Sweden and Luxembourg) that more than 50% of innovative enterprises introduced new or significantly improved products. On average in the EU-27, about one-third of innovative enterprises introduced new or improved products to the market. In South Africa, the share of innovative industrial enterprises that introduced new or significantly improved products to the market (89.4%) was substantially higher than the equivalent share of innovative service enterprises (72.5%). Table 4.8 shows that in the top four innovative countries in Europe, the percentage of service enterprises that introduced new or improved products to the market was higher than for innovative industrial enterprises, namely for Iceland (85.9% compared with 69.5%), Bulgaria (71.1% compared with 50.6%), Sweden (57.8% compared with 47.5%) and Luxembourg

(54.2% compared with 42.2%). However, for the EU-27 as a whole, innovative industrial enterprises introduced more new or improved products to the market than innovative service enterprises did (37.4% compared with 33.7%).

Table 4.8: Enterprises that introduced new or improved products to the market as a percentage of enterprises engaged in innovation activity by sector, 2002–2004

	Total	Industry	Services
South Africa	80.4	89.4	72.5
Iceland	77.6	69.5	85.9
Bulgaria	56.4	50.6	71.1
Sweden	52.4	47.5	57.8
Luxembourg	51.6	42.2	54.2
Finland	49.6	49.8	49.3
Austria	48.4	49.3	47.4
Netherlands	48.3	49.5	47.2
United Kingdom	47.8	47.1	48.4
Denmark	47.7	46.9	48.6
Slovenia	46.6	44.3	53.7
Poland	46.4	44.1	50.5
Ireland	44.5	55.5	29.8
Greece	44.4	44.3	44.5
Estonia	41.9	37.2	47.2
Slovakia	41.6	39.4	47.0
Czech Republic	41.5	42.1	40.3
Belgium	40.7	41.0	40.3
France	38.6	42.6	33.6
Norway	36.5	33.4	40.1
Hungary	36.3	37.1	35.0
EU-27	35.9	37.4	33.7
Latvia	34.5	38.0	30.8
Lithuania	34.5	39.9	27.6
Italy	31.1	32.0	28.6
Portugal	30.1	32.1	26.8
Romania	27.9	29.2	25.1
Germany	26.9	33.8	18.3
Malta	25.0	25.3	24.6
Spain	20.9	23.4	16.8
Cyprus	14.6	16.0	12.3

Source: All data, except for data pertaining to South Africa are estimates from European Communities (2007a); South African data are from Appendix Table A1.42

Figure 4.7: Percentage share of turnover from new or significantly improved products (new to the market) in the total turnover of innovative enterprises, 2002–2004

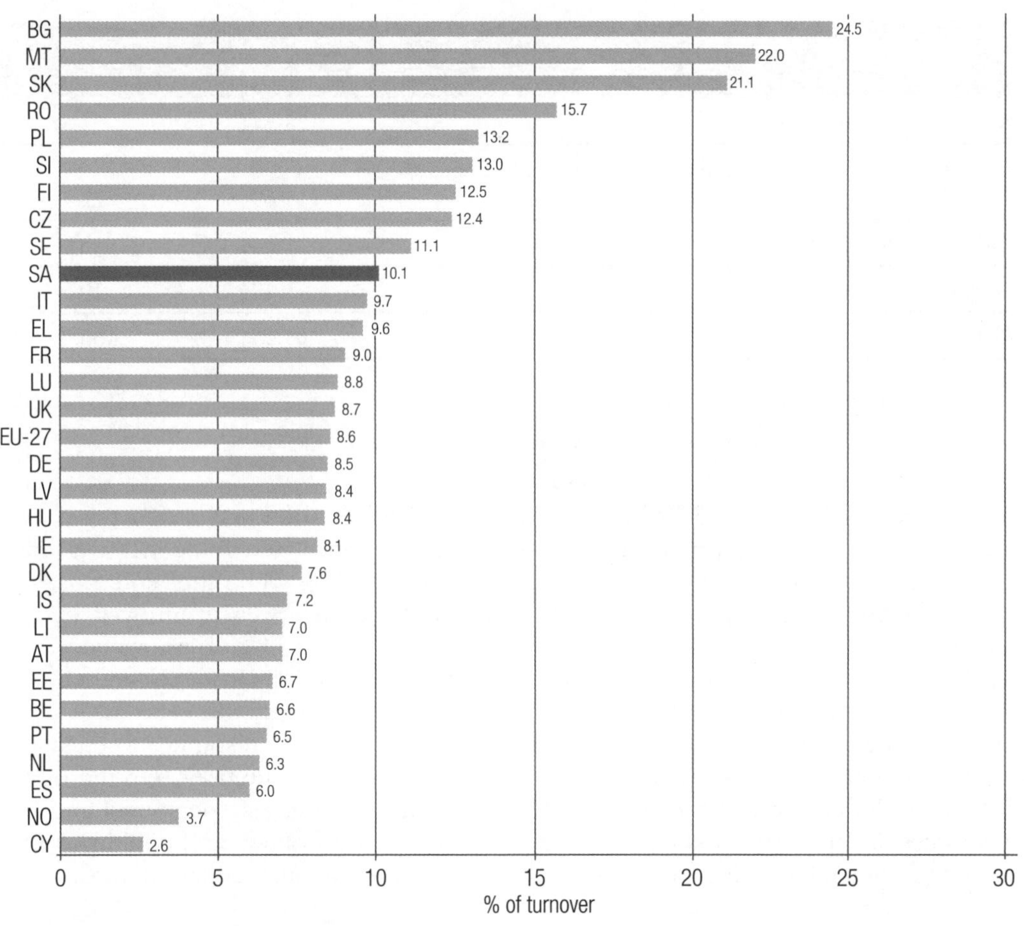

Source: All data, except for data pertaining to South Africa are estimates from European Communities (2007a); South African data are from Appendix Table A1.7

Figure 4.7 shows that South Africa performed relatively well in terms of the percentage share of turnover generated by the sale of new or significantly improved products (new to the market and not just new to the enterprise) compared with other countries. It should be noted that the leading countries on this indicator were four new members of the European Union, namely Bulgaria (24.5%), Malta (22.0%), Slovakia (21.1%) and Romania (15.7%). South Africa's 10.1% is higher than the percentages for Italy (9.7%), Greece (9.6%) and France (9.0%). For the EU-27, the average share of turnover produced by products new to the market was 8.6%. These findings could result from increased opportunities for introducing new and improved products in less mature economies.

Table 4.9 shows that product innovations developed by innovative enterprises were mainly developed by the enterprise itself (51.3%). About 23% of enterprises collaborated with other enterprises or institutions to develop product innovations, while a further 6.4% relied on other enterprises or institutions to develop their innovations.

Table 4.9: Responsibility for the development of product innovations in innovative enterprises, 2002–2004

Product innovations developed by:	Number of enterprises	% of enterprises
Mainly own enterprise	8 341	51.3
Own enterprise in collaboration with other enterprises or institutions	3 699	22.7
Other enterprises or institutions	1 041	6.4
Non-responsive enterprises*	3 183	19.6
Total	**16 264**	**100.0**

Source: Appendix Table A1.9

** Enterprises that returned the questionnaire, but did not respond to this question.*

In size class 4, just over 85% of innovative enterprises reported that product innovations were developed mainly by their own enterprise (see Table 4.10). A total of 30.7% of enterprises in size class 3 reported collaborating with other enterprises or institutions in developing product innovations, while only 5.1% of innovative enterprises in size class 4 had any such collaboration. About 11% of innovative size class 1 enterprises relied on other enterprises or institutions to develop their innovations, but this was rare (0.5%) in the smallest enterprises (size class 4). It makes sense, on the one hand, that larger enterprises have the resources to engage in such collaborative arrangements with other enterprises and institutions. On the other hand, smaller enterprises probably tend to use their own in-house personnel and resources, as they have less capacity for collaboration with others and could possibly be more vulnerable to loss of intellectual property through such collaborations.

Table 4.10: Responsibility for the development of innovations by innovative enterprises by size class, 2002–2004

Size class	1	2	3	4	Total
Product innovations developed by:					
Mainly own enterprise	48.5	57.0	33.3	85.1	51.3
Own enterprise in collaboration with other enterprises or institutions	22.4	23.8	30.7	5.1	22.7
Other enterprises or institutions	11.0	2.4	10.3	0.5	6.4
Non-responsive enterprises*	18.1	16.9	25.7	9.3	19.6
Total	**979**	**3 420**	**8 061**	**3 804**	**16 264**

Source: Appendix Table A2.9

** Enterprises that returned the questionnaire, but did not respond to this question.*

Process innovation

Process innovation is the use of new or significantly improved methods for the production or supply of goods and services. Process innovations are very important in that they often lead to better quality control, greater efficiency, better compliance with new regulations and less waste. They are less tangible than the development and sale of new innovative products and services, but they also affect the bottom line of enterprises by improving quality or saving costs in the production of goods and services.

Table 4.11: Enterprises involved in specific process innovations, 2002–2004

	Total	Industry	Services
Number of process innovators			
Methods of manufacturing or production	7 804	3 672	4 132
Delivery or distribution methods, logistics	6 689	3 548	3 142
Supporting activities	6 981	3 096	3 885
Percentage of process innovators			
Methods of manufacturing or production	24.8	26.3	23.6
Delivery or distribution methods, logistics	21.3	25.5	17.9
Supporting activities	22.2	22.2	22.2

Source: Appendix Table A1.39

About a quarter of all enterprises (24.8%) introduced process innovations involving new or significantly improved methods of manufacturing or producing new goods and services (Table 4.11). Some 21% of all enterprises developed new or significantly improved logistics, delivery or distribution methods for inputs, goods and services. In the third category of process innovation, 22.2% of enterprises produced new or significantly improved supporting activities for processes, such as maintenance and operating systems for purchasing, accounting or computing. In total, 35.4% of all enterprises produced process innovations. Industrial enterprises were more active in process innovations (41.9%) than enterprises in the services sector (30.2%). See Appendix Table A1.38.

Table 4.12: Responsibility for process innovations, 2002–2004

	Total	Industry	Services
Number of process innovators			
Mainly own	6 149	4 552	1 597
Own together with others	3 726	556	3 170
Mainly others	1 188	667	521
Percentage of process innovators			
Mainly own	19.5	32.7	9.1
Own together with others	11.8	4.0	18.1
Mainly others	3.8	4.8	3.0

Source: Appendix Table A1.40

Process innovations were mostly developed in-house, and fewer than 20% of enterprises reported that innovations were developed mainly by their enterprises. Some 11.8% of enterprises developed process innovations in collaboration with other enterprises or institutions (Table 4.12). Only 3.8% of enterprises relied mainly on other enterprises or institutions to develop process innovations for them.

Table 4.13: Origin of process innovations, 2002–2004

Size class	1	2	3	4	Total
Number of process innovators					
South Africa	575	2 675	3 512	1 848	8 610
Abroad	183	240	1 609	346	2 378
Non-process innovators	874	2 445	10 033	7 118	20 470
Percentage of process innovators					
South Africa	35.2	49.9	23.2	19.8	27.4
Abroad	11.2	4.5	10.6	3.7	7.6
Non-process innovators	53.6	45.6	66.2	76.4	65.1

Source: Appendix Table A2.41

The majority of process innovations (27.4%) were developed within South Africa (Table 4.13), while 7.6% of process innovations originated mainly from abroad. This suggests that South African enterprises are quite capable of developing their own new processes and are not as dependent on foreign technology as is sometimes believed.

Of the 16 264 innovative enterprises with product and/or process innovations, 54.9% reported that their innovations originated in South Africa, and 25.4% reported that their innovations were developed mainly abroad (see Table 4.14). A higher proportion of innovative industrial enterprises reported that their innovations were developed in South Africa (67.4%), with only 22.0% reporting that the innovations were developed mainly abroad. Fewer innovative service enterprises reported that their innovations had been developed in South Africa (43.9%), while 28.4% reported that their innovations had been developed abroad.

Table 4.14: Origin of innovations, 2002–2004

Origin (%)	Total	Industry	Services
All innovative enterprises (number of enterprises)	**16 264**	**7 637**	**8 627**
South Africa	54.9	67.4	43.9
Abroad	25.4	22.0	28.4
Non-responsive enterprises*	19.7	10.6	27.7

Source: Appendix Table A1.10

** Enterprises that returned the questionnaire, but did not respond to this question.*

Innovation activities and expenditures

Innovative enterprises spent approximately R28 billion on innovation activities, which represent about 2.4% of the total turnover of all enterprises in both the industrial and services sectors (see Table 4.15). Expenditure on innovation activities as a percentage of the turnover of innovative enterprises was 3.2% overall. The services sector had a higher share of innovation expenditure, equivalent to 3.6% of the turnover of innovative service enterprises, compared with 2.9% for industrial enterprises.

Table 4.15: Enterprises that declared innovation expenditure by sector, 2004

R million	Total	Industry	Services	% of turnover of all enterprises
Intramural (in-house) R&D	5 691	3 155	2 537	0.50
Extramural (outsourced) R&D	2 190	725	1 465	0.19
Acquisition of machinery, equipment and software	18 084	8 525	9 559	1.58
Acquisition of other external knowledge	1 841	225	1 616	0.16
Total	**27 806**	**12 630**	**15 177**	**2.43**
% of turnover of innovative enterprises	Total	Industry	Services	
Intramural (in-house) R&D	0.7	0.7	0.6	
Extramural (outsourced) R&D	0.3	0.2	0.3	
Acquisition of machinery, equipment and software	2.1	2.0	2.2	
Acquisition of other external knowledge	0.2	0.1	0.4	
Total	**3.2**	**2.9**	**3.6**	

Source: Appendix Tables A1.4 and A1.5

Table 2.15 indicates that in both the industrial and services sectors the bulk of innovation expenditure was devoted to the acquisition of new machinery, equipment and software and was equivalent to about 1.58% of the turnover of all enterprises and 2.1% of the turnover of innovative enterprises. Intramural and outsourced R&D accounted for 0.69% of the turnover of all enterprises and 1% of the turnover of innovative enterprises.

International comparisons of innovation activities in innovative enterprises provide some interesting comparisons. The proportion of innovative South African enterprises undertaking intramural R&D is similar to the average for the EU (about 52%), and South Africa ranks tenth out of 24 countries on this scale (see Table 4.16). The country is listed seventeenth in terms of the percentage of innovative enterprises that outsourced or engaged extramural R&D (19.3%). Despite relatively high expenditure on the acquisition of machinery, equipment and software, South African enterprises are not as active as enterprises in other countries in such acquisitions. Based on the 54.1% of enterprises reporting such expenditure, the country ranks only twenty-second in the world. South Africa ranks fifth in terms of the percentage of innovative enterprises engaged in the acquisition of other external knowledge (28.3%).

Table 4.16: Share of innovative enterprises by type of innovative activity, 2004 (EU member states, Norway and South Africa)

	Enterprises engaged in intramural R&D	Enterprises engaged in extramural R&D	Enterprises engaged in acquisition of machinery, equipment and software	Enterprises engaged in acquisition of other external knowledge
Ireland	85.5	22.2	71.4	23.7
France	70.2	24.9	60.0	23.9
Netherlands	67.4	35.0	63.8	24.8
Sweden	66.1	28.4	65.5	41.1
Norway	65.9	40.3	30.4	21.9
Italy	59.1	21.1	90.6	20.2
Slovakia	54.8	26.1	77.3	23.7
Germany	53.8	20.9	72.9	23.5
Belgium	53.3	26.4	73.4	19.6
EU-27	52.2	22.0	75.1	21.5
South Africa	**51.7**	**19.3**	**54.1**	**28.3**
Greece	50.6	32.0	91.6	14.7
Czech Republic	48.7	24.3	75.6	24.3
Luxembourg	45.0	25.0	75.7	24.3
Portugal	43.8	29.0	86.0	24.8
Estonia	43.2	23.0	82.6	35.9
Hungary	42.4	16.1	75.5	17.3
Malta	42.4	9.0	49.3	13.2
Denmark	40.1	23.2	63.2	35.6
Spain	34.9	20.3	66.6	12.6
Lithuania	29.6	16.8	86.5	27.2
Romania	27.7	9.1	78.9	12.8
Poland	26.2	9.2	90.7	7.8
Cyprus	24.5	15.5	97.7	33.4
Bulgaria	8.6	12.6	65.9	24.5
SA Rank (1-24)	**10**	**17**	**22**	**5**

Source: All data, except for data pertaining to South Africa are estimates from European Communities (2007b). Data for Latvia, Austria, Finland and the United Kingdom are missing, and the EU-27 average is based only on available data; South African data are from Appendix Table A1.5

In Europe, Ireland and France had the highest proportion of innovative enterprises engaged in in-house R&D, with 86% and 70% respectively. Bulgaria and Poland recorded the least amount of intramural R&D activity, with 9% and 14% respectively of innovative enterprises having in-house R&D activities.

The survey contained a question on whether intramural R&D was carried out occasionally or continuously (see Figure 4.8). The Netherlands had the highest proportion (48%) of innovative enterprises undertaking continuous R&D, followed by France (37%) and Belgium (36%). In South Africa, almost 21% of innovative enterprises undertook R&D on a continuous basis, while 26% of enterprises undertook R&D occasionally.

Figure 4.8: Share of innovative enterprises engaged in intramural R&D continuously or occasionally, 2002–2004 (EU member states and selected countries, including South Africa)

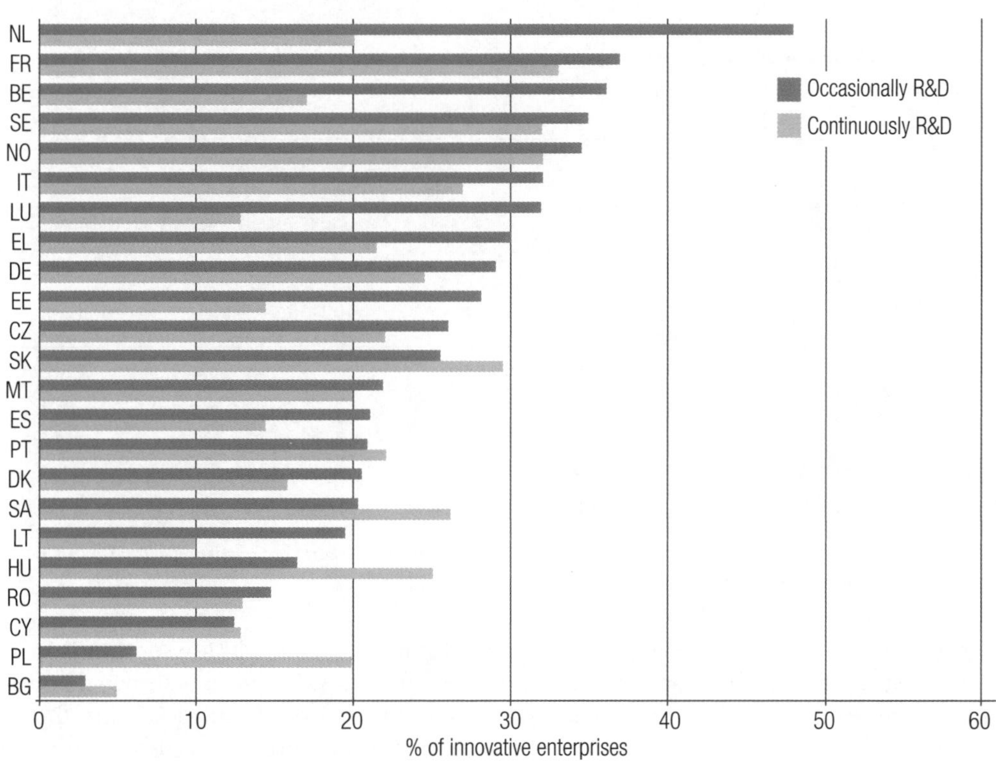

Source: All data, except for data pertaining to South Africa are from European Communities (2007a); South African data are from the Innovation Survey 2005 database

Financial support for innovation activities

National funding agencies, such as the National Research Foundation (NRF), which currently houses the Innovation Fund and the Technology and Human Resources for Industry Programme (THRIP), appear to have a stimulatory effect on innovation activities. About 6.4% of innovators in industry received funding for innovation activities from national funding agencies (see Table 4.17), while 1.1% of innovative enterprises in the services sector received funding from such sources. A further 5% of innovative enterprises in the industrial sector and 0.4% in the services sector received funding from national government. Altogether, approximately 6.5% of all innovative enterprises and 11.8% of innovative industrial enterprises received public funding for their innovation activities between 2002 and 2004.

Table 4.17: Percentage of innovative enterprises that received financial support for innovation activities from government sources, 2002–2004

Percentage of innovative enterprises	Total	Industry	Services
Metros and municipalities	0.0	0.0	0.1
Provincial government	0.2	0.3	0.1
National government	2.6	5.0	0.4
National funding agencies	3.6	6.4	1.1
Foreign government/public sources	0.1	0.1	0.0
Total	**6.5**	**11.8**	**1.7**

Source: Appendix Table A1.33

Figure 4.9: Share of innovative enterprises that received public funds, 2002–2004 (EU member states and selected countries, including South Africa)

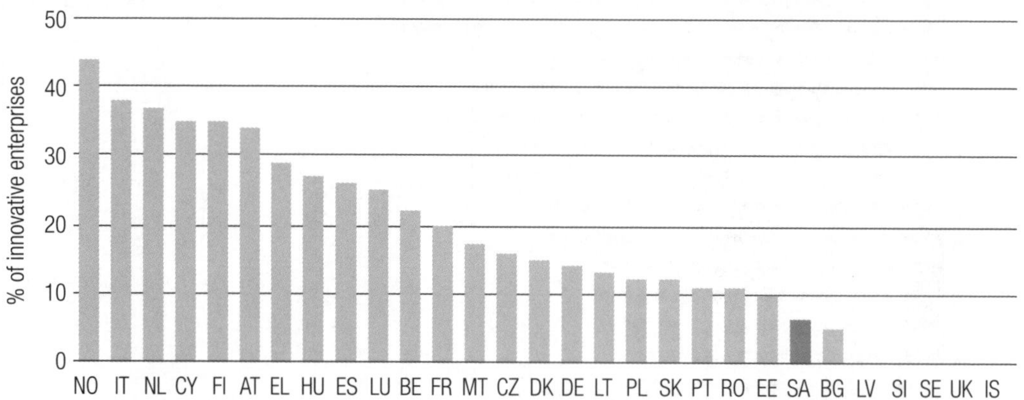

Source: All data, except for data pertaining to South Africa are estimates from European Communities (2007b); South African data are from Appendix Table A1.33

However, when considered in an international context, relatively few enterprises appear to receive public funding for innovation activities. Figure 4.9 shows that, of the countries that produce such data, innovative enterprises in Bulgaria were the only other enterprises to have received less public funding than enterprises in South Africa. In 10 out of 24 countries, more than 25% of innovative enterprises received public funding for innovation. This could possibly result from countries having favourable tax incentives for R&D and innovation or from a strong history of direct funding of R&D and innovation through grants and subsidies at both national and EU levels. For example, it would be expected that the EU's Framework Programme for Research and Technological Development, which is regarded as a major tool for supporting the creation of the European Research Area (with the Seventh Framework Programme now in place for the period 2007–2013), would be a valuable source of funding for innovation. In CIS4, however, the countries with the highest percentages of innovative enterprises indicating that they received EU funding for their innovation activities were Greece (19.7%), Austria (9.3%), Finland (8.4%) and Denmark (6.5%). Of the countries that received EU funding, relatively few received funding from the Fifth or Sixth Framework Programmes: 7.8% for Greece, 2.6% for Austria, 4.3% for Finland and 3.4% for Denmark (European Communities 2007b).

Direct measures for innovation support, such as grant funding, are more likely to lead to the development of relationships between government, industry and third parties such as higher education institutions. In the case of South Africa, the combined funding offered by the Innovation Fund, THRIP and the Support Programme for Industrial Innovation (SPII) totalled R363 million in 2004, and not all this funding went to industry (at most, possibly R250 million went to industry). Considering that the enterprises surveyed spent R27.8 billion on innovation activities, the available funding of R250 million represents only about 0.89% of the total amount used/ required. Public funding for R&D activities in the business sector appears to be more favourable and 32.9% of businesses in the 2005/06 R&D Survey accessed public sources of funding for R&D, although the monetary value of such funding was low. According to the National R&D Survey for 2004/05, the South African business sector spent a total of R6.7 billion on R&D in 2004, of which R0.48 billion (or 7.1%) came from public funding sources (DST 2006).

In order to provide public funding to 20% of innovative enterprises (equivalent to the proportion of innovative enterprises in France that received public funding in the period 2002–2004), South Africa would have to fund some 3 252 enterprises, with 196 enterprises from size class 1 (largest firms), 684 enterprises from size class 2, 1 612 enterprises from size class 3 and 760 enterprises from size class 4. Without double-counting, about 7% of enterprises in size class 1 are currently being funded from public sources, 2% in size class 2, 4.5% in size class 3 and 5.7% in size class 4 (see Appendix Table A2.33). South Africa clearly lags behind other countries in the public funding of R&D and innovation in the private sector.

Sources of information and cooperation for innovation activities

Figure 4.10: Sources of information for innovation rated as highly important by innovative enterprises, 2002–2004

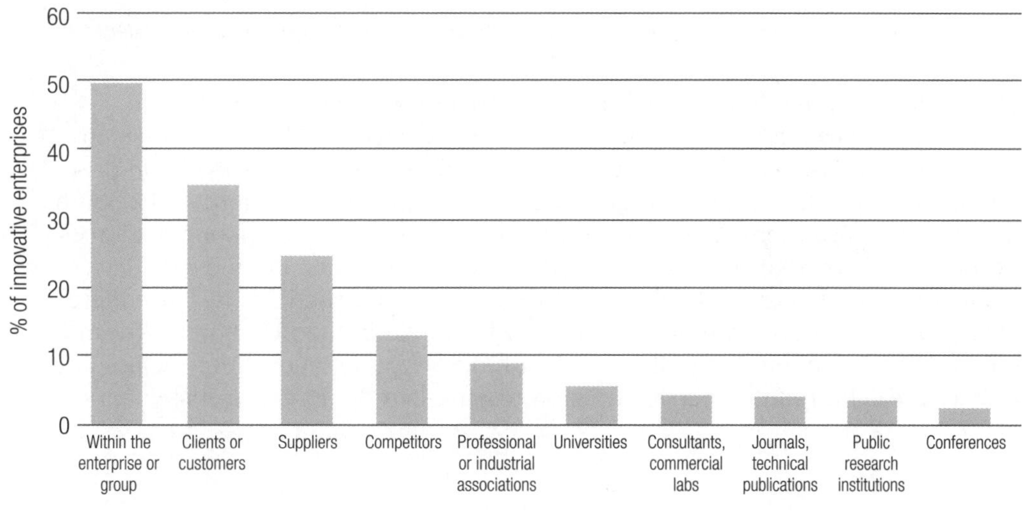

Source: Appendix Table A1.17

Almost 50% of all innovative enterprises rated sources of information within the enterprise as highly important for innovation activities (Figure 4.10). Clients and customers were rated as highly important external market sources by 35%

of innovative enterprises, followed by suppliers (24%) and competitors (13%). Universities and technikons, and government and public research institutes were rated as highly important by only 5% and 3% of enterprises respectively.

Figure 4.11: Sources of information identified by enterprises as highly important for the enterprise's innovation activities, 2002–2004

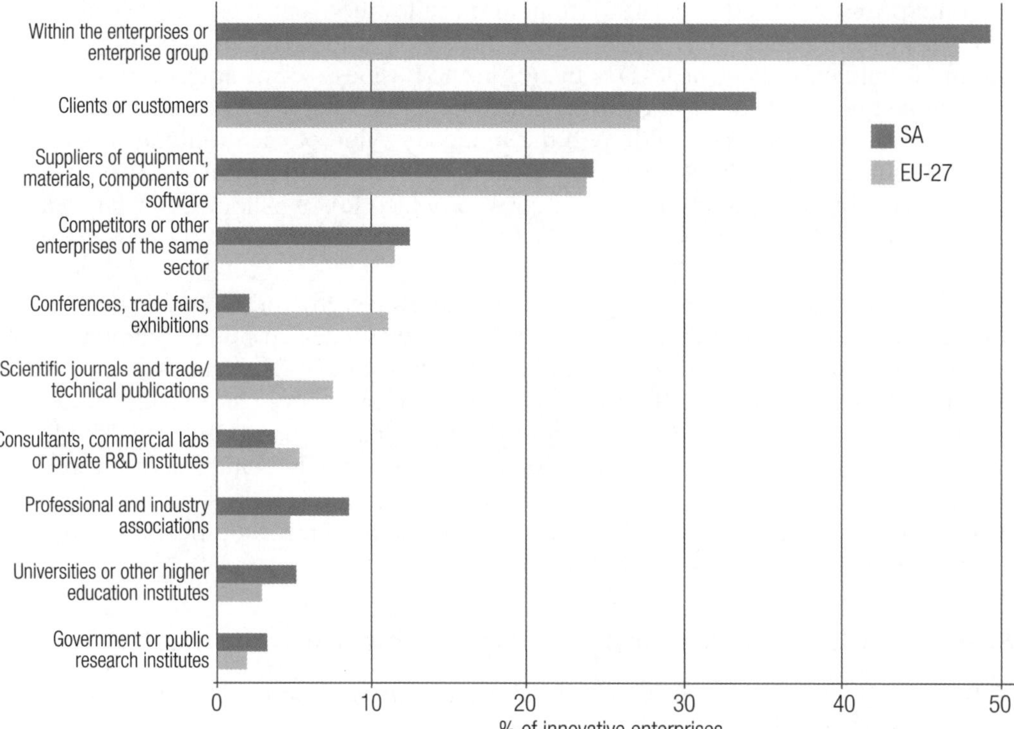

Source: Data for EU-27 are from European Communities (2007c); South African data are from Appendix Table A1.17

South Africa's profile in terms of highly important sources of information for innovation appears to be much the same as the average profile for countries in the expanded European Union (EU-27), with almost half of innovative enterprises rating internal sources of information as highly important (see Figure 4.11). South African enterprises consider clients and customers to be highly important sources of information to a greater extent than their EU counterparts, but indicate that conferences, trade fairs and exhibitions are not as useful (perhaps because there is less diversity in such resources in South Africa than in the EU). South African enterprises also report that professional and industry associations, universities and public research institutes are slightly more useful than the EU-27 average.

Table 4.18: Highly important sources of information for innovation in innovative enterprises (EU member states, Norway and South Africa), 2002–2004

	Internal sources	External: market resources			External: institutional sources			External: other sources		
	Sources within your enterprise or enterprise group	Suppliers of equipment, materials, components or software	Clients or customers	Competitors or other enterprises in your sector	Consultants, commercial laboratories or private R&D institutes	Universities and technikons	Government and public research institutes	Conferences, trade fairs, exhibitions	Scientific journals and trade/ technical publications	Professional and industry associations
Cyprus	85.9	50.6	22.1	27.9	25.3	2.3	2.8	36.4	18.5	7.0
Luxembourg	64.9	36.8	36.6	16.8	8.7	5.4	4.4	26.3	19.1	14.0
Ireland	64.3	36.4	49.9	14.6	5.7	2.7	2.8	16.1	11.2	4.7
Finland	56.9	15.8	38.1	8.3	2.4	4.9	2.4	8.0	5.3	2.0
Denmark	56.2	27.6	32.4	8.1	7.7	3.3	0.5	5.7	5.4	2.7
Belgium	54.7	30.0	38.9	18.3	4.3	3.8	2.3	12.9	8.9	7.6
France	54.5	20.3	25.6	7.9	4.6	2.3	2.0	6.9	6.9	3.5
Germany	53.3	21.6	35.0	13.9	2.6	3.4	1.4	11.0	6.5	4.8
Norway	52.1	20.0	35.0	9.4	6.2	3.1	3.2	8.7	4.7	4.6
South Africa	49.3	24.3	34.5	12.6	3.9	5.2	3.4	2.2	3.8	8.6
Malta	48.6	21.5	27.8	16.0	4.9	2.8	–	16.7	10.4	5.6
Poland	48.0	19.7	32.5	20.8	–	3.5	4.2	22.2	19.2	–
Greece	46.2	42.6	25.5	17.5	10.2	4.4	2.3	31.9	21.5	8.1
EU-27	45.7	23.2	26.7	12.2	5.7	3.6	2.7	11.5	8.3	5.5
Spain	45.1	30.2	19.6	10.5	5.5	3.2	4.4	8.6	4.3	4.5
Netherlands	45.0	20.9	27.0	11.0	3.9	2.6	2.0	6.9	3.7	5.4

	Internal sources	External: market resources			External: institutional sources			External: other sources		
	Sources within your enterprise or enterprise group	Suppliers of equipment, materials, components or software	Clients or customers	Competitors or other enterprises in your sector	Consultants, commercial laboratories or private R&D institutes	Universities and technikons	Government and public research institutes	Conferences, trade fairs, exhibitions	Scientific journals and trade/ technical publications	Professional and industry associations
Hungary	41.7	23.4	28.2	17.7	6.5	4.7	1.2	12.6	9.9	5.5
Czech Republic	39.4	23.3	32.1	14.3	4.5	3.0	1.4	14.2	7.4	3.3
Romania	38.0	37.6	30.9	19.1	4.9	2.7	2.6	23.0	22.8	6.4
Slovakia	37.1	23.7	30.1	12.4	3.0	1.8	1.1	13.3	8.3	3.4
Italy	36.3	21.8	13.8	5.6	10.7	2.0	1.0	8.9	5.6	5.8
Estonia	34.1	22.6	25.6	11.3	4.2	3.3	2.1	14.0	5.5	2.3
Bulgaria	33.1	26.7	33.1	16.7	7.0	5.4	3.3	18.5	16.3	7.9
Lithuania	32.2	15.8	19.1	8.6	7.1	1.1	2.1	13.5	6.4	2.9
SA Rank (1-24)	**10**	**10**	**7**	**13**	**21**	**3**	**4**	**24**	**23**	**3**

Note:
The EU-27 data is a Eurostat estimate that excludes missing, confidential or unreliable data for the following countries: Latvia, Austria, Portugal, Slovenia, Sweden and the United Kingdom.

Source: All data, except for data pertaining to South Africa are from European Communities (2007c); South African data are from Appendix Table A1.17

Table 4.18 shows how the various countries rated the relative importance of various sources of information. There is considerable variation, and the overall picture is not as clear as in Figure 4.11. Although some of the new members of the EU appear to rate most sources of information for innovation fairly low, enterprises in Cyprus appear to rate their own and market sources highly, but regard the importance of universities and public research institutions as not as important or valuable. It is difficult to conclude that there is any discernible pattern distinguishing particular groups of countries. However, enterprises tended to rate their own sources of information, as well as suppliers and customers, quite highly. In general, consultants, universities and public research institutions are rated quite low, which calls into question some of the current thinking and exuberance about the importance of industry, university and public sector linkages for innovation activities within national systems of innovation.

Eurostat questions why innovative enterprises do not make more use of knowledge generated by universities and public research institutes. Eurostat asks whether the research generated by these institutions is 'too theoretical to be applied for industrial purposes' or if 'public research is too expensive for industry to afford?' (European Communities 2007c). Similar questions could be raised in South Africa.

Cooperation partners for innovation activities

Figure 4.12: Innovative collaborative partnerships by type of partner, 2002–2004

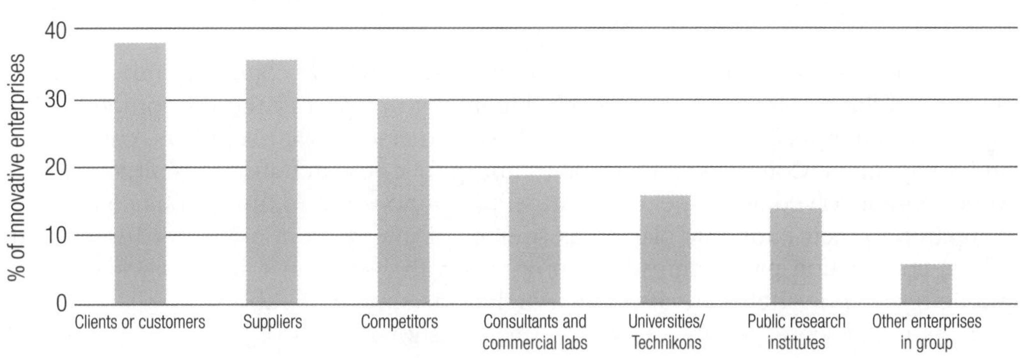

Source: Appendix Table A1.36

Table 4.19: Collaborative partnerships for innovation activities by type of partner (%), 2002–2004

Percentage of enterprises	Total	Industry	Services
Clients or customers	37.5	35.8	39.0
Suppliers of equipment, materials, components or software	35.0	34.6	35.4
Competitors or other enterprises in the sector	29.4	27.9	30.8
Consultants, commercial laboratories or private R&D institutes	18.2	24.1	13.0
Universities or technikons	15.5	23.6	8.3
Government or public research institutes	13.4	19.3	8.1
Other enterprises within the enterprise group	5.5	3.9	6.9

Source: Appendix Table A1.36

Private sector enterprises in South Africa are sometimes criticised for lacking cooperative linkages and partnerships with other organisations. However, Figures 4.12 and 4.13 and Tables 4.19 and 4.20 suggest that South African enterprises have relatively high intensities of cooperative linkages in innovation activities with other enterprises and institutions. Figure 4.12 shows that clients (or customers), suppliers and competitors (or other enterprises in the same sector) were the most important collaborative innovation partners. Collaborative partnerships with these three types of partners are slightly more prevalent in innovative services sector enterprises than in innovative industrial enterprises (see Table 4.19). The most common collaborative partnerships in the EU were suppliers (17%) and customers (14%); collaboration rates were higher in South Africa, with 35.0% for suppliers and 37.5% for customers (see Table 4.20).

Figure 4.13 shows that between 2002 and 2004, about 40% of innovative enterprises in South Africa were engaged in some sort of collaborative partnerships involving innovation activities, in comparison with 26% for the EU-27 average. In the EU, the proportion of innovative enterprises engaged in cooperative partnerships ranged from 13.0% in Italy to 56.1% in Lithuania (see Table 4.20). Lithuania, Slovenia, Finland, Sweden, Denmark and Poland all recorded higher proportions of cooperative linkages than South Africa. Austria, Germany and Italy appear to have the lowest rates of cooperative partnerships in innovative enterprises. Lithuania was the only country where more than half (56.1%) of innovative enterprises reported cooperative partnerships in innovation.

In the more detailed results for this question from individual countries, Table 4.20 shows that South Africa scores relatively highly with respect to the proportion of innovative enterprises that have collaborative partnerships with suppliers, customers and competitors. Consultants, universities and public research institutes all appear to be more involved as cooperative partners for innovation in the various countries compared to their fairly low placing as sources of information in Table 4.18. In South Africa, cooperation partnerships for innovation with consultants, universities and public research institutes are also much higher (as shown in Table 4.20) than the corresponding scores for sources of information shown in Table 4.18.

Table 4.20: Different types of cooperation partners of enterprises by country, as a percentage of innovative enterprises, 2002–2004 (EU member states and selected countries including South Africa)

	All types of cooperation	Other enterprises within your enterprise group	Suppliers of equipment, materials, components or software	Clients or customers	Competitors or other enterprises in your sector	Consultants, commercial labs or private R&D institutes	Universities and technikons	Government and public research institutes
Lithuania	56.1	16.7	45.5	34.5	25.4	24.9	12.0	9.6
Slovenia	47.3	15.0	37.5	33.0	20.4	19.7	19.5	13.2
Finland	44.4	23.5	40.8	41.4	34.2	32.7	33.2	26.4
Denmark	42.8	17.4	28.4	27.8	14.8	19.0	13.7	6.9
Sweden	42.8	17.2	32.0	27.9	10.8	19.8	17.4	6.4
Poland	42.2	12.7	28.2	16.4	8.5	7.9	6.2	8.7
South Africa	**39.9**	**5.5**	**35.0**	**37.5**	**29.4**	**18.2**	**15.5**	**13.4**
France	39.5	16.6	25.7	19.8	14.1	12.7	10.1	7.3
Netherlands	39.4	17.5	29.7	21.8	12.3	15.0	12.4	9.4
Latvia	38.8	6.1	32.6	28.7	25.1	18.3	13.8	12.2
Czech Republic	38.4	13.5	30.7	26.1	15.3	15.0	13.1	7.4
Slovakia	37.7	14.0	31.7	30.2	21.2	18.6	14.8	11.4
Cyprus	37.0	5.9	24.5	4.2	12.8	16.9	2.2	1.7
Hungary	36.8	10.1	26.2	19.6	13.6	12.6	13.7	5.0
Belgium	35.7	16.9	25.9	21.2	9.5	15.0	13.2	9.2
Estonia	34.8	15.6	23.3	22.9	18.5	10.0	8.6	6.1
Norway	33.2	14.0	23.1	22.3	11.9	20.3	14.8	16.3
Ireland	32.3	16.7	23.2	25.2	6.0	10.1	10.1	5.7

	All types of cooperation	Other enterprises within your enterprise group	Suppliers of equipment, materials, components or software	Clients or customers	Competitors or other enterprises in your sector	Consultants, commercial labs or private R&D institutes	Universities and technikons	Government and public research institutes
Malta	31.9	16.0	22.2	16.7	5.6	13.9	4.2	4.2
United Kingdom	30.6	14.8	22.6	22.3	11.1	12.6	10.0	7.6
Luxenbourg	30.5	20.3	24.0	22.2	14.9	11.0	10.0	8.2
Iceland	29.1	5.3	19.8	19.8	13.8	6.7	5.0	13.1
EU-27	25.5	9.5	16.5	13.9	8.3	8.9	8.8	5.7
Greece	24.0	3.6	11.0	7.8	11.3	6.5	6.4	2.5
Bulgaria	22.0	4.9	16.2	13.4	7.6	7.5	6.0	3.9
Portugal	19.4	5.7	13.9	11.5	6.8	8.7	7.5	4.8
Spain	18.2	3.8	9.5	4.2	3.0	4.1	4.7	5.2
Romania	17.5	8.7	13.8	10.0	6.6	4.9	3.7	4.3
Austria	17.4	8.2	7.5	7.8	3.9	7.3	10.0	5.2
Germany	16.0	5.2	7.0	8.1	4.3	2.9	8.5	4.1
Italy	13.0	3.0	7.3	5.1	4.8	6.4	4.7	1.5
SA Rank (1–30)	7	24	4	2	2	9	4	3

Source: All data, except for data pertaining to South Africa are from European Communities (2007c); South African data are from Appendix Table A1.36

Figure 4.13: Share of enterprises with cooperation partners, by country, 2002–2004 (EU member states and selected countries, including South Africa)

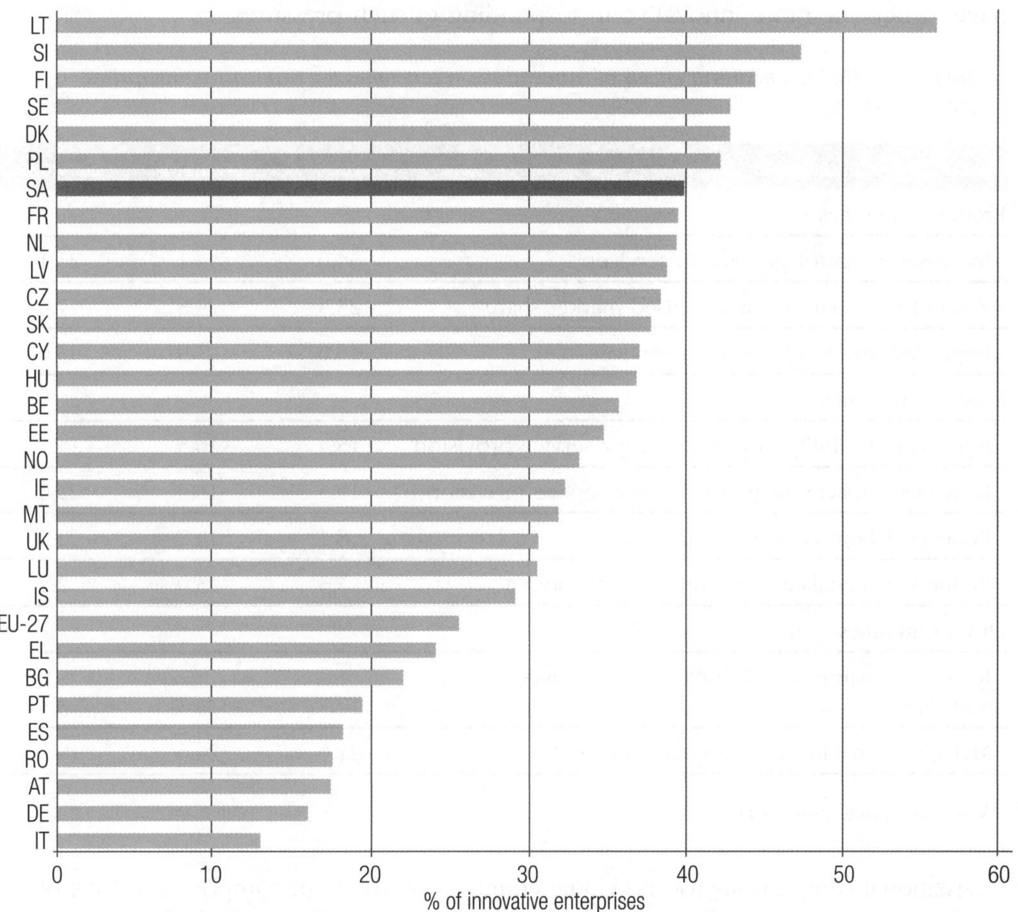

Source: All data, except for data pertaining to South Africa are from European Communities (2007a); South African data are from Appendix Table A1.36

Effects of innovation during the period 2002–2004

The Innovation Survey included a question that required innovative enterprises to qualitatively assess and classify the levels of success of their innovation activities (both product and process innovations) in various market and operational outcomes. Improved quality of goods and services was cited as a highly important effect of innovation by about 46% of innovative enterprises (Table 4.21) and was more important for industrial enterprises (49.2%) than for service enterprises (42.8%). Increasing the range of goods and services was also an important outcome for 34.3% of enterprises (44.9% for industrial enterprises), while entering new markets or increasing market share appeared less important and was cited as a highly important effect by only 22.8% of innovative enterprises. Increased capacity of production or service provision was cited as the most important effect of process innovation by 19.1% of innovative enterprises, followed by improved flexibility of production or service provision (15.1%). Other highly important effects of innovation were meeting government regulatory requirements (21.4% of innovators) and reducing environmental impacts or improving health and safety (12.8%). With South Africa tightening up on environmental regulations and health and safety in the workplace, and with the introduction of various other pieces of legislation (such as black economic empowerment and employment equity), it is expected that enterprises will have to become more innovative in responding to such pressures.

Table 4.21: Highly important effects of innovation on outcomes for innovative enterprises, 2002–2004 (%)

Percentage of enterprises	Total	Industry	Services
Product outcomes			
Increased range of goods and services	34.0	44.1	25.1
Entered new markets or increased market share	23.4	29.8	17.8
Improved quality of goods or services	45.6	47.9	43.6
Process outcomes			
Improved flexibility of production or service provision	15.4	16.5	14.5
Increased capacity of production or service provision	19.5	16.6	22.0
Reduced labour costs per unit output	8.1	14.7	2.2
Reduced materials and energy per unit output	7.3	13.0	2.2
Other outcomes			
Reduced environmental impacts or improved health and safety	12.7	23.3	3.3
Met governmental regulatory requirements	21.6	24.6	18.9

Source: Appendix Table A1.11

International comparisons for individual countries on the highly important effects of product innovations are shown in Table 4.22. South Africa lies towards the middle of the listing and has roughly the same scores as the average for the EU-27. As in the EU-27, the most frequently cited effect of product innovation in South Africa was improved quality of goods and services. The second most important effect of product innovation in both the EU-27 and South Africa was 'increased range of goods and services', which was a highly important effect for just over a third (34.3%) of all innovative enterprises. It was only in Latvia (77.3%) and France (58.6%) that enterprises ranked 'entered new markets or increased market share' as the top effect of innovation. In the EU-27, only 29.4% of innovative enterprises ranked this outcome as the most important effect of product innovation, compared with 22.8% in South Africa.

With respect to the effects of process-oriented effects of innovation, both South African and European enterprises generally reported a lower frequency of highly important outcomes than for product innovation. On all four process outcomes, South Africa's share of highly important outcomes ranked lower than the EU-27 average ratings. On the three other effects (such as reducing environmental impacts or improved health and safety), South Africa was closer to the EU-27 average. In terms of meeting regulatory requirements, 21.4% of innovative enterprises in South Africa rated this as a highly important outcome, compared with 18.4% of enterprises in the EU-27 countries. Just over 60% of innovative enterprises in Latvia rated meeting regulatory requirements as a highly important outcome of innovation activities.

Table 4.22: Percentage share of enterprises engaged in innovation activity that cited the various effects of innovation as highly important, 2004

	Product-orientated effects			Process-orientated effects				Other effects	
	Increased range of goods and services	Entered new markets or increased market share	Improved quality of goods and services	Improved flexibility of production or service provision	Increased capacity of production or service provision	Reduced labour costs per unit output	Reduced materials and energy per unit output	Reduced enviromental impacts or improved health and safety	Met regulation requirements
Latvia	76.1	77.3	74.8	72.5	71.9	60.2	56.5	45.5	60.5
France	52.6	58.6	49.5	30.9	32.3	34.9	15.9	19.1	29.1
Luxenbourg	48.2	34.5	53.2	37.6	30.3	16.3	7.6	15.3	37.6
Bulgaria	42.7	32.9	45.6	22.8	23.4	18.9	17.0	20.7	26.7
Ireland	40.7	32.8	32.7	22.1	23.5	19.3	10.1	11.1	13.8
Czech Republic	40.6	25.7	40.0	26.8	25.3	16.9	13.7	15.5	7.9
Netherlands	38.8	33.1	46.9	33.9	30.5	20.9	12.8	12.3	14.2
Slovenia	38.1	32.2	49.6	30.8	31.0	28.4	17.2	18.6	15.5
Germany	38.0	31.7	37.7	27.5	19.9	15.1	9.5	10.3	10.3
United Kingdom	37.1	36.5	40.9	23.6	23.2			15.5	25.7
Greece	36.6	29.7	58.8	43.0	40.0	13.7	9.3	21.2	18.6
Estonia	35.2	33.2	34.2	22.2	22.8	15.2	12.3	9.2	15.6
Belgium	34.8	33.3	46.6	24.7	25.8	16.6	8.8	13.3	14.4
South Africa	**34.3**	**22.8**	**45.9**	**15.1**	**19.1**	**8.0**	7.3	**12.8**	**21.4**
EU-27	34.2	29.4	37.8	24.7	24.4	15.6	8.4	14.1	18.4
Slovakia	34.1	25.3	34.8	27.1	24.5	6.8	8.8	12.2	13.7
Poland	33.4	26.7	35.1	21.1	23.2	15.0	12.0	19.2	25.4

	Product-orientated effects			Process-orientated effects				Other effects	
	Increased range of goods and services	Entered new markets or increased market share	Improved quality of goods and services	Improved flexibility of production or service provision	Increased capacity of production or service provision	Reduced labour costs per unit output	Reduced materials and energy per unit output	Reduced enviromental impacts or improved health and safety	Met regulation requirements
Hungary	31.5	19.6	35.1	20.9	21.9	4.1	6.2	13.2	19.4
Sweden	31.2	19.8	29.3	16.3	21.6	17.9	7.1	9.7	12.9
Iceland	30.5	19.3	23.4	16.0	15.3	13.8	5.7	2.9	7.2
Spain	28.1	19.6	35.2	25.2	32.5	12.7	7.0	16.2	23.0
Cyprus	26.6	17.1	29.8	64.7	56.9	27.0	8.2	29.8	46.8
Italy	25.4	15.1	34.1	18.7	23.2	18.1	4.4	14.7	19.4
Austria	25.4	20.8	35.3	23.1	19.0	7.0	4.9	8.2	13.5
Finland	25.3	21.6	24.2	15.9	17.1	13.0	5.9	7.2	9.8
Denmark	25.1	19.7	26.7	21.9	18.4	14.5	6.7	8.7	12.6
Lithuania	24.1	20.8	27.9	19.6	21.1	9.3	5.9	8.8	20.8
Norway	23.1	16.2	23.6	13.5	13.4	10.0	4.3	8.1	12.4
Malta	21.5	19.4	21.5	17.4	15.3	6.9	4.9	11.8	18.8
Romania	17.1	29.1	37.1	28.6	32.3	15.5		17.7	14.9
Portugal	9.7	15.4	9.5	8.8	6.1	17.9	25.8	12.6	12.5
SA Rank (1–30)	**15**	**17**	**9**	**28**	**23**	**25**	**17**	**16**	**9**

Source: All data, except for data pertaining to South Africa are from European Communities (2007a); South African data are from Appendix Table A1.11

Figure 4.14: Innovative enterprises that introduced organisational innovation and rated various results as highly important, 2002–2004

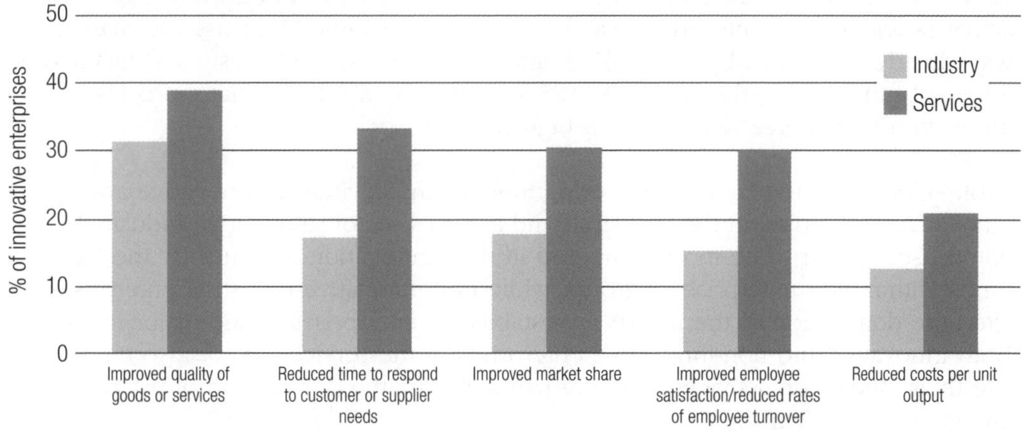

Source: Appendix Table A1.32

Innovative enterprises that introduced organisational innovations were asked to report on the most important outcomes associated with their innovation activities. Figure 4.14 shows that for 34.9% of innovative enterprises, improving the quality of their goods and services was the most important outcome. This was followed by reducing the time taken to respond to customer or supplier needs, which was reported by 25.2% of innovative enterprises. Only 16.5% of innovative enterprises considered that reducing the cost per unit output was highly important.

Factors hampering innovation activities in 2002–2004

A total of 18.9% of innovative enterprises experienced problems with certain innovation activities and reported that these activities were seriously delayed during 2002–2004 (see Table 4.23). Some 10% of innovative enterprises abandoned innovation projects in the concept stage, while 12.3% reported abandoning innovation projects once they had already begun.

Table 4.23: Enterprises with innovation activity that cited problems with their innovation activity, 2002–2004

	Total	Industry	Services
Number of innovative enterprises			
Abandoned in the concept stage	1 715	905	810
Abandoned after the activity or project was begun	1 999	855	1 144
Seriously delayed	3 070	1 164	1 906
Percentage of innovative enterprises			
Abandoned in the concept stage	10.5	11.8	9.4
Abandoned after the activity or project was begun	12.3	11.2	13.3
Seriously delayed	18.9	15.2	22.1

Source: Appendix Table A1.19

Enterprises were asked to rate the degree to which a number of specific factors hampered their innovation activities during the three-year period 2002–2004. Table 4.24 shows that 26.2% of all enterprises indicated that developing innovative activities within their enterprises was hampered or restrained because the market was already dominated by established enterprises. The second most cited factor was a lack of funds within the enterprise (25.3%), and the third was that the costs of innovation were perceived to be too high (20.4%).

Table 4.25 details the factors hampering innovation activities in innovative and non-innovative enterprises in the industrial and services sector. Innovative industrial enterprises appear to be most hampered in their innovation activities by the lack of funds within their enterprise or group, while non-innovative industrial enterprises cited the domination of the market by established enterprises as the major factor. Both innovative and non-innovative enterprises in the services sector also tended to cite their innovation activities as being hampered by the domination of established enterprises in their market.

Table 4.24: Highly important factors that hampered innovation activities of all enterprises (%), 2002–2004

Percentage of enterprises	Industry (Total)	Services (Total)	*Total	**Total Innovative	**Total Non-innovative
Cost factors					
Lack of funds within the enterprise or group	26.0	24.8	25.3	29.1	21.3
Lack of finance from sources outside the enterprise	16.6	14.4	15.4	18.7	11.9
Innovation costs too high	18.1	22.2	20.4	22.8	17.7
Knowledge factors					
Lack of qualified personnel	16.9	16.9	17	20.4	13.2
Lack of information on technology	8.3	1.0	4.3	3.5	5.1
Lack of information of markets	5.2	2.8	3.8	3.3	4.4
Difficulty in finding cooperation partners	11.2	5.6	8.1	4.0	12.5
Market factors					
Market dominated by established enterprises	20.5	30.7	26.2	23.2	29.3
Uncertain demand for innovative goods or services	6.5	12.6	9.9	9.5	10.3
Reasons not to innovate					
No need due to prior innovations	5.1	3.3	4.1	3.0	5.2
No need because of no demand for innovations	4.3	12.9	9.0	0.7	18.0

Note:
*a. *Total includes all enterprises.*
*b. ** Total = percentage of innovative or non-innovative enterprises in both services and industry.*

Source: Appendix Tables A1.20, A1.21 and A1.22

Table 4.25: Highly important factors that hampered innovation activities of innovative and non-innovative enterprises (%), 2002–2004

Percentage of enterprises	Industry		Services		Total	
	Innovative	Non-innovative	Innovative	Non-innovative	Innovative	Non-innovative
Cost factors						
Lack of funds within the enterprise or group	32.0	18.6	26.6	23.2	29.1	21.3
Lack of finance from sources outside the enterprise	16.3	17.0	20.7	8.3	18.7	11.9
Innovation costs too high	15.4	21.3	29.3	15.2	22.8	17.7
Knowledge factors						
Lack of qualified personnel	15.0	19.2	25.1	9.0	20.4	13.2
Lack of information on technology	5.9	11.3	1.3	0.7	3.5	5.1
Lack of information of markets	1.0	10.2	5.2	0.3	3.3	4.4
Difficulty in finding cooperation partners	5.4	18.4	2.8	8.3	4.0	12.5
Market factors						
Market dominated by established enterprises	14.5	27.7	30.9	30.4	23.2	29.3
Uncertain demand for innovative goods or services	3.3	10.5	14.9	10.2	9.5	10.3
Reasons not to innovate						
No need due to prior innovations	1.2	9.8	4.7	1.9	3.0	5.2
No need because of no demand for innovations	1.0	8.2	0.4	25.0	0.7	18.0

Source: Appendix Tables A1.20, A1.21 and A1.22

Figure 4.15 shows what percentage of EU and South African innovation enterprises considered high costs as a factor hampering innovation activity. South African enterprises appear in the middle cluster, with 22.8% of enterprises citing high costs as a factor hampering innovation. The highest proportion of enterprises that felt that the costs of innovation were too high were from Spain and Greece (40% and 39% of respondents respectively), while respondents from Finland (11%) and Portugal (10%) indicated that their enterprises were not really hampered by this factor.

Figure 4.15: Share of innovative enterprises that cited the high cost of innovation as a major factor hampering innovation, 2002–2004 (EU member states and selected countries, including South Africa)

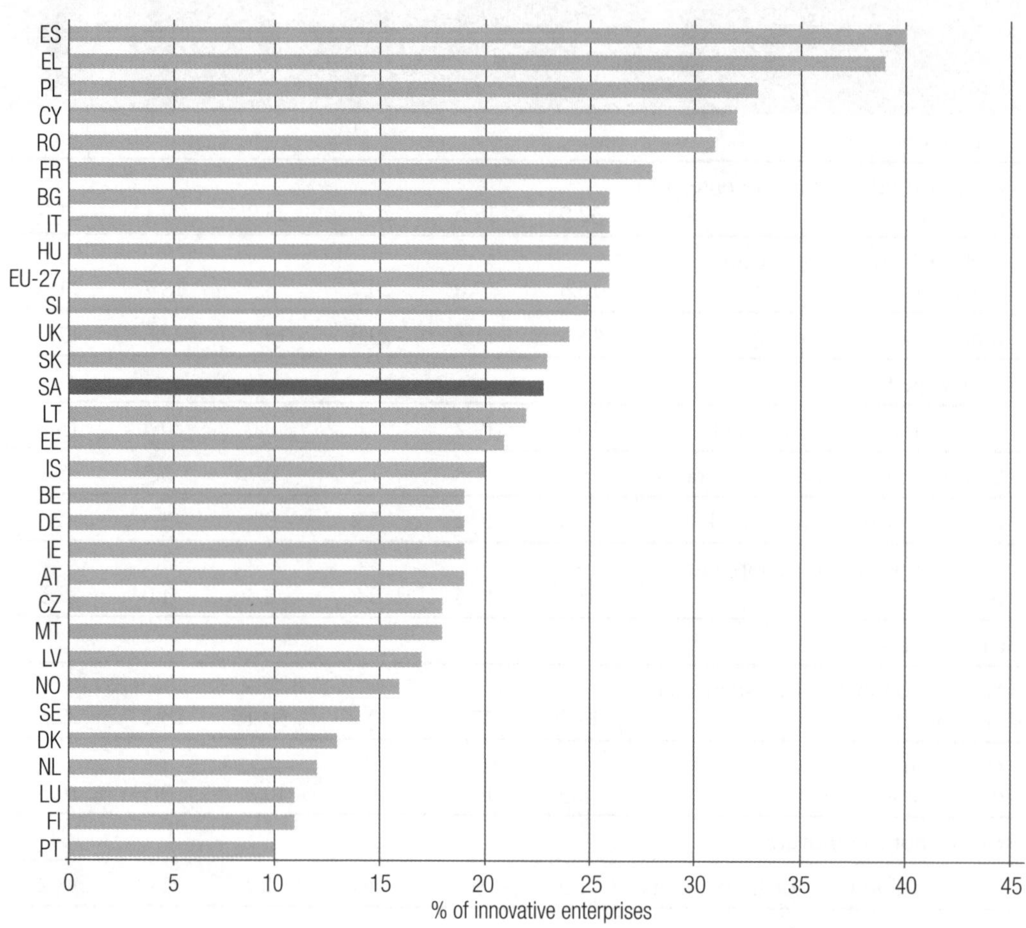

Source: All data, except for data pertaining to South Africa are estimates from European Communities (2007b); South African data are from Appendix Tables A1.20 and A1.21

Figure 4.16 shows what percentage of EU and South African innovation enterprises considered lack of finances from sources outside their enterprises as a factor hampering innovation activity.

These sources would also include public funding for R&D/innovation activities. Again, South African enterprises rank about mid-way among the countries (with 18.7% of innovative enterprises citing lack of finances as a factor hampering innovation), alongside Italy and Iceland. It appears that innovation activities of respondents from enterprises in Greece (31.9%), Romania (30.1%) and Spain (26.8%) are most hampered by the lack of finances from sources outside the enterprise. Enterprises in the Netherlands (9.8%), Denmark (9.2%) and Luxembourg (5.3%) appear to be least affected by this factor.

Figure 4.16: Share of innovative enterprises that cited the lack of external sources of finance as a major factor hampering innovation, 2002–2004 (EU member states and selected countries, including South Africa)

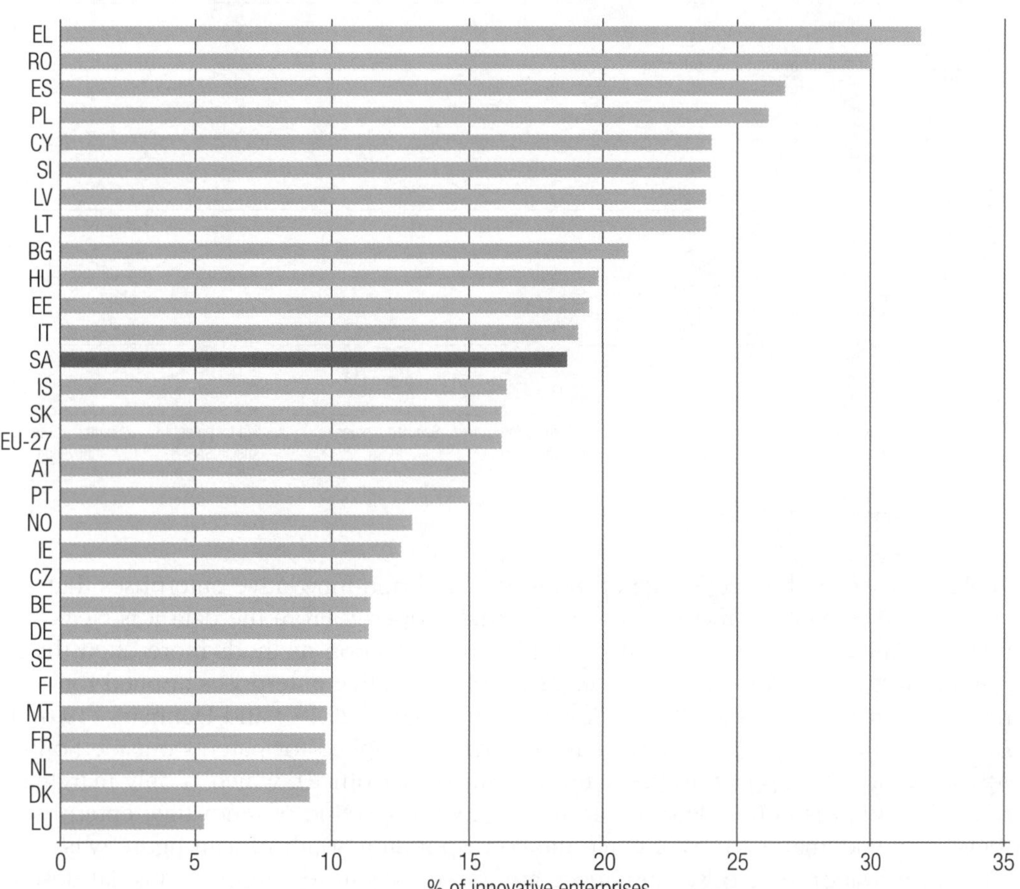

Source: All data, except for data pertaining to South Africa are estimates from European Communities (2007b); South African data are from Appendix Tables A1.20 and A1.21

Intellectual property rights

Almost 11% of innovative enterprises registered a trademark between 2002 and 2004, while about 5% claimed copyright (see Figure 4.17). A total of 3.1% of innovative enterprises secured a patent in South Africa, while 2.5% applied for a patent outside South Africa. In response to a special South African question that was not used in the equivalent section in CIS4, about 1.7% of innovative enterprises granted licences or intellectual property rights, originating from their own innovation activities, to third parties.

Figure 4.17: Enterprises with innovation activities that made use of intellectual property rights (IPR), 2002–2004

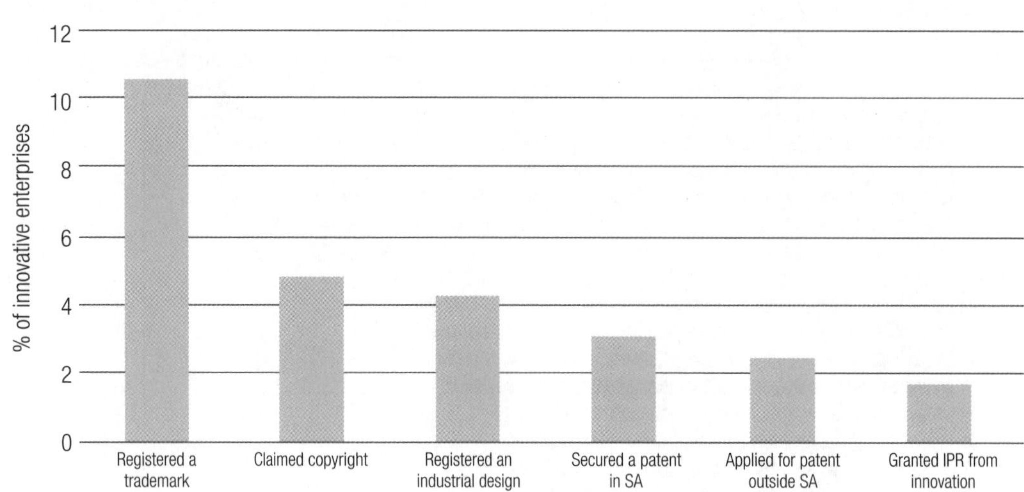

Source: Appendix Tables A1.26, A1.27 and A1.28

Table 4.26 shows the percentage of innovative and non-innovative enterprises that made use of protection methods for intellectual property. From the data it is clear that innovative enterprises made use of the four protection methods more often than non-innovative enterprises. In France, 22.2% of innovative enterprises applied for patents between 2002 and 2004, followed by Germany (20.1%) and Denmark (19.6%). In South Africa, only 2.5% of innovative enterprises applied for patents outside South Africa (while 3.1% applied to the South African patent office), which is only marginally more than Cyprus (1.0%). France had the highest proportion of innovative enterprises registering trademarks (33.5%), while the corresponding South African figure was 10.6%. Innovation enterprises in Greece are the leaders in registering industrial design (24.8% of innovative enterprises), whereas only 4.3% of South African innovative enterprises registered designs. Luxembourg had the highest percentage of innovative enterprises claiming copyright (12.3%), compared with 4.8% of South African enterprises. The different patterns of protection methods used in the various countries are interesting and reflect differences of culture and business practice.

Table 4.26: Protection methods for intellectual property used by enterprises, as a percentage of innovative enterprises and as a percentage of non-innovative enterprises, by country, 2002–2004 (EU-27 member states, Norway and South Africa), 2002–2004

	Innovative enterprises				Non-innovative enterprises			
	Applied for a patent	Registered a trademark	Registered an industrial design	Claimed copyright	Applied for a patent	Registered a trademark	Registered an industrial design	Claimed copyright
France	22.2	33.5	18.4	9.7	3.2	10.7	4.5	2.3
Germany	20.1	19.1	18.0	8.0	4.0	5.1	4.7	3.0
Denmark	19.6	25.0	9.8	9.5	3.2	7.1	3.2	4.8
Finland	18.2	19.9	9.6	2.3	0.9	2.9	0.7	0.1
Norway	17.1	22.1	8.6	11.5	2.0	4.7	0.9	1.9
Ireland	16.9	5.1	20.7	9.3	0.9	0.6	3.3	1.0
Netherlands	14.4	17.3	5.7	5.1	0.8	3.7	0.5	0.7
Italy	13.4	7.3	15.8	2.1	2.2	2.0	6.4	0.7
Spain	11.8	21.5	10.2	1.7	1.9	6.1	2.3	0.2
Belgium	11.0	13.4	4.3	3.5	0.5	3.8	0.6	0.4
Malta	9.0	7.6	3.5	c	c	1.3	c	c
Lithuania	8.9	6.4	22.8	6.4	0.6	0.1	4.5	0.5
Luxembourg	8.8	9.4	21.0	12.3	2.1	2.4	6.5	1.8
Bulgaria	7.6	18.5	6.8	3.9	0.8	2.8	0.4	0.3
Portugal	7.0	19.1	4.3	3.3	1.9	7.0	1.2	0.8
Romania	6.9	7.4	17.1	3.4	0.5	0.9	2.2	0.3
Hungary	6.5	4.8	9.5	1.9	0.7	0.4	2.5	0.7
Estonia	5.5	2.0	18.6	2.9	1.0	0.2	5.0	0.1
Czech Republic	5.1	7.9	20.8	4.3	0.7	1.3	5.9	0.9
Poland	4.9	18.8	9.8	6.7	0.3	3.1	0.9	0.6
Slovakia	3.7	7.1	18.4	6.0	0.6	1.1	5.5	1.4
Greece	3.0	5.5	24.8	9.0	0.0	1.6	8.9	2.6
South Africa	*****2.5**	**10.6**	**4.3**	**4.8**	*****0.2**	**2.9**	**0.0**	**0.5**
Cyprus	1.0	4.8	1.0	1.3	0.0	0.0	0.0	0.0
SA Rank (1-24)	**23**	**12**	**20**	**12**	**21**	**10**	**22**	**16**

Note:
c confidential data

**** Applied for a patent outside South Africa*

Source: Data for the EU-27 are from European Communities (2007d); South African data are from Appendix Table A1.28

CHAPTER 5

Conclusions and policy recommendations

'All wealthy nations have the following in common: free markets, the rule of law and technology-based innovation' (Chait 2007). South Africa has all these characteristics, and there is a healthy outlook for the future of the economy. However, the country faces several pressing problems, particularly the underdevelopment of disadvantaged communities and associated poverty, widespread crime and violence and the HIV/AIDS pandemic. These problems are difficult and complex, and will require innovative solutions involving technology, education and appropriate approaches to the social aspects of these problems. One thing that is clear, however, is that economic growth and employment opportunities are an important basis for providing solutions to social problems. It is a widely held belief that innovation is a primary driver of economic growth, so this report will attempt to provide some recommendations for better understanding the processes of innovation and the means of encouraging the further development and growth of innovation in the private sector.

It is acknowledged that countries are still learning to understand the determinants and processes of innovation. In contrast, the concept of R&D and its measurement in R&D surveys is far better understood. This will be readily admitted by the experienced practitioners that administer national R&D and innovation surveys and participate in the meetings, task teams and discussion groups of the OECD National Experts on Science and Technology Indicators (NESTI). A useful outcome of innovation surveys is that they provide common ground for discussing issues that affect innovation in countries. Such discussions help guide further understanding of the dynamics and processes of innovation.

In this study, we surveyed innovation only in the private sector, and the innovation survey instrument we used is still fairly blunt, providing limited insight into the extent, costs and types of innovation in the country and the linkages between them. This is South Africa's first official innovation survey based on a proper random stratified sample from the official business register. It is not strictly comparable with the innovation survey covering the period 1998–2000 (Oerlemans et al. 2004), because that survey was based on a sample from a commercial source, and the questions used in the questionnaire were mostly different from those used in the present survey. It is difficult to draw policy conclusions based on a single official innovation survey, but some more obvious conclusions can be reached.

The first two innovation surveys in the EU (CIS1 and CIS2) were carried out in the early 1990s and were largely a learning exercise for most countries that undertook them. Countries had to learn the suggested methodology and apply it to their local systems. They also had to learn to interpret the results of the surveys. Systems for statistical collection are fairly similar across EU countries, and they receive considerable assistance from Eurostat in obtaining conformance between countries. Nevertheless, there are still many unexplained and sometimes puzzling differences between the results obtained for the various countries (Abramovsky et al. 2004).

In the case of South Africa, this is the first government-commissioned national innovation survey (commissioned by the Department of Science and Technology).

It is also the first time that the survey has been undertaken using the official business register of the national statistical agency (Statistics South Africa), as recommended in Eurostat's CIS4 methodology. The survey was administered as closely as possible in accordance with the core questionnaire and guidelines prescribed for EU members in order to provide direct comparability with the results from other countries. Because administering the CIS4 in South Africa is a novel experience, however, we have also had to learn along the way, as did the Europeans in CIS1 and CIS2. However, South Africa does not have the benefit of the centralised and standardised statistical systems and procedures that are being implemented in Europe. Some of the South African procedures are quite different from those in Europe. For example, our official size class classification procedures for enterprises are very different from those in Europe. Compared to European countries, the willingness of South African enterprises to engage in surveys (apart from official Statistics South Africa surveys) is very low. It required considerable persistence to obtain the eventual response rate to the Innovation Survey. Low response rates generally detract from the generalisability of survey results to disaggregated levels below national and major sectoral totals. Nevertheless, for a developing country, the survey should be regarded as a success, and subsequent innovation surveys will benefit from the learning experience and build the database resource, as has been the experience of CeSTII with successive R&D surveys.

The outputs of innovation surveys in both developed and developing countries are seldom used to design innovation policy instruments (Mani 2007). Mani (2007) and Arundel (2006) both report that innovation surveys have not been effectively used for policy purposes. In an evaluation of 162 academic papers using CIS data and information, Arundel (2006) found that only 13% made any policy recommendations. However, Mani believes that the results of innovation surveys in developing countries should be used to point out any systemic failures in innovation activities in the country. We discuss some of the implications and policy recommendations arising from the results of the South African Innovation Survey 2005, given the limitations associated with having the results of only a single survey in the country. However, the richness comes from having undertaken an internationally comparable survey, the results of which are readily comparable with the results of innovation surveys in many other countries. In interpreting the South African Innovation Survey 2005, the local relevance of the findings must be taken into account, for instance, their relevance to the implementation of the Small Business Amendment Act of 2003.

Innovation is no longer regarded as the outcome only of the performance of R&D, and it is more common for a variety of non-R&D activities and expenditures to result in innovation outcomes. Activities that lead to innovation can include the acquisition of machinery, equipment, software and knowledge from outside the enterprise in the form of licences, patents or other know-how. Public funding has traditionally been provided for S&T and R&D activities in South Africa. Intramural R&D accounts for only 20% of innovation expenditure, although 51.7% of innovative enterprises engage in R&D. Public funds do not appear to have much penetration into the activities of innovative enterprises in most of the countries for which such data are available, despite the best intentions of governments to stimulate innovation through funding. The reason may be that innovation is part of the business activities of successful enterprises, which are reluctant to seek public funding if, in doing so, they risk disclosing secret information to their competition. Enterprises appear to be more open about engaging in publicly funded R&D where the application of activities is possibly less obvious to those outside the business. However, government should note the low percentage of innovative enterprises receiving public funds in South Africa compared with EU countries. This finding suggests that, in consultation with industry, the current public funding programmes could be intensified and more widely publicised.

What is to be made of South Africa's relatively high rate of innovation activity compared with European countries? The high rate of innovation was noted in the previous innovation survey undertaken by the University of Pretoria in partnership with the Eindhoven University of Technology covering the period 1998–2000. The extent of national innovation activities measured in innovation surveys is entirely dependent on the collective self-assessment by enterprises of whether or not they are innovative. This assessment is partly determined by the national psyche and perceptions about how innovative and inventive the society and its enterprises actually are, and the levels of business confidence in a country. The rate of innovation is also directly affected by the challenges and changes in the national business environment. In the case of South Africa, in particular, substantial new policies and regulations are changing the ways in which enterprises conduct their business. These changes range from compliance with equity and BEE regulations to stricter environmental regulation and adherence to international standards. Indeed, more than 21% of innovative enterprises in South Africa reported that a highly important effect of their innovation activity was to meet government regulatory requirements. It should also be noted that according to the Business Confidence Index of the South African Chamber of Business (SACOB), business confidence levels increased sharply between 2002 and 2004. Business confidence levels remained high during the time of the survey. When business confidence levels are high, enterprises are more likely to invest in innovative new ventures and activities. The levels of confidence in the economic climate in a country will also positively affect respondents' perceptions of levels of innovation in their enterprises.

It is clear that expenditure on innovation activities results in the sale of new and improved products for enterprises. Enterprises invested R27.8 billion in innovation activities in 2004, including intramural R&D expenditure of R5.7 billion and extramural R&D expenditure of R2.2 billion. In the same year, they grossed R67.8 billion from the sale of products that were new to the market, and a total of R147 billion from the sale of products new to the enterprise (but not new to the market). These returns on prior investment in innovation activities do not include the benefits to the enterprise of innovative processes or organisational innovations. Businesses and government need to be made aware of these tangible benefits of innovation in order to further encourage innovation. The close similarity between the estimate of intramural expenditure on R&D obtained in the 2005 Innovation Survey (R5.7 billion) and the 2004/05 R&D Survey for the equivalent business sectors (R5.9 billion) is encouraging. In most countries, the reported amounts of expenditure in these two surveys varied quite widely (Mortensen 2007).

A particular area of focus of policies designed to nurture national systems of innovation has been the linkages between institutions, particularly universities, and industry. The results of innovation surveys both in South Africa and abroad suggest that such linkages may not be as important sources of information and collaboration for innovation as they had been considered. The most important links and collaborations for businesses are with other enterprises, including customers, suppliers and even competitors. These linkages form part of the market-driven business environment of enterprises and are more difficult for government to stimulate. It appears that South Africa is far from unusual in this regard, and the lack of innovation-related linkages between public and private sector institutions in the EU is noted (European Communities 2007c).

It is apparent that it is more important for government to create an enabling environment for innovation than to attempt to boost innovation through funding programmes. For example, establishing a more efficient system for South African patents could be part of such an enabling environment. Recognition in the form of media coverage of innovations and awards for innovative enterprises also appears to be a means of encouraging further innovation.

In the case of Brazil, one of the government interventions in technology policy in the 1970s and 1980s was to place restrictions on importing foreign technology in order to stimulate the development of local technology (Mani 2001). Ironically, the sanctions that resulted from the response of the international community to the South African apartheid regime had a similar effect on local technology development in this country (although sanctions-busting was supported by government at the time). Most of the restrictions on importing technology into Brazil were lifted as part of the liberalisation strategy during the 1990s, which led to a general increase in expenditure on foreign technology agreements and imports (Mani 2001). In a recent paper, however, economists argue that import tariffs in Brazil are still too high and should be gradually eliminated on capital goods and intermediate imports in order to facilitate access to productivity-enhancing technologies embodied in imports (De Brito Cruz & De Mello 2006). South Africa has relatively moderate import tariffs, as recommended by the World Trade Organization, and this generally helps stimulate technology imports and innovation in the country.

The results of the South African Innovation Survey 2005 clearly show that South African enterprises have much in common with enterprises in many European countries. For example, the close similarities between the results for South Africa and the EU-27 profile on questions such as the factors hampering innovation and the most important outcomes of innovation for enterprises (see Tables 4.22, 4.24 and 4.25 and Figures 4.14, 4.15 and 4.16). This is important to note and indicates that, on the one hand, South Africa can learn much from innovation-support policies that are applied in the EU and does not necessarily have to do things differently. On the other hand, it is clear that the South African Innovation Survey 2005 results have considerable local relevance and can provide insight into many of the issues that concern policymakers, such as the apparent limited collaboration in innovation between public institutions and private enterprises.

Finally, the results of the 2005 Innovation Survey clearly indicate that South Africa is not a 'technology colony' dependent on foreign technology. Most innovations are developed by enterprises in South Africa, and the influence of foreign partners is similar to the experience of other countries. South Africans should stop berating themselves and acknowledge that our industry and services are among the most innovative in the world.

REFERENCES AND ADDITIONAL READING

Abramovsky L, Jaumandreu J, Kremp E & Peter B (2004) National differences in innovation behaviour: facts and explanations. Results using basic statistics from CIS3 for France, Germany, Spain and United Kingdom. Paper from the European Commission Fifth Framework Programme-funded Research Project on Innovation and Employment in European Firms: Macroeconometric Evidence

Arundel A (2006) Innovation survey indicators: Any progress since 1996? Paper presented at the Blue Sky Conference, Ottawa

Australian Bureau of Statistics (2006) *Innovation in Australian Business 2005*. Sydney: Australian Bureau of Statistics

Blankley W & Kaplan D (1997) *Innovation patterns in South African manufacturing firms: Report on the survey of innovative activity in South African manufacturing firms.* Pretoria: Foundation for Research Development, and Cape Town: Industrial Strategy Project

Chait G (2007) Zim's only hope lies in restoring global funders' confidence, *Cape Argus*, 20 July

Chudnovsky D, Lopez A & Pupato G (2006) Innovation and productivity in developing countries: A study of Argentine manufacturing firms' behaviour (1992–2001). *Research Policy* 35(2): 266–288

De Brito Cruz CH & De Mello L (2006) *Boosting innovation performance in Brazil.* Economics Department Working Paper No. 532. Economics Department, OECD. Paris

Department of Enterprise, Trade and Investment (2006) *UK Innovation Survey 2005: Northern Ireland results*. Belfast: Department of Enterprise, Trade and Investment

DST (Department of Science and Technology) (2006) *National Survey of Research and Experimental Development (R&D) 2004/05*. Cape Town: Centre for Science, Technology and Innovation Indicators (CeSTII) for DST

EC (European Commission) (2004) *Innovation in Europe: Results for the EU, Iceland and Norway. Data 1998–2001.* Eurostat, Theme Nine: Science and Technology. Luxembourg: European Commission

European Communities (2004) Sources and resources for EU innovation. *Statistics in Focus: Science and Technology*, 5/2004

European Communities (2007a) Community innovation statistics: Is Europe growing more innovative? *Statistics in Focus: Science and Technology*, 61/2007

European Communities (2007b) Community innovation statistics: More than half of the innovative enterprises in the EU do inhouse R&D. *Statistics in Focus: Science and Technology*, 72/2007

European Communities (2007c) Community innovation statistics: Weak link between innovative enterprises and public research institutes/universities. *Statistics in Focus: Science and Technology*, 81/2007

European Communities (2007d) Innovative enterprises and the use of patents and other intellectual property rights: Patents and Community Innovation Survey (CIS) statistics. *Statistics in Focus: Science and Technology*, 91/2007

European Communities (2007e) Community innovation statistics: Innovation activities and their effects. *Statistics in Focus: Science and Technology*, 113/2007

Forfás Innovation Survey (2006) *The Fourth Community Innovation Survey: First findings.* Dublin: Forfás

Gaude, M (2007) Eurostat: from the CIS3 to the CIS2008. Keynote address at the 32nd CEIES Seminar (European Advisory Committee on Statistical Information in the Economic and Social Spheres), Aarhus, Denmark

Kremp E & Rousseau S (2006) One-fourth of enterprises are innovation active; innovation-active enterprises are often mid-sized or large; they account for 60% of total turnover. Le 4 Pages No. 222. Available at http://www.industrie.gouv.fr/sessi/4pages

Mani S (2001) *Government, innovation and technology policy: An analysis of the Brazilian experience during the 1990s.* Discussion Paper No. 11, United Nations University, Institute for New Technologies

Mani S (2007) Innovation surveys in developing countries: What can we learn from them for public innovation policies. Paper presented at the Conference on Micro Evidence on Innovation in Developing Countries 2007. Maastricht, The Netherlands

Mortensen PS (2007) Response ability and willingness. Paper presented at the 32nd CEIES Seminar (The European Advisory Committee on Statistical Information in the Economic and Social Spheres), Aarhus, Denmark

OECD/EC (Organisation for Economic Cooperation and Development/European Commission (2005) *Oslo manual* (3rd edition). Paris: OECD Publishing. Available at http://www.oecd.org/dataoecd/35/61/2367580.pdf

Oerlemans LAG, Pretorius TP, Buys A & Rooks G (2004) *Industrial innovation in South Africa, 1998–2000.* Pretoria: University of Pretoria

Robson S & Ortmans L (2006) First findings from the UK Innovation Survey, 2005. *Economic Trends* 628: 58–64

Statistics South Africa (2004) Final sample innovation survey 2004: Quality and methodology. Document created by Dr DF Molefe, Analysis and Consulting Department, Statistics South Africa

Statistics New Zealand (2007) *Innovation in New Zealand 2005.* Available at http://www.stats.govt.nz/analytical-reports/innovation-in-nz-2005.htm

Statistik Austria (2006) Main results of the 4th Community Innovation Survey (CIS4) in Austria. Accessed 2/11/2006 at http://www.statistik.at

Trendchart Innovation Policy in Europe (2006) *Hungary: Almost one in five enterprises are innovative, reveals CIS4. Trendchart Newsletter.* Accessed 9/11/2006 at http://www.proinno-europe.eu

Appendix 1 Main tabular results of the SAIS 2002–2004, by main SIC sector

Table A1.1: Number and percentage of enterprises, 2004

	Total	Industry	Mining and quarrying	Manufacturing	Electricity, gas and water supply	Services	Wholesale and retail trade	Transport, storage and communication	Financial intermediation	Computer and related, R&D, architectural & engineering, technical testing
Number of enterprises										
All enterprises	**31,456**	**13,939**	350	13,518	71	**17,517**	13,654	2,300	245	1,319
Enterprises with innovation activity	**16,264**	**7,637**	184	7,410	43	**8,627**	6,968	838	42	779
Product only innovators	**3,749**	**1,516**	8	1,503	4	**2,233**	2,039	85	26	83
Process only innovators	**1,801**	**529**	44	470	15	**1,272**	688	390	2	192
Product and process innovators	**9,332**	**5,313**	104	5,186	24	**4,019**	3,156	353	14	496
Enterprises with only ongoing or abandoned activities	**1,383**	**279**	28	251	0	**1,103**	1,084	10	0	8
Enterprises without innovation activity	**15,192**	**6,302**	166	6,108	28	**8,890**	6,686	1,462	202	539
Percentage of enterprises										
All enterprises	**100.0**	**100.0**	100.0	100.0	100.0	**100.0**	100.0	100.0	100.0	100.0
Enterprises with innovation activity	**51.7**	**54.8**	52.6	54.8	60.8	**49.3**	51.0	36.4	17.3	59.1
Product only innovators	**11.9**	**10.9**	2.3	11.1	6.0	**12.7**	14.9	3.7	10.8	6.3
Process only innovators	**5.7**	**3.8**	12.5	3.5	21.6	**7.3**	5.0	16.9	0.7	14.6
Product and process innovators	**29.7**	**38.1**	29.6	38.4	33.2	**22.9**	23.1	15.4	5.8	37.6
Enterprises with only ongoing or abandoned activities	**4.4**	**2.0**	8.1	1.9	0.0	**6.3**	7.9	0.4	0.0	0.6
Enterprises without innovation activity	**48.3**	**45.2**	47.4	45.2	39.2	**50.7**	49.0	63.6	82.7	40.9

Table A1.2: Summary of number and percenage of enterprises, 2004

	Total	Industry	Mining and quarrying	Manufacturing	Electricity, gas and water supply	Services	Wholesale and retail trade	Transport, storage and communication	Financial intermediation	Computer and related, R&D, architectural & engineering, technical testing
Number of enterprises										
All enterprises	**31,456**	**13,939**	350	13,518	71	**17,517**	13,654	2,300	245	1,319
Enterprises with innovation activity	**16,264**	**7,637**	184	7,410	43	**8,627**	6,968	838	42	779
Enterprises without innovation activity	**15,192**	**6,302**	166	6,108	28	**8,890**	6,686	1,462	202	539
Percentage of enterprises										
All enterprises	**100.0**	**100.0**	100.0	100.0	100.0	**100.0**	100.0	100.0	100.0	100.0
Enterprises with innovation activity	**51.7**	**54.8**	52.6	54.8	60.8	**49.3**	51.0	36.4	17.3	59.1
Enterprises without innovation activity	**48.3**	**45.2**	47.4	45.2	39.2	**50.7**	49.0	63.6	82.7	40.9

Table A1.3: Number and percentage of employees, 2004

	Total	Industry	Mining and quarrying	Manufacturing	Electricity, gas and water supply	Services	Wholesale and retail trade	Transport, storage and communication	Financial intermediation	Computer and related, R&D, architectural & engineering, technical testing
Number of employees										
All enterprises	**1,770,745**	**1,011,516**	239,550	769,760	2,206	**759,229**	427,489	91,688	207,023	33,028
Enterprises with innovation activity	**1,381,976**	**792,517**	228,959	561,557	2,001	**589,460**	313,341	60,319	200,829	14,971
Enterprises without innovation activity	**388,769**	**219,000**	10,591	208,204	205	**169,769**	114,148	31,369	6,194	18,057
Percentage of all employees										
All enterprises	**100.0**	**100.0**	100.0	100.0	100.0	**100.0**	100.0	100.0	100.0	100.0
Enterprises with innovation activity	**78.0**	**78.3**	95.6	73.0	90.7	**77.6**	73.3	65.8	97.0	45.3
Enterprises without innovation activity	**22.0**	**21.7**	4.4	27.0	9.3	**22.4**	26.7	34.2	3.0	54.7

Table A1.4: Turnover, 2004

	Total	Industry	Mining and quarrying	Manufacturing	Electricity, gas and water supply	Services	Wholesale and retail trade	Transport, storage and communication	Financial intermediation	Computer and related, R&D, architectural & engineering, technical testing
Turnover (R millions)										
All enterprises	**1,144,445**	**515,608**	90,962	423,792	854	**628,837**	322,016	129,126	160,141	17,555
Enterprises with innovation activity	**863,632**	**436,845**	85,254	350,924	667	**426,787**	210,333	73,185	135,238	8,031
Enterprises without innovation activity	**280,812**	**78,763**	5,708	72,868	187	**202,050**	111,683	55,941	24,902	9,524
Percentage of total turnover										
All enterprises	**100.0**	**100.0**	100.0	100.0	100.0	**100.0**	100.0	100.0	100.0	100.0
Enterprises with innovation activity	**75.5**	**84.7**	93.7	82.8	78.1	**67.9**	65.3	56.7	84.4	45.7
Enterprises without innovation activity	**24.5**	**15.3**	6.3	17.2	21.9	**32.1**	34.7	43.3	15.6	54.3

Table A1.5: Enterprises with innovation activities: expenditure on innovation, 2004

	Total	Industry	Mining and quarrying	Manufacturing	Electricity, gas and water supply	Services	Wholesale and retail trade	Transport, storage and communication	Financial intermediation	Computer and related, R&D, architectural & engineering, technical testing
Expenditure (R millions)										
Intramural (in-house) R&D	**5,691**	**3,155**	685	2,457	13	**2,537**	1,190	305	375	666
Extramural (outsourced) R&D	**2,190**	**725**	152	572	1	**1,465**	644	128	194	499
Acquisition of machinery, equipment and software	**18,084**	**8,525**	579	7,933	13	**9,559**	2,030	4,490	1,077	1,963
Acquisition of other external knowledge	**1,841**	**225**	52	171	1	**1,616**	602	135	284	595
Total expenditure	**27,806**	**12,629**	1,467	11,134	29	**15,177**	4,466	5,058	1,930	3,723
Proportion of innovation expenditure (%)										
Intramural (in-house) R&D	**20.5**	**25.0**	46.7	22.1	45.4	**16.7**	26.7	6.0	19.4	17.9
Extramural (outsourced) R&D	**7.9**	**5.7**	10.4	5.1	4.3	**9.7**	14.4	2.5	10.1	13.4
Acquisition of machinery, equipment and software	**65.0**	**67.5**	39.4	71.3	45.0	**63.0**	45.4	88.8	55.8	52.7
Acquisition of other external knowledge	**6.6**	**1.8**	3.5	1.5	5.3	**10.6**	13.5	2.7	14.7	16.0

Table A1.6: Number and percentage of innovative enterprises having engaged in specific innovation expenditure, 2004

	Total	Industry	Mining and quarrying	Manufacturing	Electricity, gas and water supply	Services	Wholesale and retail trade	Transport, storage and communication	Financial intermediation	Computer and related, R&D, architectural & engineering, technical testing
Number of innovative enterprises										
Intramural (in-house) R&D	**8,411**	**4,885**	95	4,756	33	**3,527**	2,755	351	41	380
Extramural (outsourced) R&D	**3,140**	**1,241**	90	1,140	12	**1,899**	1,602	88	11	199
Acquisition of machinery, equipment and software	**8,794**	**3,570**	130	3,417	23	**5,225**	4,232	452	14	526
Acquisition of other external knowledge	**4,604**	**1,633**	102	1,520	11	**2,971**	2,638	159	7	167
Percemtage of innovative enterprises										
Intramural (in-house) R&D	**51.7**	**64.0**	51.7	64.2	76.6	**40.9**	39.5	41.9	95.8	48.7
Extramural (outsourced) R&D	**19.3**	**16.3**	48.8	15.4	26.9	**22.0**	23.0	10.5	25.0	25.6
Acquisition of machinery, equipment and software	**54.1**	**46.7**	70.5	46.1	54.2	**60.6**	60.7	54.0	33.4	67.5
Acquisition of other external knowledge	**28.3**	**21.4**	55.4	20.5	25.0	**34.4**	37.9	19.0	16.7	21.4

Table A1.7: Product (goods and services) innovators: number breakdown of turnover by product type, 2004

	Total	Industry	Mining and quarrying	Manufacturing	Electricity, gas and water supply	Services	Wholesale and retail trade	Transport, storage and communication	Financial intermediation	Computer and related, R&D, architectural & engineering, technical testing
Turnover breakdown (R millions)										
All product innovators	673,746	280,063	6,838	272,601	623	393,684	181,537	69,449	135,148	7,550
Innovations new to the market	67,848	37,750	275	37,392	83	30,098	13,194	2,137	13,838	929
Innovations new to the firm	79,194	41,738	1,208	40,444	86	37,455	18,732	4,267	12,220	2,236
Unchanged or marginally modified	526,705	200,574	5,356	194,765	453	326,130	149,611	63,045	109,090	4,384
Product only innovators	80,779	32,478	165	32,127	186	48,301	44,937	472	2,170	723
Innovations new to the market	6,290	2,399	1	2,390	8	3,891	3,677	95	0	118
Innovations new to the firm	8,572	2,986	22	2,926	38	5,586	5,057	89	325	115
Unchanged or marginally modified	65,917	27,093	142	26,811	139	38,824	36,203	288	1,844	489
Product and process innovators	592,967	247,585	6,673	240,474	437	345,382	136,600	68,977	132,978	6,827
Innovations new to the market	61,558	35,351	274	35,002	75	26,207	9,516	2,042	13,838	811
Innovations new to the firm	70,622	38,753	1,186	37,519	48	31,869	13,676	4,178	11,894	2,121
Unchanged or marginally modified	460,788	173,481	5,214	167,954	314	287,306	113,408	62,757	107,246	3,896

Table A1.8: Product (goods and services) innovators: percentage breakdown of turnover by product type, 2004

	Total	Industry	Mining and quarrying	Manufacturing	Electricity, gas and water supply	Services	Wholesale and retail trade	Transport, storage and communication	Financial intermediation	Computer and related, R&D, architectural & engineering, technical testing
Turnover breakdown (% of total turnover)										
All product innovators	100.0	100.0	100.0	100.0	100.0	100.0	100.0	100.0	100.0	100.0
Innovations new to the market	**10.1**	**13.5**	4.0	13.7	13.4	**7.6**	7.3	3.1	10.2	12.3
Innovations new to the firm	**11.8**	**14.9**	17.7	14.8	13.8	**9.5**	10.3	6.1	9.0	29.6
Unchanged or marginally modified	**78.2**	**71.6**	78.3	71.4	72.8	**82.8**	82.4	90.8	80.7	58.1
Product only innovators	**100.0**	**100.0**	**100.0**	**100.0**	**100.0**	**100.0**	**100.0**	**100.0**	**100.0**	**100.0**
Innovations new to the market	**7.8**	**7.4**	0.6	7.4	4.4	**8.1**	8.2	20.2	0.0	16.4
Innovations new to the firm	**10.6**	**9.2**	13.1	9.1	20.7	**11.6**	11.3	18.8	15.0	16.0
Unchanged or marginally modified	**81.6**	**83.4**	86.3	83.5	74.9	**80.4**	80.6	61.0	85.0	67.6
Product and process innovators	**100.0**	**100.0**	**100.0**	**100.0**	**100.0**	**100.0**	**100.0**	**100.0**	**100.0**	**100.0**
Innovations new to the market	**10.4**	**14.3**	4.1	14.6	17.2	**7.6**	7.0	3.0	10.4	11.9
Innovations new to the firm	**11.9**	**15.7**	17.8	15.6	10.9	**9.2**	10.0	6.1	8.9	31.1
Unchanged or marginally modified	77.7	**70.1**	78.1	69.8	71.8	**83.2**	83.0	91.0	80.6	57.1

Table A1.9: Innovative enterprises: responsibility for the development of innovations, 2002–2004

	Total	Industry	Mining and quarrying	Manufacturing	Electricity, gas and water supply	Services	Wholesale and retail trade	Transport, storage and communication	Financial intermediation	Computer and related, R&D, architectural & engineering, technical testing
Total number of innovative enterprises										
All innovative enterprises	**16,264**	**7,637**	184	7,410	43	**8,627**	6,968	838	42	779
Mainly own enterprise	**8,341**	**5,367**	86	5,268	13	**2,974**	2,365	266	37	306
Own enterprise in collaboration with other enterprises or institutions	**3,699**	**1,264**	24	1,229	11	**2,435**	2,035	162	4	235
Other enterprises or institutions	**1,041**	**198**	1	192	4	**843**	795	10	0	38
Non-responsive firms*	**3,183**	**809**	72	721	15	**2,375**	1,772	400	2	201
Percentage of innovative enterprises										
All innovative enterprises	**100.0**	**100.0**	100.0	100.0	100.0	**100.0**	100.0	100.0	100.0	100.0
Mainly own enterprise	**51.3**	**70.3**	46.8	71.1	29.4	**34.5**	33.9	31.7	87.5	39.3
Own enterprise in collaboration with other enterprises or institutions	**22.7**	**16.5**	13.2	16.6	24.8	**28.2**	29.2	19.3	8.3	30.2
Other enterprises or institutions	**6.4**	**2.6**	0.8	2.6	10.3	**9.8**	11.4	1.2	0.0	4.8
Non-responsive firms*	**19.6**	**10.6**	39.2	9.7	35.5	**27.5**	25.4	47.7	4.2	25.7

** Enterprises that returned the questionnaire, but did not respond to this question.*

Table A1.10: Origin of innovation, 2002–2004

	Total	Industry	Mining and quarrying	Manufacturing	Electricity, gas and water supply	Services	Wholesale and retail trade	Transport, storage and communication	Financial intermediation	Computer and related, R&D, architectural & engineering, technical testing
Origin of innovation										
All innovative enterprises	**16,264**	**7,637**	184	7,410	43	**8,627**	6,968	838	42	779
South Africa	**8,935**	**5,145**	109	5,013	23	**3,789**	2,879	422	37	452
Abroad	**4,125**	**1,679**	2	1,671	5	**2,446**	2,316	16	4	110
No response	**3,205**	**813**	72	726	15	**2,392**	1,772	400	2	218
Percentage of innovation origin										
All innovative enterprises	**100.0**	**100.0**	100.0	100.0	100.0	**100.0**	100.0	100.0	100.0	100.0
South Africa	**54.9**	**67.4**	59.5	67.7	53.0	**43.9**	41.3	50.3	87.5	58.0
Abroad	**25.4**	**22.0**	1.3	22.6	11.6	**28.4**	33.2	1.9	8.3	14.1
No response	**19.7**	**10.6**	39.2	9.8	35.5	**27.7**	25.4	47.7	4.2	27.9

Table A1.11: Highly important effects of innovation on outcomes for enterprises (number), 2002–2004

	Total	Industry	Mining and quarrying	Manufacturing	Electricity, gas and water supply	Services	Wholesale and retail trade	Transport, storage and communication	Financial intermediation	Computer and related, R&D, architectural & engineering, technical testing
Product outcomes										
Increased range of goods and services	**5,529**	**3,365**	55	3,302	8	**2,164**	1,747	187	5	225
Entered new markets or increased market share	**3,811**	**2,277**	56	2,214	8	**1,533**	1,271	131	2	129
Improved quality of goods or services	**7,416**	**3,658**	53	3,578	26	**3,758**	3,181	268	5	304
Process outcomes										
Improved flexibility of production or service provision	**2,509**	**1,262**	67	1,191	4	**1,247**	843	187	5	212
Increased capacity of production or service provision	**3,173**	**1,271**	74	1,189	8	**1,902**	1,577	138	4	184
Reduced labour costs per unit output	**1,312**	**1,124**	56	1,065	4	**188**	49	57	2	81
Reduced materials and energy per unit output	**1,183**	**989**	3	983	4	**193**	45	57	2	90
Other outcomes										
Reduced environmental impacts or improved health and safety	**2,065**	**1,781**	35	1,724	22	**284**	54	102	0	127
Met governmental regulatory requirements	**3,507**	**1,877**	80	1,776	21	**1,630**	1,183	301	4	144

Table A1.12: Highly important effects of innovation on outcomes for enterprises (%), 2002–2004

	Total	Industry	Mining and quarrying	Manufacturing	Electricity, gas and water supply	Services	Wholesale and retail trade	Transport, storage and communication	Financial intermediation	Computer and related, R&D, architectural & engineering, technical testing
Product outcomes										
Increased range of goods and services	**34.0**	**44.1**	29.8	44.6	18.4	**25.1**	25.1	22.3	12.5	28.9
Entered new markets or increased market share	**23.4**	**29.8**	30.3	29.9	18.4	**17.8**	18.2	15.7	4.2	16.6
Improved quality of goods or services	**45.6**	**47.9**	28.9	48.3	61.0	**43.6**	45.7	31.9	12.5	39.0
Process outcomes										
Improved flexibility of production or service provision	**15.4**	**16.5**	36.3	16.1	8.9	**14.5**	12.1	22.3	12.5	27.2
Increased capacity of production or service provision	**19.5**	**16.6**	40.2	16.0	19.0	**22.0**	22.6	16.4	8.3	23.6
Reduced labour costs per unit output	**8.1**	**14.7**	30.2	14.4	8.2	**2.2**	0.7	6.8	4.2	10.4
Reduced materials and energy per unit output	**7.3**	**13.0**	1.6	13.3	8.4	**2.2**	0.6	6.8	4.2	11.5
Other outcomes										
Reduced environmental impacts or improved health and safety	**12.7**	**23.3**	18.9	23.3	51.6	**3.3**	0.8	12.2	0.0	16.3
Met governmental regulatory requirements	**21.6**	**24.6**	43.4	24.0	48.2	**18.9**	17.0	35.9	8.3	18.4

Table A1.13: Enterprises with innovation activity: number of enterprises that introduced new goods or services, 2002–2004

	Total	Industry	Mining and quarrying	Manufacturing	Electricity, gas and water supply	Services	Wholesale and retail trade	Transport, storage and communication	Financial intermediation	Computer and related, R&D, architectural & engineering, technical testing
All product innovators										
Introduced new goods	**7,835**	**4,217**	70	4,127	19	**3,617**	3,208	154	11	245
Introduced new services	**9,941**	**5,118**	104	4,988	26	**4,823**	3,850	376	35	562
Product only innovators										
Introduced new goods	**1,843**	**948**	2	941	4	**895**	833	51	0	11
Introduced new services	**2,614**	**832**	7	823	2	**1,782**	1,596	76	26	83
Product and process innovators										
Introduced new goods	**5,992**	**3,269**	68	3,186	15	**2,722**	2,376	102	11	234
Introduced new services	**7,328**	**4,286**	97	4,165	24	**3,042**	2,254	300	9	479

Table A1.14: Enterprises with innovation activity: percentage of enterprises that introduced new goods or services, 2002–2004

	Total	Industry	Mining and quarrying	Manufacturing	Electricity, gas and water supply	Services	Wholesale and retail trade	Transport, storage and communication	Financial intermediation	Computer and related, R&D, architectural & engineering, technical testing
All product innovators										
Introduced new goods	**48.2**	**55.2**	38.3	55.7	45.2	**41.9**	46.0	18.3	25.0	31.4
Introduced new services	**61.1**	**67.0**	56.7	67.3	59.6	**55.9**	55.3	44.8	83.3	72.1
Product only innovators										
Introduced new goods	**11.3**	**12.4**	1.3	12.7	9.9	**10.4**	11.9	6.1	0.0	1.4
Introduced new services	**16.1**	**10.9**	3.9	11.1	5.0	**20.7**	22.9	9.0	62.5	10.7
Product and process innovators										
Introduced new goods	**36.8**	**42.8**	37.0	43.0	35.3	**31.6**	34.1	12.2	25.0	30.0
Introduced new services	**45.1**	**56.1**	52.8	56.2	54.6	**35.3**	32.3	35.8	20.8	61.4

Table A1.15: Innovative enterprises that received financial support for innovation activities from government sources (number), 2002–2004

	Total	Industry	Mining and quarrying	Manufacturing	Electricity, gas and water supply	Services	Wholesale and retail trade	Transport, storage and communication	Financial intermediation	Computer and related, R&D, architectural & engineering, technical testing
Enterprises with innovation activity	**1,029**	**895**	13	881	1	**134**	30	11	2	91
Successful innovators	**973**	**856**	10	845	0	**117**	25	8	2	83
Enterprises with only ongoing and/or abandoned innovations	**5**	**5**	0	5	0	**0**	0	0	0	0

Table A1.16: Innovative enterprises that received financial support for innovation activities from government sources (%), 2002–2004

	Total	Industry	Mining and quarrying	Manufacturing	Electricity, gas and water supply	Services	Wholesale and retail trade	Transport, storage and communication	Financial intermediation	Computer and related, R&D, architectural & engineering, technical testing
Enterprises with innovation activity	**6.3**	**11.7**	6.8	11.9	3.2	**1.6**	0.4	1.3	4.2	11.7
Successful innovators	**6.0**	**11.2**	5.6	11.4	0.0	**1.4**	0.4	0.9	4.2	10.6
Enterprises with only ongoing and/or abandoned innovations	**0.0**	**0.1**	0.0	0.1	0.0	**0.0**	0.0	0.0	0.0	0.0

Table A1.17: Sources of information for innovation rated as 'highly important' by innovative enterprises (number), 2002–2004

	Total	Industry	Mining and quarrying	Manufacturing	Electricity, gas and water supply	Services	Wholesale and retail trade	Transport, storage and communication	Financial intermediation	Computer and related, R&D, architectural & engineering, technical testing
Internal sources										
Sources within your enterprise or enterprise group	8,021	4,148	103	4,025	19	3,873	3,124	345	32	373
External - market resources										
Suppliers of equipment, materials, components or software	3,953	1,960	26	1,922	12	1,993	1,601	158	5	228
Clients or customers	5,613	3,350	83	3,236	30	2,264	1,903	151	4	206
Competitors or other enterprises in your sector	2,052	1,212	61	1,145	6	840	686	78	2	74
Consultants, commercial labs or private R&D institutes	634	476	19	452	5	158	46	53	2	56
External - institutional sources										
Universities and technikons	853	760	0	760	0	93	7	38	0	48
Government and public research institutes	546	465	1	464	0	80	7	36	0	37
External - other sources										
Conferences, trade fairs, exhibitions	363	266	0	265	1	97	57	19	0	20
Scientific journals and trade/technical publications	620	432	3	427	2	188	35	80	0	74
Professional and industry associations	1,404	65	4	59	2	1,339	1,122	102	0	115

Table A1.18: Sources of information for innovation rated as 'highly important' by innovative enterprises (%), 2002–2004

	Total	Industry	Mining and quarrying	Manufacturing	Electricity, gas and water supply	Services	Wholesale and retail trade	Transport, storage and communication	Financial intermediation	Computer and related, R&D, architectural & engineering, technical testing
Internal sources										
Sources within your enterprise or enterprise group	**49.3**	**54.3**	56.1	54.3	45.1	**44.9**	44.8	41.2	75.0	47.8
External – market resources										
Suppliers of equipment, materials, components or software	**24.3**	**25.7**	14.0	25.9	28.7	**23.1**	23.0	18.9	12.5	29.3
Clients or customers	**34.5**	**43.9**	45.2	43.7	70.6	**26.2**	27.3	18.0	8.3	26.4
Competitors or other enterprises in your sector	**12.6**	**15.9**	33.0	15.5	14.1	**9.7**	9.8	9.3	4.2	9.5
Consultants, commercial labs or private R&D institutes	**3.9**	**6.2**	10.2	6.1	11.4	**1.8**	0.7	6.4	4.2	7.2
External – institutional sources										
Universities and technikons	**5.2**	**9.9**	0.0	10.2	0.0	**1.1**	0.1	4.5	0.0	6.2
Government and public research institutes	**3.4**	**6.1**	0.8	6.3	0.0	**0.9**	0.1	4.3	0.0	4.8
External – other sources										
Conferences, trade fairs, exhibitions	**2.2**	**3.5**	0.0	3.6	3.2	**1.1**	0.8	2.3	0.0	2.6
Scientific journals and trade/technical publications	**3.8**	**5.7**	1.4	5.8	5.2	**2.2**	0.5	9.6	0.0	9.4
Professional and industry associations	**8.6**	**0.8**	2.0	0.8	5.0	**15.5**	16.1	12.2	0.0	14.8

Table A1.19: Enterprises with innovation activity citing the following problems with their innovation activity, 2002–2004

	Total	Industry	Mining and quarrying	Manufacturing	Electricity, gas and water supply	Services	Wholesale and retail trade	Transport, storage and communication	Financial intermediation	Computer and related, R&D, architectural & engineering, technical testing
Number of innovative enterprises										
Abandoned in the concept stage	**1,715**	**905**	60	838	8	**810**	451	168	12	178
Abandoned after the activity or project was begun	**1,999**	**855**	28	803	25	**1,144**	811	134	12	187
Seriously delayed	**3,070**	**1,164**	21	1,118	25	**1,906**	1,462	233	11	200
Percentage of innovative enterprises										
Abandoned in the concept stage	**10.5**	**11.8**	32.4	11.3	18.0	**9.4**	6.5	20.0	29.2	22.9
Abandoned after the activity or project was begun	**12.3**	**11.2**	15.2	10.8	57.4	**13.3**	11.6	16.0	29.2	23.9
Seriously delayed	**18.9**	**15.2**	11.3	15.1	58.6	**22.1**	21.0	27.8	25.0	25.6

Table A1.20: Highly important factors that hampered innovation activities of innovative enterprises (number), 2002–2004

	Total	Industry	Mining and quarrying	Manufacturing	Electricity, gas and water supply	Services	Wholesale and retail trade	Transport, storage and communication	Financial intermediation	Computer and related, R&D, architectural & engineering, technical testing
Cost factors										
Lack of funds within your enterprise or group	4,737	2,446	20	2,403	23	2,291	1,864	123	0	303
Lack of finance from sources outside your enterprise	3,036	1,247	13	1,206	28	1,790	1,485	111	0	194
Innovation costs too high	3,710	1,180	10	1,149	21	2,530	2,203	161	5	161
Knowledge factors										
Lack of qualified personnel	3,316	1,148	16	1,131	1	2,168	1,873	177	4	115
Lack of information on technology	564	448	4	439	5	116	22	58	2	34
Lack of information on markets	532	79	1	78	0	452	393	12	2	46
Difficulty in finding cooperation partners	653	409	8	381	20	243	22	107	0	114
Market factors										
Market dominated by established enterprises	3,776	1,111	53	1,038	21	2,665	2,226	209	2	229
Uncertain demand for innovative goods or services	1,542	253	7	242	3	1,289	1,123	110	2	55
Reasons not to innovate										
No need due to prior innovations	495	89	31	56	3	406	389	0	0	17
No need because of no demand for innovations	111	79	28	51	0	32	10	0	0	22

Table A1.21: Highly important factors that hampered innovation activities of innovative enterprises (%), 2002–2004

	Total	Industry	Mining and quarrying	Manufacturing	Electricity, gas and water supply	Services	Wholesale and retail trade	Transport, storage and communication	Financial intermediation	Computer and related, R&D, architectural & engineering, technical testing
Cost factors										
Lack of funds within your enterprise or group	**29.1**	**32.0**	10.7	32.4	54.2	**26.6**	26.8	14.7	0.0	38.9
Lack of finance from sources outside your enterprise	**18.7**	**16.3**	7.0	16.3	65.0	**20.7**	21.3	13.2	0.0	24.9
Innovation costs too high	**22.8**	**15.4**	5.6	15.5	47.7	**29.3**	31.6	19.2	12.5	20.6
Knowledge factors										
Lack of qualified personnel	**20.4**	**15.0**	8.7	15.3	3.2	**25.1**	26.9	21.1	8.3	14.7
Lack of information on technology	**3.5**	**5.9**	2.2	5.9	10.9	**1.3**	0.3	7.0	4.2	4.3
Lack of information on markets	**3.3**	**1.0**	0.8	1.1	0.0	**5.2**	5.6	1.4	4.2	5.9
Difficulty in finding cooperation partners	**4.0**	**5.4**	4.4	5.1	45.7	**2.8**	0.3	12.8	0.0	14.6
Market factors										
Market dominated by established enterprises	**23.2**	**14.5**	28.6	14.0	48.8	**30.9**	31.9	24.9	4.2	29.4
Uncertain demand for innovative goods or services	**9.5**	**3.3**	4.0	3.3	7.6	**14.9**	16.1	13.1	4.2	7.1
Reasons not to innovate										
No need due to prior innovations	**3.0**	**1.2**	16.6	0.8	6.4	**4.7**	5.6	0.0	0.0	2.2
No need because of no demand for innovations	**0.7**	**1.0**	15.4	0.7	0.0	**0.4**	0.1	0.0	0.0	2.8

Table A1.22: Highly important factors that hampered innovation activities of non-innovative enterprises (number), 2002–2004

	Total	Industry	Mining and quarrying	Manufacturing	Electricity, gas and water supply	Services	Wholesale and retail trade	Transport, storage and communication	Financial intermediation	Computer and related, R&D, architectural & engineering, technical testing
Cost factors										
Lack of funds within your enterprise or group	3,235	1,175	23	1,153	0	2,059	1,808	166	0	85
Lack of finance from sources outside your enterprise	1,810	1,069	23	1,047	0	741	544	112	0	85
Innovation costs too high	2,695	1,344	20	1,324	0	1,350	1,172	66	2	111
Knowledge factors										
Lack of qualified personnel	2,004	1,208	20	1,176	11	796	549	155	30	62
Lack of information on technology	777	715	0	709	6	62	17	0	2	43
Lack of information on markets	673	643	0	643	0	30	10	0	2	18
Difficulty in finding cooperation partners	1,897	1,157	0	1,157	0	740	644	59	2	36
Market factors										
Market dominated by established enterprises	4,453	1,748	0	1,737	11	2,705	2,360	218	2	126
Uncertain demand for innovative goods or services	1,570	659	0	648	11	911	638	159	2	111
Reasons not to innovate										
No need due to prior innovations	790	619	0	619	0	171	39	59	2	71
No need because of no demand for innovations	2,734	514	0	514	0	2,220	1,662	421	55	82

Table A1.23: Highly important factors that hampered innovation activities of non-innovative enterprises (%), 2002–2004

	Total	Industry	Mining and quarrying	Manufacturing	Electricity, gas and water supply	Services	Wholesale and retail trade	Transport, storage and communication	Financial intermediation	Computer and related, R&D, architectural & engineering, technical testing
Cost factors										
Lack of funds within your enterprise or group	**21.3**	**18.6**	13.6	18.9	0.0	**23.2**	27.0	11.4	0.0	15.8
Lack of finance from sources outside your enterprise	**11.9**	**17.0**	13.6	17.1	0.0	**8.3**	8.1	7.6	0.0	15.8
Innovation costs too high	**17.7**	**21.3**	12.2	21.7	0.0	**15.2**	17.5	4.5	0.9	20.6
Knowledge factors										
Lack of qualified personnel	**13.2**	**19.2**	12.2	19.3	40.0	**9.0**	8.2	10.6	14.7	11.5
Lack of information on technology	**5.1**	**11.3**	0.0	11.6	20.0	**0.7**	0.3	0.0	0.9	8.0
Lack of information on markets	**4.4**	**10.2**	0.0	10.5	0.0	**0.3**	0.2	0.0	0.9	3.4
Difficulty in finding cooperation partners	**12.5**	**18.4**	0.0	18.9	0.0	**8.3**	9.6	4.0	0.9	6.7
Market factors										
Market dominated by established enterprises	**29.3**	**27.7**	0.0	28.4	40.0	**30.4**	35.3	14.9	0.9	23.4
Uncertain demand for innovative goods or services	**10.3**	**10.5**	0.0	10.6	40.0	**10.2**	9.5	10.9	0.9	20.7
Reasons not to innovate										
No need due to prior innovations	**5.2**	**9.8**	0.0	10.1	0.0	**1.9**	0.6	4.0	0.9	13.2
No need because of no demand for innovations	**18.0**	**8.2**	0.0	8.4	0.0	**25.0**	24.9	28.8	27.2	15.3

Table A1.24: Number of innovative and non-innovative enterprises that introduced organisational or marketing innovations, 2002–2004

	Total	Industry	Mining and quarrying	Manufacturing	Electricity, gas and water supply	Services	Wholesale and retail trade	Transport, storage and communication	Financial intermediation	Computer and related, R&D, architectural & engineering, technical testing
Enterprises with innovation activities										
Organisational innovations										
Knowledge management systems to better use or exchange information	8,552	3,688	122	3,532	34	4,863	3,812	651	9	391
Major changes to the organisation of work	8,803	2,769	83	2,669	18	6,033	5,241	435	16	342
External relations with other firms or public institutions	4,443	1,047	71	941	35	3,396	2,713	381	12	289
Marketing innovations										
Design or packaging of a good or service	5,916	2,355	22	2,310	22	3,562	3,214	106	35	206
Sales or distribution methods	3,681	1,427	21	1,389	18	2,253	1,990	145	9	109
Enterprises without innovation activities										
Organisational innovations										
Knowledge management systems to better use or exchange information	1,160	493	2	479	11	668	67	534	2	65
Major changes to the organisation of work	1,838	772	7	765	0	1,066	606	371	2	87
External relations with other firms or public institutions	1,641	571	7	564	0	1,070	694	313	2	62
Marketing innovations										
Design or packaging of a good or service	1,146	759	2	757	0	387	22	309	2	54
Sales or distribution methods	991	560	0	560	0	431	39	364	4	24

Table A1.25: Percentage of innovative and non-innovative enterprises that introduced organisational or marketing innovations, 2002–2004

	Total	Industry	Mining and quarrying	Manufacturing	Electricity, gas and water supply	Services	Wholesale and retail trade	Transport, storage and communication	Financial intermediation	Computer and related, R&D, architectural & engineering, technical testing
Enterprises with innovation activities										
Organisational innovations										
Knowledge management systems to better use or exchange information	**52.6**	**48.3**	66.4	47.7	78.9	**56.4**	54.7	77.7	20.8	50.2
Major changes to the organisation of work	**54.1**	**36.3**	45.1	36.0	41.3	**69.9**	75.2	51.9	37.5	43.9
External relations with other firms or public institutions	**27.3**	**13.7**	38.5	12.7	80.7	**39.4**	38.9	45.5	29.2	37.1
Marketing innovations										
Design or packaging of a good or service	**36.4**	**30.8**	12.2	31.2	51.3	**41.3**	46.1	12.7	83.3	26.4
Sales or distribution methods	**22.6**	**18.7**	11.2	18.7	41.2	**26.1**	28.6	17.3	20.8	14.0
Enterprises without innovation activities										
Organisational innovations										
Knowledge management systems to better use or exchange information	**7.6**	**7.8**	1.3	7.8	40.0	**7.5**	1.0	36.5	0.9	12.1
Major changes to the organisation of work	**12.1**	**12.2**	4.0	12.5	0.0	**12.0**	9.1	25.4	0.9	16.1
External relations with other firms or public institutions	**10.8**	**9.1**	4.0	9.2	0.0	**12.0**	10.4	21.4	0.9	11.5
Marketing innovations										
Design or packaging of a good or service	**7.5**	**12.0**	1.3	12.4	0.0	**4.3**	0.3	21.1	0.9	10.0
Sales or distribution methods	**6.5**	**8.9**	0.0	9.2	0.0	**4.8**	0.6	24.9	1.9	4.5

Table A1.26: Number of enterprises that secured a patent in SA or applied for at least one patent outside SA, 2002–2004

	Total	Industry	Mining and quarrying	Manufacturing	Electricity, gas and water supply	Services	Wholesale and retail trade	Transport, storage and communication	Financial intermediation	Computer and related, R&D, architectural & engineering, technical testing
Enterprises that secured a patent in SA										
All enterprises	**528**	**337**	5	327	5	**192**	57	13	2	120
Enterprises with innovation activity	**498**	**333**	5	322	5	**166**	52	13	2	99
Enterprises without innovation activity	**30**	**4**	0	4	0	**26**	5	0	0	21
Enterprises that applied for a patent outside SA										
All enterprises	**444**	**316**	4	311	1	**129**	37	2	0	90
Enterprises with innovation activity	**413**	**307**	4	302	1	**106**	35	2	0	69
Enterprises without innovation activity	**31**	**8**	0	8	0	**23**	2	0	0	21

Table A1.27: Percentage of enterprises that secured a patent in SA or applied for at least one patent outside SA, 2002–2004

	Total	Industry	Mining and quarrying	Manufacturing	Electricity, gas and water supply	Services	Wholesale and retail trade	Transport, storage and communication	Financial intermediation	Computer and related, R&D, architectural & engineering, technical testing
Enterprises that secured a patent in SA										
All enterprises	**1.7**	**2.4**	1.5	2.4	7.0	**1.1**	0.4	0.5	0.7	9.1
Enterprises with innovation activity	**3.1**	**4.4**	2.8	4.4	11.6	**1.9**	0.7	1.5	4.2	12.8
Enterprises without innovation activity	**0.2**	**0.1**	0.0	0.1	0.0	**0.3**	0.1	0.0	0.0	3.8
Enterprises that applied for a patent outside SA										
All enterprises	**1.4**	**2.3**	1.0	2.3	1.9	**0.7**	0.3	0.1	0.0	6.8
Enterprises with innovation activity	**2.5**	**4.0**	2.0	4.1	3.2	**1.2**	0.5	0.2	0.0	8.9
Enterprises without innovation activity	**0.2**	**0.1**	0.0	0.1	0.0	**0.3**	0.0	0.0	0.0	3.8

Table A1.28: Number of enterprises that made use of intellectual property rights, 2002–2004

	Total	Industry	Mining and quarrying	Manufacturing	Electricity, gas and water supply	Services	Wholesale and retail trade	Transport, storage and communication	Financial intermediation	Computer and related, R&D, architectural & engineering, technical testing
Enterprises with innovation activity										
Registered an industrial design	705	263	3	258	1	443	399	0	4	40
Registered a trademark	1,720	723	1	720	1	997	887	60	12	38
Claimed copyright	788	233	3	229	1	554	418	63	9	65
Granted a license on any intellectual property rights resulting from innovation	279	146	3	141	1	134	12	3	7	111
Enterprises without innovation activity										
Registered an industrial design	2	0	0	0	0	2	2	0	0	0
Registered a trademark	441	387	2	385	0	54	33	0	2	19
Claimed copyright	73	61	2	59	0	12	2	0	0	10
Granted a license on any intellectual property rights resulting from innovation	2	0	0	0	0	2	2	0	0	0

Table A1.29: Percentage of enterprises that made use of intellectual property rights, 2002–2004

	Total	Industry	Mining and quarrying	Manufacturing	Electricity, gas and water supply	Services	Wholesale and retail trade	Transport, rtorage and communication	Financial intermediation	Computer and related, R&D, architectural & engineering, technical testing
Enterprises with innovation activity										
Registered and industrial design	**4.3**	**3.4**	1.6	3.5	3.2	**5.1**	5.7	0.0	8.3	5.2
Registered a trademark	**10.6**	**9.5**	0.8	9.7	3.2	**11.6**	12.7	7.1	29.2	4.9
Claimed copyright	**4.8**	**3.1**	1.6	3.1	3.2	**6.4**	6.0	7.5	20.8	8.3
Granted a license on any intellectual property rights resulting from innovation	**1.7**	**1.9**	1.6	1.9	3.2	**1.5**	0.2	0.4	16.7	14.2
Enterprises without innovation activity										
Registered and industrial design	**0.0**	**0.0**	0.0	0.0	0.0	**0.0**	0.0	0.0	0.0	0.0
Registered a trademark	**2.9**	**6.1**	1.3	6.3	0.0	**0.6**	0.5	0.0	0.9	3.6
Claimed copyright	**0.5**	**1.0**	1.3	1.0	0.0	**0.1**	0.0	0.0	0.0	1.8
Granted a license on any intellectual property rights resulting from innovation	**0.0**	**0.0**	0.0	0.0	0.0	**0.0**	0.0	0.0	0.0	0.0

Table A1.30: Geographic distribution of goods and services sold by innovative and non-innovative enterprises (number), 2002–2004

Number of enterprises	Total	Industry	Mining and quarrying	Manufacturing	Electricity, gas and water supply	Services	Wholesale and retail trade	Transport, storage and communication	Financial intermediation	Computer and related, R&D, architectural & engineering, technical testing
All enterprises										
South Africa (only some provinces)	**18,952**	**8,492**	249	8,194	49	**10,460**	9,123	451	139	747
South Africa (national)	**9,835**	**4,813**	82	4,710	22	**5,022**	2,759	1,566	104	593
Rest of Africa	**4,412**	**2,264**	54	2,180	30	**2,148**	1,256	532	61	298
Europe	**1,319**	**729**	29	697	4	**590**	76	435	7	71
United States	**935**	**559**	18	540	1	**376**	32	287	0	57
Asia	**1,298**	**356**	11	338	7	**942**	424	478	0	40
Other countries	**1,706**	**1,174**	25	1,138	11	**532**	90	375	2	65
Enterprises with innovation activity										
South Africa (only some provinces)	**8,843**	**3,881**	109	3,739	32	**4,962**	4,474	110	2	376
South Africa (national)	**6,106**	**3,134**	59	3,064	11	**2,971**	2,014	541	41	376
Rest of Africa	**3,134**	**1,537**	39	1,473	25	**1,597**	1,188	150	32	227
Europe	**828**	**569**	15	550	4	**258**	50	130	7	71
United States	**635**	**471**	4	465	1	**165**	25	83	0	57
Asia	**883**	**278**	9	262	7	**605**	398	169	0	38
Other countries	**883**	**600**	3	591	6	**282**	66	164	2	51
Enterprises without innovation activity										
South Africa (only some provinces)	**10,109**	**4,610**	140	4,454	17	**5,498**	4,649	340	137	372
South Africa (national)	**3,729**	**1,679**	22	1,646	11	**2,050**	745	1,025	63	217
Rest of Africa	**1,278**	**728**	16	707	6	**550**	68	382	30	71
Europe	**491**	**160**	13	146	0	**331**	26	305	0	0
United States	**300**	**89**	13	75	0	**212**	7	205	0	0
Asia	**415**	**77**	2	75	0	**337**	26	309	0	2
Other countries	**823**	**574**	22	546	6	**249**	24	212	0	14

Table A1.31: Geographic distribution of goods and services sold by innovative and non-innovative enterprises (%), 2002–2004

Proportion of enterprises (%)	Total	Industry	Mining and quarrying	Manufacturing	Electricity, gas and water supply	Services	Wholesale and retail trade	Transport, storage and communication	Financial intermediation	Computer and related, R&D, architectural & engineering, technical testing
All enterprises										
South Africa (only some provinces)	**60.2**	**60.9**	71.1	60.6	69.1	**59.7**	66.8	19.6	56.8	56.7
South Africa (national)	**31.3**	**34.5**	23.3	34.8	30.9	**28.7**	20.2	68.1	42.4	45.0
Rest of Africa	**14.0**	**16.2**	15.5	16.1	42.7	**12.3**	9.2	23.1	25.1	22.6
Europe	**4.2**	**5.2**	8.2	5.2	5.4	**3.4**	0.6	18.9	2.9	5.4
United States	**3.0**	**4.0**	5.1	4.0	1.5	**2.1**	0.2	12.5	0.0	4.3
Asia	**4.1**	**2.6**	3.1	2.5	10.1	**5.4**	3.1	20.8	0.0	3.0
Other countries	**5.4**	**8.4**	7.2	8.4	16.0	**3.0**	0.7	16.3	0.7	4.9
Enterprises with innovation activity										
South Africa (only some provinces)	**54.4**	**50.8**	59.5	50.5	75.0	**57.5**	64.2	13.2	4.2	48.2
South Africa (national)	**37.5**	**41.0**	32.3	41.4	25.0	**34.4**	28.9	64.5	95.8	48.3
Rest of Africa	**19.3**	**20.1**	21.2	19.9	57.3	**18.5**	17.0	17.9	75.0	29.2
Europe	**5.1**	**7.5**	8.3	7.4	8.9	**3.0**	0.7	15.5	16.7	9.2
United States	**3.9**	**6.2**	2.4	6.3	2.5	**1.9**	0.4	9.9	0.0	7.3
Asia	**5.4**	**3.6**	4.7	3.5	16.6	**7.0**	5.7	20.1	0.0	4.9
Other countries	**5.4**	**7.9**	1.6	8.0	13.4	**3.3**	0.9	19.5	4.2	6.6
Enterprises without innovation activity										
South Africa (only some provinces)	**66.5**	**73.2**	84.1	72.9	60.0	**61.8**	69.5	23.3	67.8	68.9
South Africa (national)	**24.5**	**26.6**	13.3	26.9	40.0	**23.1**	11.1	70.1	31.2	40.2
Rest of Africa	**8.4**	**11.5**	9.3	11.6	20.0	**6.2**	1.0	26.1	14.7	13.1
Europe	**3.2**	**2.5**	8.0	2.4	0.0	**3.7**	0.4	20.9	0.0	0.0
United States	**2.0**	**1.4**	8.0	1.2	0.0	**2.4**	0.1	14.0	0.0	0.0
Asia	**2.7**	**1.2**	1.3	1.2	0.0	**3.8**	0.4	21.1	0.0	0.4
Other countries	**5.4**	**9.1**	13.4	8.9	20.0	**2.8**	0.4	14.5	0.0	2.5

Table A1.32: Innovative enterprises that introduced organisational innovation that rated the following results as having a 'high' level of importance, 2002–2004

	Total	Industry	Mining and quarrying	Manufacturing	Electricity, gas and water supply	Services	Wholesale and retail trade	Transport, storage and communication	Financial intermediation	Computer and related, R&D, architectural & engineering, technical testing
Number of innovative enterprises										
Improved market share	**3,862**	**1,298**	89	1,204	5	**2,564**	2,242	137	7	178
Reduced time to respond to customer or supplier needs	**4,104**	**1,275**	75	1,195	6	**2,829**	2,351	208	5	264
Improved quality of your goods or services	**5,671**	**2,350**	91	2,250	9	**3,320**	2,633	294	9	385
Reduced costs per unit output	**2,680**	**918**	81	827	9	**1,762**	1,446	124	4	188
Improved employee satisfaction/turnover	**3,681**	**1,134**	80	1,049	5	**2,547**	2,188	160	4	196
Percentage of innovative enterprises										
Improved market share	**23.7**	**17.0**	48.4	16.2	12.6	**29.7**	32.2	16.3	16.7	22.8
Reduced time to respond to customer or supplier needs	**25.2**	**16.7**	40.7	16.1	14.0	**32.8**	33.7	24.8	12.5	33.9
Improved quality of your goods or services	**34.9**	**30.8**	49.2	30.4	21.0	**38.5**	37.8	35.0	20.8	49.3
Reduced costs per unit output	**16.5**	**12.0**	44.3	11.2	21.1	**20.4**	20.8	14.8	8.3	24.2
Improved employee satisfaction/turnover	**22.6**	**14.9**	43.5	14.2	12.1	**29.5**	31.4	19.1	8.3	25.1
Percentage of all enterprises										
Improved market share	**12.3**	**9.3**	25.4	8.9	7.7	**14.6**	16.4	6.0	2.9	13.5
Reduced time to respond to customer or supplier needs	**13.0**	**9.2**	21.4	8.8	8.5	**16.1**	17.2	9.0	2.2	20.0
Improved quality of your goods or services	**18.0**	**16.9**	25.9	16.6	12.7	**19.0**	19.3	12.8	3.6	29.2
Reduced costs per unit output	**8.5**	**6.6**	23.3	6.1	12.8	**10.1**	10.6	5.4	1.4	14.3
Improved employee satisfaction/turnover	**11.7**	**8.1**	22.9	7.8	7.4	**14.5**	16.0	7.0	1.4	14.8

Table A1.33: Innovative enterprises that received financial support for innovation activities from government sources, 2002–2004

	Total	Industry	Mining and quarrying	Manufacturing	Electricity, gas and water supply	Services	Wholesale and retail trade	Transport, storage and communication	Financial intermediation	Computer and related, R&D, architectural & engineering, technical testing
Number of innovative enterprises										
Metros and municipalities	**6**	**0**	0	0	0	**6**	2	3	0	0
Provincial government	**31**	**25**	1	23	0	**6**	2	3	0	0
National government	**416**	**382**	2	379	1	**34**	12	11	0	10
National funding agencies	**588**	**490**	7	483	0	**98**	15	0	2	81
Foreign government/ public sources	**10**	**7**	4	4	0	**2**	2	0	0	0
Percentage of innovative enterprises										
Metros and municipalities	**0.0**	**0.0**	0.0	0.0	0.0	**0.1**	0.0	0.4	0.0	0.0
Provincial government	**0.2**	**0.3**	0.8	0.3	0.0	**0.1**	0.0	0.4	0.0	0.0
National government	**2.6**	**5.0**	1.2	5.1	3.2	**0.4**	0.2	1.3	0.0	1.3
National funding agencies	**3.6**	**6.4**	4.0	6.5	0.0	**1.1**	0.2	0.0	4.2	10.4
Foreign government/ public sources	**0.1**	**0.1**	2.0	0.0	0.0	**0.0**	0.0	0.0	0.0	0.0

*Table A1.34: Number and percentage of staff with a degree or diploma, 2004**

	Total	Industry	Mining and quarrying	Manufacturing	Electricity, gas and water supply	Services	Wholesale and retail trade	Transport, storage and communication	Financial intermediation	Computer and related, R&D, architectural & engineering, technical testing
Total number of staff										
Enterprises with innovation activity	**1,290,157**	**769,230**	220,034	547,196	2,001	**520,926**	253,346	51,780	200,829	14,971
Enterprises without innovation activity	**365,055**	**217,039**	10,591	206,243	205	**148,016**	92,395	31,369	6,194	18,057
Number of staff with a degree or diploma										
Enterprises with innovation activity	**179,072**	**111,268**	23,607	87,411	250	**67,805**	23,157	3,820	33,610	7,217
Enterprises without innovation activity	**30,973**	**10,357**	416	9,912	29	**20,617**	7,608	5,070	3,228	4,710
Percentage of staff with a degree or diploma										
Enterprises with innovation activity	**13.9**	**14.5**	10.7	16.0	12.5	**13.0**	9.1	7.4	16.7	48.2
Enterprises without innovation activity	**8.5**	**4.8**	3.9	4.8	14.4	**13.9**	8.2	16.2	52.1	26.1

** Only includes enterprises that entered both staff number and percentage of staff with a degree or diploma.*

Table A1.35: Enterprises with organisational and/or marketing innovations, 2002–2004

	Total	Industry	Mining and quarrying	Manufacturing	Electricity, gas and water supply	Services	Wholesale and retail trade	Transport, storage and communication	Financial intermediation	Computer and related, R&D, architectural & engineering, technical testing
Number of enterprises with organisational and/or marketing innovations										
Enterprises with organisational innovation	**14,318**	**5,489**	135	5,307	47	**8,828**	6,610	1,561	18	640
Enterprises with marketing innovation	**8,770**	**3,985**	30	3,931	23	**4,784**	3,688	726	41	330
Innovative enterprises with organisational and/ or marketing innovation	**13,433**	**5,498**	128	5,330	40	**7,936**	6,526	828	42	539
Product only innovative enterprises with organisational and/or marketing innovation	**2,464**	**687**	5	678	4	**1,776**	1,633	85	26	32
Process only innovative enterprises with organisational and/or marketing innovation	**1,609**	**436**	40	381	15	**1,173**	681	386	2	104
Product and process innovative enterprises with organisational and/ or marketing innovation	**8,016**	**4,123**	55	4,047	20	**3,893**	3,131	353	14	395
Non-innovative enterprises with organisational innovation	**3,261**	**1,089**	9	1,069	11	**2,172**	1,293	738	2	139
Non-innovative enterprises with marketing innovation	**1,591**	**888**	2	886	0	**702**	56	565	4	78
Non-innovative enterprises with organisational **or** marketing innovation	**3,613**	**1,411**	9	1,391	11	**2,202**	1,303	738	4	157
Non-innovative enterprises with organisational **and** marketing innovation	**1,239**	**567**	2	564	0	**672**	46	565	2	60

	Total	Industry	Mining and quarrying	Manufacturing	Electricity, gas and water supply	Services	Wholesale and retail trade	Transport, storage and communication	Financial intermediation	Computer and related, R&D, architectural & engineering, technical testing
Percentage enterprises with organisational and/or marketing innovations										
Enterprises with organisational innovation	**45.5**	**39.4**	38.6	39.3	66.7	**50.4**	48.4	67.8	7.3	48.5
Enterprises with marketing innovation	**27.9**	**28.6**	8.6	29.1	33.1	**27.3**	27.0	31.6	16.7	25.0
Innovative enterprises with organisational and/ or marketing innovation	**82.6**	**72.0**	69.8	71.9	92.3	**92.0**	93.7	98.8	100.0	69.2
Product only innovative enterprises with organisational and/or marketing innovation	**15.1**	**9.0**	2.6	9.2	9.9	**20.6**	23.4	10.1	62.5	4.1
Process only innovative enterprises with organisational and/or marketing innovation	**9.9**	**5.7**	21.8	5.1	35.5	**13.6**	9.8	46.1	4.2	13.4
Product and process innovative enterprises with organisational and/ or marketing innovation	**49.3**	**54.0**	30.0	54.6	46.8	**45.1**	44.9	42.1	33.4	50.6
Non-innovative enterprises with organisational innovation	**21.5**	**17.3**	5.3	17.5	40.0	**24.4**	19.3	50.5	0.9	25.7
Non-innovative enterprises with marketing innovation	**10.5**	**14.1**	1.3	14.5	0.0	**7.9**	0.8	38.6	1.9	14.4
Non-innovative enterprises with organisational **or** marketing innovation	**23.8**	**22.4**	5.3	22.8	40.0	**24.8**	19.5	50.5	1.9	29.1
Non-innovative enterprises with organisational **and** marketing innovation	**8.2**	**9.0**	1.3	9.2	0.0	**7.6**	0.7	38.6	0.9	11.0

Table A1.36: Collaborative partnerships for innovation activities by type of partner and their location (number), 2002–2004

	Total	Industry	Mining and quarrying	Manufacturing	Electricity, gas and water supply	Services	Wholesale and retail trade	Transport, storage and communication	Financial intermediation	Computer and related, R&D, architectural & engineering, technical testing
Other enterprises within your enterprise group										
South Africa	646	139	8	131	0	508	405	54	7	42
Rest of Africa	35	13	1	10	1	22	5	15	2	0
Europe	609	186	0	185	1	423	401	17	4	2
USA	555	125	0	125	0	431	381	41	0	8
Asia	81	21	1	19	0	60	10	50	0	0
Other countries	32	20	3	17	0	12	10	0	0	3
Suppliers of equipment, materials, components or software										
South Africa	4,824	2,274	44	2,215	15	2,550	2,029	276	9	236
Rest of Africa	107	10	0	9	1	97	0	96	2	0
Europe	1,396	713	11	696	6	683	526	77	7	72
USA	541	339	5	332	2	201	17	82	4	98
Asia	64	43	0	40	3	21	19	0	0	2
Other countries	447	39	5	33	1	408	389	0	2	17
Clients or customers										
South Africa	5,993	2,707	38	2,649	20	3,287	2,765	159	7	355
Rest of Africa	676	55	3	52	1	621	400	151	2	67
Europe	323	153	6	145	2	170	17	64	2	87
USA	176	80	2	78	0	96	10	61	0	26
Asia	145	52	0	51	1	93	10	54	0	29
Other countries	167	55	0	53	2	111	22	53	0	36
Competitors or other enterprises in your sector										
South Africa	4,734	2,102	10	2,076	16	2,632	2,372	71	9	180
Rest of Africa	92	14	1	13	0	77	7	56	4	11
Europe	408	269	1	266	1	139	17	52	5	65
USA	355	239	4	233	1	116	12	50	5	48
Asia	478	42	1	36	5	435	374	50	0	11
Other countries	43	25	1	23	0	18	10	4	2	2

	Total	Industry	Mining and quarrying	Manufacturing	Electricity, gas and water supply	Services	Wholesale and retail trade	Transport, storage and communication	Financial intermediation	Computer and related, R&D, architectural & engineering, technical testing
Consultants, commercial labs or private R&D institutes										
South Africa	2,911	1,814	12	1,791	12	1,097	827	67	9	194
Rest of Africa	11	5	0	5	0	6	2	0	4	0
Europe	159	50	2	46	1	109	15	48	7	39
USA	84	30	4	24	1	55	5	46	4	0
Asia	32	9	0	9	0	23	2	0	0	21
Other countries	45	35	6	29	0	10	2	0	2	5
Universities or technikons										
South Africa	2,506	1,786	9	1,767	10	720	431	101	2	185
Rest of Africa	2	2	0	2	0	0	0	0	0	0
Europe	93	14	2	10	1	79	7	46	0	26
USA	58	4	2	0	1	54	2	46	0	5
Asia	2	0	0	0	0	2	2	0	0	0
Other countries	28	20	4	17	0	8	2	0	0	5
Government or public research institutes										
South Africa	2,148	1,461	8	1,439	14	688	424	101	4	159
Rest of Africa	13	0	0	0	0	13	2	0	2	9
Europe	63	4	2	2	0	59	2	46	2	9
USA	51	0	0	0	0	51	5	46	0	0
Asia	2	0	0	0	0	2	2	0	0	0
Other countries	26	22	2	18	1	4	2	0	2	0

Table A1.37: Collaborative partnerships for innovation activities by type of partner and their location (%), 2002–2004

	Total	Industry	Mining and quarrying	Manufacturing	Electricity, gas and water supply	Services	Wholesale and retail trade	Transport, storage and communication	Financial intermediation	Computer and related, R&D, architectural & engineering, technical testing
Other enterprises within your enterprise group										
South Africa	4.0	1.8	4.3	1.8	0.0	5.9	5.8	6.4	16.7	25.3
Rest of Africa	0.2	0.2	0.8	0.1	3.2	0.3	0.1	1.8	4.2	0.0
Europe	3.7	2.4	0.0	2.5	3.2	4.9	5.8	2.0	8.3	0.2
USA	3.4	1.6	0.0	1.7	0.0	5.0	5.5	4.8	0.0	1.1
Asia	0.5	0.3	0.8	0.3	0.0	0.7	0.1	6.0	0.0	0.0
Other countries	0.2	0.3	1.6	0.2	0.0	0.1	0.1	0.0	0.0	0.3
Suppliers of equipment, materials, components or software										
South Africa	29.7	29.8	23.7	29.9	34.9	29.6	29.1	32.9	20.8	30.2
Rest of Africa	0.7	0.1	0.0	0.1	3.2	1.1	0.0	11.4	4.2	0.0
Europe	8.6	9.3	6.1	9.4	14.8	7.9	7.5	9.2	16.7	9.3
USA	3.3	4.4	2.8	4.5	5.0	2.3	0.2	9.8	8.3	12.6
Asia	0.4	0.6	0.0	0.5	7.7	0.2	0.3	0.0	0.0	0.2
Other countries	2.7	0.5	2.8	0.4	2.5	4.7	5.6	0.0	4.2	2.2
Clients or customers										
South Africa	36.8	35.4	20.5	35.8	45.9	38.1	39.7	19.0	16.7	45.6
Rest of Africa	4.2	0.7	1.4	0.7	2.5	7.2	5.7	18.1	4.2	8.6
Europe	2.0	2.0	3.2	2.0	5.2	2.0	0.2	7.6	4.2	11.1
USA	1.1	1.0	1.2	1.1	0.0	1.1	0.1	7.2	0.0	3.3
Asia	0.9	0.7	0.0	0.7	3.2	1.1	0.1	6.4	0.0	3.7
Other countries	1.0	0.7	0.0	0.7	5.7	1.3	0.3	6.3	0.0	4.7
Competitors or other enterprises in your sector										
South Africa	29.1	27.5	5.5	28.0	36.2	30.5	34.0	8.5	20.8	23.1
Rest of Africa	0.6	0.2	0.8	0.2	0.0	0.9	0.1	6.7	8.3	1.4
Europe	2.5	3.5	0.8	3.6	3.2	1.6	0.2	6.2	12.5	8.3
USA	2.2	3.1	2.2	3.1	3.2	1.3	0.2	6.0	12.5	6.1
Asia	2.9	0.6	0.8	0.5	10.9	5.0	5.4	6.0	0.0	1.4
Other countries	0.3	0.3	0.8	0.3	0.0	0.2	0.1	0.5	4.2	0.2

	Total	Industry	Mining and quarrying	Manufacturing	Electricity, gas and water supply	Services	Wholesale and retail trade	Transport, storage and communication	Financial intermediation	Computer and related, R&D, architectural & engineering, technical testing
Consultants, commercial labs or private R&D institutes										
South Africa	**17.9**	**23.8**	6.3	24.2	27.3	**12.7**	11.9	8.0	20.8	24.9
Rest of Africa	**0.1**	**0.1**	0.0	0.1	0.0	**0.1**	0.0	0.0	8.3	0.0
Europe	**1.0**	**0.7**	1.2	0.6	3.2	**1.3**	0.2	5.7	16.7	5.1
USA	**0.5**	**0.4**	2.0	0.3	3.2	**0.6**	0.1	5.5	8.3	0.0
Asia	**0.2**	**0.1**	0.0	0.1	0.0	**0.3**	0.0	0.0	0.0	2.6
Other countries	**0.3**	**0.5**	3.2	0.4	0.0	**0.1**	0.0	0.0	4.2	0.7
Universities or technikons										
South Africa	**15.4**	**23.4**	4.7	23.8	24.1	**8.3**	6.2	12.0	4.2	23.8
Rest of Africa	**0.0**	**0.0**	0.0	0.0	0.0	**0.0**	0.0	0.0	0.0	0.0
Europe	**0.6**	**0.2**	1.2	0.1	3.2	**0.9**	0.1	5.5	0.0	3.3
USA	**0.4**	**0.0**	1.2	0.0	3.2	**0.6**	0.0	5.5	0.0	0.7
Asia	**0.0**	**0.0**	0.0	0.0	0.0	**0.0**	0.0	0.0	0.0	0.0
Other countries	**0.2**	**0.3**	2.0	0.2	0.0	**0.1**	0.0	0.0	0.0	0.7
Government or public research institutes										
South Africa	**13.2**	**19.1**	4.3	19.4	31.8	**8.0**	6.1	12.0	8.3	20.4
Rest of Africa	**0.1**	**0.0**	0.0	0.0	0.0	**0.2**	0.0	0.0	4.2	1.1
Europe	**0.4**	**0.1**	1.2	0.0	0.0	**0.7**	0.0	5.5	4.2	1.1
USA	**0.3**	**0.0**	0.0	0.0	0.0	**0.6**	0.1	5.5	0.0	0.0
Asia	**0.0**	**0.0**	0.0	0.0	0.0	**0.0**	0.0	0.0	0.0	0.0
Other countries	**0.2**	**0.3**	1.2	0.2	3.2	**0.0**	0.0	0.0	4.2	0.0

Table A1.38: Innovative enterprises performing process innovations, 2002–2004

	Total	Industry	Mining and quarrying	Manufacturing	Electricity, gas and water supply	Services	Wholesale and retail trade	Transport, storage and communication	Financial intermediation	Computer and related, R&D, architectural & engineering, technical testing
Number of process innovators	**11,133**	**5,842**	147	5,656	39	**5,291**	3,844	743	182	521
Percentage of process innovators	**35.4**	**41.9**	42.1	41.8	54.8	**30.2**	28.2	32.3	74.6	39.5

Table A1.39: Innovative enterprises performing specific process innovations, 2002–2004

	Total	Industry	Mining and quarrying	Manufacturing	Electricity, gas and water supply	Services	Wholesale and retail trade	Transport, storage and communication	Financial intermediation	Computer and related, R&D, architectural & engineering, technical testing
Number of specific process innovators										
Methods of manufacturing or production	**7,804**	**3,672**	122	3,537	14	**4,132**	3,414	272	11	435
Delivery or distribution methods	**6,689**	**3,548**	100	3,431	17	**3,142**	2,395	442	11	294
Supporting activities	**6,981**	**3,096**	137	2,922	36	**3,885**	2,705	635	14	530
Percentage of specific process innovators										
Methods of manufacturing or production	**24.8**	**26.3**	34.9	26.2	19.1	**23.6**	25.0	11.8	4.3	33.0
Delivery or distribution methods	**21.3**	**25.5**	28.6	25.4	23.4	**17.9**	17.5	19.2	4.3	22.3
Supporting activities	**22.2**	**22.2**	39.2	21.6	51.3	**22.2**	19.8	27.6	5.8	40.2

Table A1.40: Responsibility for process innovations, 2002–2004

	Total	Industry	Mining and quarrying	Manufacturing	Electricity, gas and water supply	Services	Wholesale and retail trade	Transport, storage and communication	Financial intermediation	Computer and related, R&D, architectural & engineering, technical testing
Number of process innovators										
Mainly own	**6,149**	**4,552**	118	4,426	8	**1,597**	1,123	155	5	313
Own together with others	**3,726**	**556**	28	499	29	**3,170**	2,442	391	11	327
Mainly others	**1,188**	**667**	1	662	4	**521**	280	201	0	41
Percentage of process innovators										
Mainly own	**19.5**	**32.7**	33.8	32.7	11.7	**9.1**	8.2	6.8	2.2	23.8
Own together with others	**11.8**	**4.0**	7.9	3.7	41.1	**18.1**	17.9	17.0	4.3	24.8
Mainly others	**3.8**	**4.8**	0.4	4.9	5.1	**3.0**	2.0	8.7	0.0	3.1

Table A1.41: Origin of process innovation, 2002–2004

	Total	Industry	Mining and quarrying	Manufacturing	Electricity, gas and water supply	Services	Wholesale and retail trade	Transport, storage and communication	Financial intermediation	Computer and related, R&D, architectural & engineering, technical testing
Number of process innovators										
South Africa	**8,608**	**4,583**	121	4,428	35	**4,025**	2,705	742	14	564
Abroad	**2,378**	**1,115**	27	1,082	6	**1,263**	1,139	5	2	117
Non-process innovators	**20,470**	**8,241**	203	8,009	30	**12,229**	9,809	1,553	229	638
Percentage of process innovators										
South Africa	**27.4**	**32.9**	34.5	32.8	49.2	**23.0**	19.8	32.2	5.8	42.8
Abroad	**7.6**	**8.0**	7.6	8.0	8.6	**7.2**	8.3	0.2	0.7	8.9
Non-process innovators	**65.1**	**59.1**	57.9	59.2	42.2	**69.8**	71.8	67.5	93.5	48.4

Table A1.42: Enterprises which introduced new or improved products to the market as a percentage of enterprises engaged in innovation activity by sector, 2004

	Total	Industry	Mining and quarrying	Manufacturing	Electricity, gas and water supply	Services	Wholesale and retail trade	Transport, storage and communication	Financial intermediation	Computer and related, R&D, architectural & engineering, technical testing
Number of enterprises	**13,081**	**6,828**	112	6,689	28	**6,253**	5,195	438	41	579
Percentage enterprises	**80.4**	**89.4**	60.8	90.3	64.5	**72.5**	74.6	52.3	95.8	74.3

Appendix 2 Main tabular results of the SAIS 2002–2004, by size class

Table A2.1: Number and percentage of enterprises, 2004

Size classes	Total				Industry				Services			
	1	2	3	4	1	2	3	4	1	2	3	4
Number of enterprises												
All enterprises	1,632	5,360	15,153	9,312	656	3,423	4,575	5,285	976	1,937	10,578	4,027
Enterprises with innovation activity	979	3,420	8,061	3,804	429	2,090	2,845	2,274	551	1,331	5,216	1,530
Product only innovators	192	427	1,732	1,398	73	380	905	157	119	46	827	1,241
Process only innovators	146	554	960	141	65	290	161	14	81	264	800	127
Product and process innovators	610	2,415	4,255	2,053	277	1,395	1,751	1,891	333	1,020	2,504	162
Enterprises with only ongoing and/or abandoned innovations	32	25	1,114	212	14	25	28	212	18	0	1,085	0
Enterprises without innovation activity	652	1,939	7,092	5,508	227	1,333	1,731	3,011	425	606	5,362	2,497
Percentage of enterprises												
All enterprises	100.0	100.0	100.0	100.0	100.0	100.0	100.0	100.0	100.0	100.0	100.0	100.0
Enterprises with innovation activity	60.0	63.8	53.2	40.9	65.3	61.1	62.2	43.0	56.4	68.7	49.3	38.0
Product only innovators	11.8	8.0	11.4	15.0	11.2	11.1	19.8	3.0	12.2	2.4	7.8	30.8
Process only innovators	8.9	10.3	6.3	1.5	9.9	8.5	3.5	0.3	8.3	13.6	7.6	3.2
Product and process innovators	37.4	45.1	28.1	22.0	42.1	40.8	38.3	35.8	34.2	52.7	23.7	4.0
Enterprises with only ongoing and/or abandoned innovations	1.9	0.5	7.4	2.3	2.1	0.7	0.6	4.0	1.8	0.0	10.3	0.0
Enterprises without innovation activity	40.0	36.2	46.8	59.1	34.7	38.9	37.8	57.0	43.6	31.3	50.7	62.0

Table A2.2: Summary of number and percentage of enterprises, 2004

	Total				Industry				Services			
Size classes	1	2	3	4	1	2	3	4	1	2	3	4
Number of enterprises												
All enterprises	1,632	5,360	15,153	9,312	656	3,423	4,575	5,285	976	1,937	10,578	4,027
Enterprises with innovation activity	979	3,420	8,061	3,804	429	2,090	2,845	2,274	551	1,331	5,216	1,530
Enterprises without innovation activity	652	1,939	7,092	5,508	227	1,333	1,731	3,011	425	606	5,362	2,497
Percentage of enterprises												
All enterprises	100.0	100.0	100.0	100.0	100.0	100.0	100.0	100.0	100.0	100.0	100.0	100.0
Enterprises with innovation activity	60.0	63.8	53.2	40.9	65.3	61.1	62.2	43.0	56.4	68.7	49.3	38.0
Enterprises without innovation activity	40.0	36.2	46.8	59.1	34.7	38.9	37.8	57.0	43.6	31.3	50.7	62.0

Table A2.3: Number and percentage of employees, 2004

	Total				Industry				Services			
Size classes	1	2	3	4	1	2	3	4	1	2	3	4
Number of employees												
All enterprises	1,059,947	342,685	298,183	100,388	541,306	244,103	171,669	84,895	518,641	98,581	126,514	15,493
Enterprises with innovation activity	923,970	213,494	203,060	70,973	485,970	153,170	116,254	66,642	438,000	60,323	86,807	4,330
Enterprises without innovation activity	135,977	129,191	95,123	29,415	55,336	90,933	55,416	18,252	80,641	38,258	39,707	11,163
Percentage of employees												
All enterprises	100.0	100.0	100.0	100.0	100.0	100.0	100.0	100.0	100.0	100.0	100.0	100.0
Enterprises with innovation activity	87.2	62.3	68.1	70.7	89.8	62.7	67.7	78.5	84.5	61.2	68.6	27.9
Enterprises without innovation activity	12.8	37.7	31.9	29.3	10.2	37.3	32.3	21.5	15.5	38.8	31.4	72.1

Table A2.4: Turnover, 2004

	Total				Industry				Services			
Size classes	1	2	3	4	1	2	3	4	1	2	3	4
Turnover (R millions)												
All enterprises	899,169	120,860	104,764	19,651	404,071	70,888	28,646	12,002	495,098	49,972	76,118	7,649
Enterprises with innovation activity	708,875	72,982	72,422	9,353	366,398	41,059	21,834	7,553	342,477	31,923	50,587	1,800
Enterprises without innovation activity	190,294	47,878	32,342	10,298	37,673	29,829	6,812	4,449	152,621	18,050	25,530	5,849
Percentage of total turnover												
All enterprises	100.0	100.0	100.0	100.0	100.0	100.0	100.0	100.0	100.0	100.0	100.0	100.0
Enterprises with innovation activity	78.8	60.4	69.1	47.6	90.7	57.9	76.2	62.9	69.2	63.9	66.5	23.5
Enterprises without innovation activity	21.2	39.6	30.9	52.4	9.3	42.1	23.8	37.1	30.8	36.1	33.5	76.5

Table A2.5: Enterprises with innovation activities: expenditure on innovation, 2004

	Total				Industry				Services			
Size classes	1	2	3	4	1	2	3	4	1	2	3	4
Expenditure (R millions)												
Intramural (in-house) R&D	2,981	1,606	834	270	1,923	557	434	241	1,058	1,049	400	29
Extramural (outsourced) R&D	1,286	635	235	34	521	55	142	8	765	581	93	26
Acquisition of machinery, equipment and software	7,764	2,633	5,992	1,695	4,987	1,546	1,141	850	2,776	1,087	4,851	845
Acquisition of other external knowledge	1,047	448	231	114	152	50	11	11	895	398	220	103
Percentage of innovation expenditure												
Intramural (in-house) R&D	52.4	28.2	14.7	4.7	61.0	17.7	13.8	7.6	41.7	41.4	15.8	1.1
Extramural (outsourced) R&D	58.7	11.2	10.7	0.6	71.8	7.6	19.6	1.0	52.2	39.6	6.3	1.8
Acquisition of machinery, equipment and software	42.9	46.3	33.1	29.8	58.5	18.1	13.4	10.0	29.0	11.4	50.7	8.8
Acquisition of other external knowledge	56.9	7.9	12.6	2.0	67.7	22.5	4.8	5.0	55.4	24.6	13.6	6.4

Table A2.6: Number and percentage of innovative enterprises having engaged in specific innovation expenditure, 2004

	Total				Industry				Services			
Size classes	1	2	3	4	1	2	3	4	1	2	3	4
Number of innovative enterprises												
Intramural (in-house) R&D	575	2,462	3,386	1,989	291	1,416	1,288	1,889	283	1,046	2,098	99
Extramural (outsourced) R&D	339	1,000	1,216	586	151	194	422	474	188	805	794	112
Acquisition of machinery, equipment and software	645	2,410	3,554	2,185	326	1,260	1,176	808	319	1,150	2,378	1,377
Acquisition of other external knowledge	252	1,071	2,075	1,206	106	264	97	1,166	146	807	1,978	41
Percentage of innovative enterprises												
Intramural (in-house) R&D	58.7	72.0	42.0	52.3	67.9	67.8	45.3	83.1	51.5	78.6	40.2	6.5
Extramural (outsourced) R&D	34.6	29.2	15.1	15.4	35.2	9.3	14.8	20.8	34.1	60.5	15.2	7.3
Acquisition of machinery, equipment and software	65.8	70.5	44.1	57.4	76.0	60.3	41.3	35.5	57.9	86.4	45.6	90.0
Acquisition of other external knowledge	25.7	31.3	25.7	31.7	24.7	12.7	3.4	51.3	26.4	60.7	37.9	2.7

Table A2.7: Product (goods and services) innovators: breakdown of turnover by product type, 2004

	Total				Industry				Services			
Size classes	1	2	3	4	1	2	3	4	1	2	3	4
Turnover breakdown (R millions)												
All product innovators	**551,496**	**57,826**	**55,217**	**9,208**	**222,388**	**36,097**	**14,030**	**7,548**	**329,108**	**21,729**	**41,187**	**1,660**
Innovations new to the market	55,762	6,935	3,936	1,215	30,409	5,089	1,089	1,163	25,353	1,846	2,847	52
Innovations new to the firm	54,065	10,313	13,043	1,772	26,853	6,644	6,718	1,524	27,212	3,670	6,325	248
Unchanged or marginally modified	441,669	40,577	38,238	6,221	165,126	24,364	6,223	4,861	276,543	16,213	32,014	1,360
Product only innovators	**53,844**	**7,102**	**18,343**	**1,491**	**24,725**	**4,648**	**3,036**	**69**	**29,119**	**2,454**	**15,307**	**1,422**
Innovations new to the market	4,960	660	670	1	1,553	641	204	1	3,406	19	466	0
Innovations new to the firm	4,170	879	3,311	211	1,551	529	905	0	2,619	350	2,406	211
Unchanged or marginally modified	44,714	5,562	14,361	1,279	21,620	3,478	1,926	69	23,094	2,084	12,435	1,210
Product and process innovators	**497,652**	**50,724**	**36,874**	**7,717**	**197,663**	**31,449**	**10,994**	**7,479**	**299,988**	**19,275**	**25,880**	**239**
Innovations new to the market	50,802	6,275	3,266	1,214	28,856	4,448	884	1,162	21,947	1,827	2,382	52
Innovations new to the firm	49,895	9,434	9,732	1,561	25,302	6,115	5,812	1,524	24,593	3,319	3,919	37
Unchanged or marginally modified	396,954	35,015	23,876	4,942	143,506	20,886	4,297	4,792	253,449	14,129	19,579	150

Table A2.8: Product (goods and services) innovators: percentage breakdown of turnover by product type, 2004

	Total				Industry				Services			
Size classes	1	2	3	4	1	2	3	4	1	2	3	4
Turnover breakdown (% of total turnover)												
All product innovators	**100.0**	**100.0**	**100.0**	**100.0**	**100.0**	**100.0**	**100.0**	**100.0**	**100.0**	**100.0**	**100.0**	**100.0**
Innovations new to the market	10.1	12.0	7.1	13.2	13.7	14.1	7.8	15.4	7.7	8.5	6.9	3.1
Innovations new to the firm	9.8	17.8	23.6	19.2	12.1	18.4	47.9	20.2	8.3	16.9	15.4	15.0
Unchanged or marginally modified	80.1	70.2	69.2	67.6	74.3	67.5	44.4	64.4	84.0	74.6	77.7	81.9
Product only innovators	**100.0**	**100.0**	**100.0**	**100.0**	**100.0**	**100.0**	**100.0**	**100.0**	**100.0**	**100.0**	**100.0**	**100.0**
Innovations new to the market	9.2	9.3	3.7	0.0	6.3	13.8	6.7	1.0	11.7	0.8	3.0	0.0
Innovations new to the firm	7.7	12.4	18.1	14.2	6.3	11.4	29.8	0.0	9.0	14.3	15.7	14.9
Unchanged or marginally modified	83.0	78.3	78.3	85.8	87.4	74.8	63.4	99.0	79.3	84.9	81.2	85.1
Product and process innovators	**100.0**	**100.0**	**100.0**	**100.0**	**100.0**	**100.0**	**100.0**	**100.0**	**100.0**	**100.0**	**100.0**	**100.0**
Innovations new to the market	10.2	12.4	8.9	15.7	14.6	14.1	8.0	15.5	7.3	9.5	9.2	21.7
Innovations new to the firm	10.0	18.6	26.4	20.2	12.8	19.4	52.9	20.4	8.2	17.2	15.1	15.6
Unchanged or marginally modified	79.8	69.0	64.8	64.0	72.6	66.4	39.1	64.1	84.5	73.3	75.7	62.7

Table A2.9: Innovative enterprises: responsibility for the development of innovations, 2002–2004

	Total				Industry				Services			
Size classes	1	2	3	4	1	2	3	4	1	2	3	4
Total number of innovative enterprises												
All innovative enterprises	979	3,420	8,061	3,804	429	2,090	2,845	2,274	551	1,331	5,216	1,530
Mainly own enterprise	475	1,948	2,682	3,236	240	1,430	1,755	1,942	235	518	927	1,294
Own enterprise in collaboration with other enterprises or institutions	219	813	2,473	194	74	273	811	106	145	540	1,662	88
Other enterprises or institutions	108	81	831	21	36	72	90	0	72	9	742	21
Non-responsive firms*	178	578	2,074	353	79	314	189	226	99	264	1,885	127
Percentage of innovative enterprises												
All innovative enterprises	100.0	100.0	100.0	100.0	100.0	100.0	100.0	100.0	100.0	100.0	100.0	100.0
Mainly own enterprise	48.5	57.0	33.3	85.1	56.0	68.4	61.7	85.4	42.6	38.9	17.8	84.6
Own enterprise in collaboration with other enterprises or institutions	22.4	23.8	30.7	5.1	17.3	13.1	28.5	4.6	26.4	40.6	31.9	5.8
Other enterprises or institutions	11.0	2.4	10.3	0.5	8.3	3.5	3.2	0.0	13.1	0.7	14.2	1.3
Non-responsive firms*	18.1	16.9	25.7	9.3	18.4	15.0	6.7	10.0	17.9	19.8	36.1	8.3

* *Enterprises that returned the questionnaire, but did not respond to this question*

Table A2.10: Origin of innovation, 2002–2004

	Total				Industry				Services			
Size classes	1	2	3	4	1	2	3	4	1	2	3	4
Origin of innovation												
All innovative enterprises	979	3,420	8,061	3,804	429	2,090	2,845	2,274	551	1,331	5,216	1,530
South Africa	510	2,442	2,855	3,129	213	1,396	1,790	1,746	297	1,046	1,065	1,383
Abroad	288	391	3,123	322	133	379	865	302	155	12	2,258	21
No response	182	587	2,083	353	83	314	189	226	99	273	1,893	127
Percentage of innovation origin												
All innovative enterprises	100.0	100.0	100.0	100.0	100.0	100.0	100.0	100.0	100.0	100.0	100.0	100.0
South Africa	52.0	71.4	35.4	82.2	49.6	66.8	62.9	76.8	53.9	78.6	20.4	90.4
Abroad	29.4	11.4	38.7	8.5	31.0	18.1	30.4	13.3	28.2	0.9	43.3	1.3
No response	18.6	17.2	25.8	9.3	19.4	15.0	6.7	10.0	17.9	20.5	36.3	8.3

Table A2.11: Highly important effects of innovation on outcomes for enterprises (number), 2002–2004

	Total				Industry				Services			
Size classes	1	2	3	4	1	2	3	4	1	2	3	4
Product outcomes												
Increased range of goods and services	384	1,457	2,319	1,369	166	814	1,077	1,307	218	643	1,242	62
Entered new markets or increased market share	355	1,966	1,289	201	152	1,123	831	172	203	843	458	29
Improved quality of goods or services	386	1,922	3,326	1,780	184	1,224	572	1,678	203	698	2,755	102
Process outcomes												
Improved flexibility of production or service provision	246	749	1,265	249	108	575	392	187	138	175	873	62
Increased capacity of production or service provision	291	1,441	1,114	327	145	600	249	278	146	841	865	50
Reduced labour costs per unit output	148	662	211	292	91	607	163	263	57	55	47	29
Reduced materials and energy per unit output	118	606	141	318	65	545	133	247	53	62	8	70
Other outcomes												
Reduced environmental impacts or improved health and safety	156	841	377	691	88	788	296	609	68	53	81	82
Met governmental regulatory requirements	217	1,787	821	682	114	803	350	609	103	983	471	73

Table A2.12: Highly important effects of innovation on outcomes for enterprises (%), 2002–2004

	Total				Industry				Services			
Size classes	1	2	3	4	1	2	3	4	1	2	3	4
Product outcomes												
Increased range of goods and services	6.9	26.4	41.9	24.8	4.9	24.2	32.0	38.9	10.1	29.7	57.4	2.8
Entered new markets or increased market share	9.3	51.6	33.8	5.3	6.7	49.3	36.5	7.6	13.2	55.0	29.9	1.9
Improved quality of goods or services	5.2	25.9	44.9	24.0	5.0	33.5	15.6	45.9	5.4	18.6	73.3	2.7
Process outcomes												
Improved flexibility of production or service provision	9.8	29.9	50.4	9.9	8.5	45.5	31.1	14.8	11.1	14.0	70.0	4.9
Increased capacity of production or service provision	9.2	45.4	35.1	10.3	11.4	47.2	19.6	21.8	7.7	44.2	45.5	2.6
Reduced labour costs per unit output	11.3	50.4	16.1	22.2	8.1	54.0	14.5	23.4	30.1	29.2	25.2	15.5
Reduced materials and energy per unit output	10.0	51.3	11.9	26.9	6.6	55.0	13.4	25.0	27.3	32.0	4.3	36.3
Other outcomes												
Reduced environmental impacts or improved health and safety	7.6	40.7	18.3	33.5	4.9	44.2	16.6	34.2	24.0	18.7	28.6	28.8
Met governmental regulatory requirements	6.2	50.9	23.4	19.5	6.1	42.8	18.6	32.5	6.3	60.3	28.9	4.5

Table A2.13: Enterprises with innovation activity: number of enterprises that introduced new goods or services, 2002–2004

	Total				Industry				Services			
Size classes	1	2	3	4	1	2	3	4	1	2	3	4
Number of enterprises												
All product innovators												
Introduced new goods	668	2,403	3,853	910	311	1,573	1,505	828	357	830	2,348	82
Introduced new services	505	1,811	4,332	3,294	204	1,273	1,751	1,891	301	539	2,581	1,403
Product only innovators												
Introduced new goods	171	389	1,126	157	67	379	344	157	104	9	782	0
Introduced new services	71	238	1,063	1,241	28	201	603	0	43	37	461	1,241
Product and process innovators												
Introduced new goods	497	2,014	2,727	753	244	1,194	1,161	671	254	820	1,567	82
Introduced new services	434	1,573	3,268	2,053	176	1,071	1,148	1,891	258	502	2,120	162

Table A2.14: Enterprises with innovation activity: percentage of enterprises that introduced new goods or services, 2002–2004

	Total				Industry				Services			
Size classes	1	2	3	4	1	2	3	4	1	2	3	4
All product innovators												
Introduced new goods	8.5	30.7	49.2	11.6	7.4	37.3	35.7	19.6	9.9	22.9	64.9	2.3
Introduced new services	5.1	18.2	43.6	33.1	4.0	24.9	34.2	36.9	6.2	11.2	53.5	29.1
Product only innovators												
Introduced new goods	9.3	21.1	61.1	8.5	7.1	40.0	36.3	16.6	11.6	1.1	87.3	0.0
Introduced new services	2.7	9.1	40.7	47.5	3.3	24.2	72.5	0.0	2.4	2.1	25.8	69.7
Product and process innovators												
Introduced new goods	8.3	33.6	45.5	12.6	7.5	36.5	35.5	20.5	9.3	30.1	57.5	3.0
Introduced new services	5.9	21.5	44.6	28.0	4.1	25.0	26.8	44.1	8.5	16.5	69.7	5.3

Table A2.15: Innovative enterprises that received financial support for innovation activities from government sources (number), 2002–2004

	Total				Industry				Services			
Size classes	1	2	3	4	1	2	3	4	1	2	3	4
Enterprises with innovation activity	109	83	638	198	68	81	588	157	41	2	50	41
Successful innovators	92	53	630	198	59	52	588	157	32	2	42	41
Enterprises with only ongoing and/or abandoned innovations	0	5	0	0	0	5	0	0	0	0	0	0

Table A2.16: Innovative enterprises that received financial support for innovation activities from government sources (%), 2002–2004

	Total				Industry				Services			
Size classes	1	2	3	4	1	2	3	4	1	2	3	4
Enterprises with innovation activity	10.6	8.1	62.0	19.2	7.7	9.1	65.7	17.5	30.5	1.3	37.6	30.7
Successful innovators	9.4	5.5	64.7	20.4	6.9	6.0	68.7	18.3	27.7	1.5	35.8	35.0
Enterprises with only ongoing and/or abandoned innovations	0.0	100.0	0.0	0.0	0.0	100.0	0.0	0.0	0.0	0.0	0.0	0.0

Table A2.17: Sources of information for innovation rated as 'highly important' by innovative enterprises (number), 2002–2004

	Total				Industry				Services			
Size classes	1	2	3	4	1	2	3	4	1	2	3	4
Internal sources												
Sources within your enterprise or enterprise group	537	2,152	3,942	1,390	261	1,101	1,515	1,270	276	1,051	2,427	120
External - market resources												
Suppliers of equipment, materials, components or software	318	883	2,489	263	136	816	836	172	182	67	1,653	91
Clients or customers	392	1,171	2,303	1,747	170	775	763	1,642	222	396	1,540	105
Competitors or other enterprises in your sector	126	851	473	602	45	528	60	579	81	323	413	23
Consultants, commercial labs or private R&D institutes	83	118	63	370	28	72	47	329	55	46	15	41
External - institutional sources												
Universities and technikons	18	335	102	397	9	335	47	368	9	0	55	29
Government and public research institutes	15	301	53	177	8	301	0	157	7	0	53	21
External - other sources												
Conferences, trade fairs, exhibitions	106	236	21	0	44	223	0	0	63	13	21	0
Scientific journals and trade/ technical publications	69	194	170	186	31	194	50	157	38	0	121	29
Professional and industry associations	69	62	1,209	64	16	5	44	0	53	57	1,165	64

Table A2.18: Sources of information for innovation rated as 'highly important' by innovative enterprises (%), 2002–2004

	Total				Industry				Services			
Size classes	1	2	3	4	1	2	3	4	1	2	3	4
Internal sources												
Sources within your enterprise or enterprise group	6.7	26.8	49.1	17.3	6.3	26.5	36.5	30.6	7.1	27.1	62.7	3.1
External – market resources												
Suppliers of equipment, materials, components or software	8.0	22.3	63.0	6.6	6.9	41.6	42.6	8.8	9.1	3.4	82.9	4.6
Clients or customers	7.0	20.9	41.0	31.1	5.1	23.1	22.8	49.0	9.8	17.5	68.0	4.7
Competitors or other enterprises in your sector	6.1	41.5	23.1	29.4	3.7	43.5	5.0	47.8	9.6	38.5	49.2	2.8
Consultants, commercial labs or private R&D institutes	13.1	18.6	9.9	58.4	5.9	15.1	9.9	69.1	34.9	29.3	9.8	26.0
External – institutional sources												
Universities and Technikons	2.1	39.3	12.0	46.6	1.2	44.1	6.2	48.5	9.9	0.0	58.7	31.3
Government and public research institutes	2.8	55.1	9.6	32.5	1.6	64.6	0.0	33.7	9.2	0.0	65.3	25.5
External – other sources												
Conferences, trade fairs, exhibitions	29.3	64.9	5.8	0.0	16.4	83.6	0.0	0.0	64.8	13.4	21.8	0.0
Scientific journals and trade/ technical publications	11.2	31.3	27.5	30.0	7.2	44.9	11.5	36.4	20.4	0.0	64.1	15.5
Professional and industry associations	4.9	4.4	86.1	4.6	24.2	7.9	68.0	0.0	4.0	4.2	87.0	4.8

Table A2.19: Enterprises with innovation activity citing the following problems with their innovation activity, 2002–2004

	Total				Industry				Services			
Size classes	1	2	3	4	1	2	3	4	1	2	3	4
Number of innovative enterprises												
Abandoned in the concept stage	253	680	543	239	127	570	51	157	126	110	492	82
Abandoned after the activity or project was begun	236	1,400	98	265	119	541	9	186	117	859	89	79
Seriously delayed	324	878	1,470	398	152	459	226	328	172	420	1,244	70
Percentage of innovative enterprises												
Abandoned in the concept stage	1.6	4.2	3.3	1.5	1.7	7.5	0.7	2.1	1.5	1.3	5.7	1.0
Abandoned after the activity or project was begun	1.5	8.6	0.6	1.6	1.6	7.1	0.1	2.4	1.4	10.0	1.0	0.9
Seriously delayed	2.0	5.4	9.0	2.4	2.0	6.0	3.0	4.3	2.0	4.9	14.4	0.8

Table A2.20: Highly important factors that hampered innovation activities of innovative enterprises (number), 2002–2004

	Total				Industry				Services			
Size classes	1	2	3	4	1	2	3	4	1	2	3	4
Cost factors												
Lack of funds within your enterprise or group	159	680	2,356	1,543	69	606	409	1,362	89	73	1,947	181
Lack of finance from sources outside your enterprise	143	481	1,909	503	71	426	367	383	73	55	1,542	120
Innovation costs too high	159	678	2,555	317	79	519	356	226	80	159	2,200	91
Knowledge factors												
Lack of qualified personnel	203	715	2,156	242	102	612	222	212	101	104	1,934	29
Lack of information on technology	74	168	133	189	38	122	131	157	36	46	2	32
Lack of information on markets	65	50	376	41	29	50	0	0	35	0	376	41
Difficulty in finding cooperation partners	73	321	151	107	40	227	128	14	33	94	23	94
Market factors												
Market dominated by established enterprises	149	517	2,547	564	78	304	277	452	71	212	2,270	111
Uncertain demand for innovative goods or services	124	164	1,225	29	54	107	92	0	70	57	1,132	29
Reasons not to innovate												
No need due to prior innovations	38	3	454	0	16	3	71	0	22	0	383	0
No need because of no demand for innovations	18	0	93	0	8	0	71	0	10	0	22	0

Table A2.21: Highly important factors that hampered innovation activities of innovative enterprises (%), 2002–2004

	Total				Industry				Services			
Size classes	1	2	3	4	1	2	3	4	1	2	3	4
Cost factors												
Lack of funds within your enterprise or group	1.0	4.2	14.5	9.5	0.9	7.9	5.4	17.8	1.0	0.8	22.6	2.1
Lack of finance from sources outside your enterprise	0.9	3.0	11.7	3.1	0.9	5.6	4.8	5.0	0.8	0.6	17.9	1.4
Innovation costs too high	1.0	4.2	15.7	1.9	1.0	6.8	4.7	3.0	0.9	1.8	25.5	1.1
Knowledge factors												
Lack of qualified personnel	1.2	4.4	13.3	1.5	1.3	8.0	2.9	2.8	1.2	1.2	22.4	0.3
Lack of information on technology	0.5	1.0	0.8	1.2	0.5	1.6	1.7	2.1	0.4	0.5	0.0	0.4
Lack of information on markets	0.4	0.3	2.3	0.3	0.4	0.7	0.0	0.0	0.4	0.0	4.4	0.5
Difficulty in finding cooperation partners	0.4	2.0	0.9	0.7	0.5	3.0	1.7	0.2	0.4	1.1	0.3	1.1
Market factors												
Market dominated by established enterprises	0.9	3.2	15.7	3.5	1.0	4.0	3.6	5.9	0.8	2.5	26.3	1.3
Uncertain demand for innovative goods or services	0.8	1.0	7.5	0.2	0.7	1.4	1.2	0.0	0.8	0.7	13.1	0.3
Reasons not to innovate												
No need due to prior innovations	0.2	0.0	2.8	0.0	0.2	0.0	0.9	0.0	0.3	0.0	4.4	0.0
No need because of no demand for innovations	0.1	0.0	0.6	0.0	0.1	0.0	0.9	0.0	0.1	0.0	0.3	0.0

Table A2.22: Highly important factors that hampered innovation activities of non-innovative enterprises (number), 2002–2004

	Total				Industry				Services			
Size classes	1	2	3	4	1	2	3	4	1	2	3	4
Cost factors												
Lack of funds within your enterprise or group	65	417	1,587	1,165	35	363	284	493	29	55	1,303	672
Lack of finance from sources outside your enterprise	46	245	601	918	19	245	558	247	27	0	42	672
Innovation costs too high	51	375	961	1,307	17	304	284	740	35	71	677	567
Knowledge factors												
Lack of qualified personnel	41	183	689	1,090	17	128	570	493	25	55	120	597
Lack of information on technology	32	176	280	290	12	176	280	247	19	0	0	43
Lack of information on markets	16	117	284	255	4	117	275	247	12	0	10	9
Difficulty in finding cooperation partners	38	177	934	749	25	117	275	740	13	59	659	9
Market factors												
Market dominated by established enterprises	84	302	2,003	2,065	25	176	560	987	59	126	1,442	1,078
Uncertain demand for innovative goods or services	56	172	785	557	37	117	11	493	19	55	774	63
Reasons not to innovate												
No need due to prior innovations	66	406	71	247	21	351	0	247	45	55	71	0
No need because of no demand for innovations	104	615	1,423	592	33	234	0	247	71	381	1,423	345

Table A2.23: Highly important factors that hampered innovation activities of non-innovative enterprises (%), 2002–2004

	Total				Industry				Services			
Size classes	1	2	3	4	1	2	3	4	1	2	3	4
Cost factors												
Lack of funds within your enterprise or group	0.4	2.7	10.4	7.7	0.6	5.8	4.5	7.8	0.3	0.6	14.7	7.6
Lack of finance from sources outside your enterprise	0.3	1.6	4.0	6.0	0.3	3.9	8.9	3.9	0.3	0.0	0.5	7.6
Innovation costs too high	0.3	2.5	6.3	8.6	0.3	4.8	4.5	11.7	0.4	0.8	7.6	6.4
Knowledge factors												
Lack of qualified personnel	0.3	1.2	4.5	7.2	0.3	2.0	9.0	7.8	0.3	0.6	1.3	6.7
Lack of information on technology	0.2	1.2	1.8	1.9	0.2	2.8	4.4	3.9	0.2	0.0	0.0	0.5
Lack of information on markets	0.1	0.8	1.9	1.7	0.1	1.9	4.4	3.9	0.1	0.0	0.1	0.1
Difficulty in finding cooperation partners	0.3	1.2	6.1	4.9	0.4	1.9	4.4	11.7	0.1	0.7	7.4	0.1
Market factors												
Market dominated by established enterprises	0.6	2.0	13.2	13.6	0.4	2.8	8.9	15.7	0.7	1.4	16.2	12.1
Uncertain demand for innovative goods or services	0.4	1.1	5.2	3.7	0.6	1.9	0.2	7.8	0.2	0.6	8.7	0.7
Reasons not to innovate												
No need due to prior innovations	0.4	2.7	0.5	1.6	0.3	5.6	0.0	3.9	0.5	0.6	0.8	0.0
No need because of no demand for innovations	0.7	4.0	9.4	3.9	0.5	3.7	0.0	3.9	0.8	4.3	16.0	3.9

Table A2.24: Number of innovative and non-innovative enterprises that introduced organisational or marketing innovations, 2002–2004

	Total				Industry				Services			
Size classes	1	2	3	4	1	2	3	4	1	2	3	4
Enterprises with innovation activities												
Organisational innovations												
Knowledge management systems to better use or exchange information	604	2,189	4,127	1,632	254	1,018	935	1,482	350	1,171	3,192	150
Major changes to the organisation of work	621	2,344	5,531	307	271	1,166	1,145	187	350	1,178	4,386	119
External relations with other firms or public institutions	399	685	2,942	417	160	413	183	292	239	272	2,759	125
Marketing innovations												
Design or packaging of a good or service	417	1,866	1,759	1,874	179	1,009	557	609	238	857	1,202	1,265
Sales or distribution methods	310	1,201	1,420	750	115	350	262	700	196	850	1,158	50
Enterprises without innovation activities												
Organisational innovations												
Knowledge management systems to better use or exchange information	124	314	618	104	31	176	286	0	92	138	332	104
Major changes to the organisation of work	157	540	266	875	56	469	0	247	100	71	266	629
External relations with other firms or public institutions	104	297	889	351	32	293	0	247	72	4	889	104
Marketing innovations												
Design or packaging of a good or service	62	234	243	606	31	234	0	493	30	0	243	113
Sales or distribution methods	67	372	201	351	21	293	0	247	46	79	201	104

Table A2.25: Percentage of innovative and non-innovative enterprises that introduced organisational or marketing innovations, 2002–2004

	Total				Industry				Services			
Size classes	1	2	3	4	1	2	3	4	1	2	3	4
Enterprises with innovation activities												
Organisational innovations												
Knowledge management systems to better use or exchange information	3.7	13.5	25.4	10.0	3.3	13.3	12.2	19.4	4.1	13.6	37.0	1.7
Major changes to the organisation of work	3.8	14.4	34.0	1.9	3.6	15.3	15.0	2.5	4.1	13.7	50.8	1.4
External relations with other firms or public institutions	2.5	4.2	18.1	2.6	2.1	5.4	2.4	3.8	2.8	3.2	32.0	1.5
Marketing innovations												
Design or packaging of a good or service	2.6	11.5	10.8	11.5	2.3	13.2	7.3	8.0	2.8	9.9	13.9	14.7
Sales or distribution methods	1.9	7.4	8.7	4.6	1.5	4.6	3.4	9.2	2.3	9.9	13.4	0.6
Enterprises without innovation activities												
Organisational innovations												
Knowledge management systems to better use or exchange information	0.8	1.9	3.8	0.6	0.4	2.3	3.7	0.0	1.1	1.6	3.9	1.2
Major changes to the organisation of work	1.0	3.3	1.6	5.4	0.7	6.1	0.0	3.2	1.2	0.8	3.1	7.3
External relations with other firms or public institutions	0.6	1.8	5.5	2.2	0.4	3.8	0.0	3.2	0.8	0.1	10.3	1.2
Marketing innovations												
Design or packaging of a good or service	0.4	1.4	1.5	3.7	0.4	3.1	0.0	6.5	0.4	0.0	2.8	1.3
Sales or distribution methods	0.4	2.3	1.2	2.2	0.3	3.8	0.0	3.2	0.5	0.9	2.3	1.2

Table A2.26: Number of enterprises that secured a patent in SA or applied for at least one patent outside SA, 2002–2004

	Total				Industry				Services			
Size classes	1	2	3	4	1	2	3	4	1	2	3	4
Enterprises that secured a patent in SA												
All enterprises	151	222	64	92	84	206	47	0	67	16	17	92
Enterprises with innovation activity	141	222	64	71	79	206	47	0	62	16	17	71
Enterprises without innovation activity	10	0	0	21	4	0	0	0	5	0	0	21
Enterprises that applied for a patent outside SA												
All enterprises	114	204	64	62	73	196	47	0	41	9	17	62
Enterprises with innovation activity	103	204	64	41	64	196	47	0	39	9	17	41
Enterprises without innovation activity	11	0	0	21	8	0	0	0	2	0	0	21

Table A2.27: Percentage of enterprises that secured a patent in SA or applied for at least one patent outside SA, 2002–2004

	Total				Industry				Services			
Size classes	1	2	3	4	1	2	3	4	1	2	3	4
Enterprises that secured a patent in SA												
All enterprises	0.5	0.7	0.2	0.3	0.6	1.5	0.3	0.0	0.4	0.1	0.1	0.5
Enterprises with innovation activity	0.9	1.4	0.4	0.4	1.0	2.7	0.6	0.0	0.7	0.2	0.2	0.8
Enterprises without innovation activity	0.1	0.0	0.0	0.1	0.1	0.0	0.0	0.0	0.1	0.0	0.0	0.2
Enterprises that applied for a patent outside SA												
All enterprises	0.4	0.6	0.2	0.2	0.5	1.4	0.3	0.0	0.2	0.1	0.1	0.4
Enterprises with innovation activity	0.6	1.3	0.4	0.3	0.8	2.6	0.6	0.0	0.5	0.1	0.2	0.5
Enterprises without innovation activity	0.1	0.0	0.0	0.1	0.1	0.0	0.0	0.0	0.0	0.0	0.0	0.2

Table A2.28: Number of enterprises that made use of intellectual property rights, 2002–2004

	Total				Industry				Services			
Size classes	1	2	3	4	1	2	3	4	1	2	3	4
Enterprises with innovation activity												
Registered an industrial design	91	172	422	21	53	163	47	0	38	9	375	21
Registered a trademark	334	409	931	46	139	401	184	0	195	9	747	46
Claimed copyright	127	156	455	50	51	138	44	0	76	18	411	50
Granted a license on any intellectual property rights resulting from innovation	52	119	67	41	27	119	0	0	25	0	67	41
Enterprises without innovation activity												
Registered an industrial design	2	0	0	0	0	0	0	0	2	0	0	0
Registered a trademark	58	117	19	247	23	117	0	247	35	0	19	0
Claimed copyright	5	59	10	0	2	59	0	0	2	0	10	0
Granted a license on any intellectual property rights resulting from innovation	2	0	0	0	0	0	0	0	2	0	0	0

Table A2.29: Percentage of enterprises that made use of intellectual property rights, 2002–2004

	Total				Industry				Services			
Size classes	1	2	3	4	1	2	3	4	1	2	3	4
Enterprises with innovation activity												
Registered an industrial design	0.6	1.1	2.6	0.1	0.7	2.1	0.6	0.0	0.4	0.1	4.3	0.2
Registered a trademark	2.1	2.5	5.7	0.3	1.8	5.2	2.4	0.0	2.3	0.1	8.7	0.5
Claimed copyright	0.8	1.0	2.8	0.3	0.7	1.8	0.6	0.0	0.9	0.2	4.8	0.6
Granted a license on any intellectual property rights resulting from innovation	0.3	0.7	0.4	0.3	0.3	1.6	0.0	0.0	0.3	0.0	0.8	0.5
Enterprises without innovation activity												
Registered an industrial design	0.0	0.0	0.0	0.0	0.0	0.0	0.0	0.0	0.0	0.0	0.0	0.0
Registered a trademark	0.4	0.8	0.1	1.6	0.4	1.9	0.0	3.9	0.4	0.0	0.2	0.0
Claimed copyright	0.0	0.4	0.1	0.0	0.0	0.9	0.0	0.0	0.0	0.0	0.1	0.0
Granted a license on any intellectual property rights resulting from innovation	0.0	0.0	0.0	0.0	0.0	0.0	0.0	0.0	0.0	0.0	0.0	0.0

Table A2.30: Geographic distribution of goods and services sold by innovative and non-innovative enterprises (number), 2002–2004

	Total				Industry				Services			
Size classes	1	2	3	4	1	2	3	4	1	2	3	4
All enterprises												
South Africa (only some provinces)	537	2,131	8,544	7,740	170	1,273	2,657	4,392	367	858	5,887	3,348
South Africa (national)	1,031	2,591	4,773	1,440	463	1,969	1,661	721	567	622	3,113	720
Rest of Africa	621	1,666	1,426	699	276	1,199	286	503	345	467	1,140	196
Europe	303	436	559	21	185	325	220	0	118	112	339	21
United States	184	276	446	29	116	223	220	0	68	53	226	29
Asia	217	317	658	106	127	178	51	0	90	138	607	106
Other countries	294	579	807	26	158	468	548	0	137	110	259	26
Enterprises with innovation activity												
South Africa (only some provinces)	233	1,043	4,301	3,266	83	712	1,212	1,874	150	331	3,089	1,392
South Africa (national)	723	1,739	3,257	386	336	1,196	1,375	228	388	543	1,882	159
Rest of Africa	477	1,166	1,193	298	222	778	280	257	255	388	913	41
Europe	241	308	258	21	153	196	220	0	88	112	38	21
United States	155	207	245	29	98	153	220	0	57	53	25	29
Asia	168	258	457	0	108	120	51	0	60	138	406	0
Other countries	222	322	312	26	120	212	268	0	102	110	44	26
Enterprises without innovation activity												
South Africa (only some provinces)	304	1,088	4,243	4,474	87	560	1,445	2,518	217	527	2,798	1,956
South Africa (national)	307	852	1,516	1,054	127	772	286	493	180	79	1,231	561
Rest of Africa	144	500	232	401	54	421	6	247	90	79	227	155
Europe	61	128	301	0	31	128	0	0	30	0	301	0
United States	30	70	201	0	19	70	0	0	11	0	201	0
Asia	49	59	201	106	19	59	0	0	30	0	201	106
Other countries	72	257	495	0	37	257	280	0	35	0	214	0

Table A2.31: Geographic distribution of goods and services sold by innovative and non-innovative enterprises (%), 2002–2004

	Total				Industry				Services			
Size classes	1	2	3	4	1	2	3	4	1	2	3	4
All enterprises												
South Africa (only some provinces)	32.9	39.8	56.4	83.1	25.9	37.2	58.1	83.1	37.6	44.3	55.7	83.1
South Africa (national)	63.1	48.3	31.5	15.5	70.6	57.5	36.3	13.6	58.2	32.1	29.4	17.9
Rest of Africa	38.1	31.1	9.4	7.5	42.1	35.0	6.2	9.5	35.4	24.1	10.8	4.9
Europe	18.6	8.1	3.7	0.2	28.1	9.5	4.8	0.0	12.1	5.8	3.2	0.5
United States	11.3	5.2	2.9	0.3	17.7	6.5	4.8	0.0	6.9	2.7	2.1	0.7
Asia	13.3	5.9	4.3	1.1	19.3	5.2	1.1	0.0	9.2	7.1	5.7	2.6
Other countries	18.0	10.8	5.3	0.3	24.0	13.7	12.0	0.0	14.0	5.7	2.4	0.6
Enterprises with innovation activity												
South Africa (only some provinces)	23.8	30.5	53.4	85.9	19.3	34.1	42.6	82.4	27.3	24.9	59.2	91.0
South Africa (national)	73.9	50.8	40.4	10.2	78.3	57.2	48.3	10.0	70.4	40.8	36.1	10.4
Rest of Africa	48.7	34.1	14.8	7.8	51.7	37.2	9.9	11.3	46.3	29.2	17.5	2.7
Europe	24.7	9.0	3.2	0.5	35.7	9.4	7.7	0.0	16.0	8.4	0.7	1.3
United States	15.8	6.0	3.0	0.8	22.8	7.3	7.7	0.0	10.3	4.0	0.5	1.9
Asia	17.1	7.5	5.7	0.0	25.2	5.7	1.8	0.0	10.9	10.4	7.8	0.0
Other countries	22.7	9.4	3.9	0.7	28.1	10.1	9.4	0.0	18.5	8.3	0.8	1.7
Enterprises without innovation activity												
South Africa (only some provinces)	46.6	56.1	59.8	81.2	38.4	42.0	83.5	83.6	51.0	87.0	52.2	78.4
South Africa (national)	47.1	43.9	21.4	19.1	56.0	58.0	16.5	16.4	42.3	13.0	23.0	22.5
Rest of Africa	22.1	25.8	3.3	7.3	23.9	31.6	0.3	8.2	21.2	13.0	4.2	6.2
Europe	9.4	6.6	4.2	0.0	13.8	9.6	0.0	0.0	7.1	0.0	5.6	0.0
United States	4.5	3.6	2.8	0.0	8.3	5.2	0.0	0.0	2.5	0.0	3.7	0.0
Asia	7.5	3.0	2.8	1.9	8.3	4.4	0.0	0.0	7.1	0.0	3.7	4.3
Other countries	11.1	13.2	7.0	0.0	16.5	19.2	16.2	0.0	8.2	0.0	4.0	0.0

Table A2.32: Innovative enterprises that introduced organisational innovation that rated the following results as having a 'high' level of importance, 2002–2004

	Total				Industry				Services			
Size classes	1	2	3	4	1	2	3	4	1	2	3	4
Number of innovative enterprises												
Improved market share	366	1,784	1,415	296	171	665	237	226	195	1,120	1,178	70
Reduced time to respond to customer or supplier needs	366	1,462	1,902	373	172	597	281	226	195	865	1,622	147
Improved quality of your goods or services	450	2,292	2,587	341	220	1,036	868	226	230	1,256	1,719	115
Reduced costs per unit output	261	638	1,673	107	142	289	471	15	119	349	1,202	92
Improved employee satisfaction/ turnover	209	1,701	1,600	171	92	573	364	106	118	1,128	1,236	65
Percentage of innovative enterprises												
Improved market share	2.3	11.0	8.7	1.8	2.2	8.7	3.1	3.0	2.3	13.0	13.7	0.8
Reduced time to respond to customer or supplier needs	2.3	9.0	11.7	2.3	2.2	7.8	3.7	3.0	2.3	10.0	18.8	1.7
Improved quality of your goods or services	2.8	14.1	15.9	2.1	2.9	13.6	11.4	3.0	2.7	14.6	19.9	1.3
Reduced costs per unit output	1.6	3.9	10.3	0.7	1.9	3.8	6.2	0.2	1.4	4.0	13.9	1.1
Improved employee satisfaction/ turnover	1.3	10.5	9.8	1.1	1.2	7.5	4.8	1.4	1.4	13.1	14.3	0.8
Percentage of all enterprises												
Improved market share	1.2	5.7	4.5	0.9	1.2	4.8	1.7	1.6	1.1	6.4	6.7	0.4
Reduced time to respond to customer or supplier needs	1.2	4.6	6.0	1.2	1.2	4.3	2.0	1.6	1.1	4.9	9.3	0.8
Improved quality of your goods or services	1.4	7.3	8.2	1.1	1.6	7.4	6.2	1.6	1.3	7.2	9.8	0.7
Reduced costs per unit output	0.8	2.0	5.3	0.3	1.0	2.1	3.4	0.1	0.7	2.0	6.9	0.5
Improved employee satisfaction/ turnover	0.7	5.4	5.1	0.5	0.7	4.1	2.6	0.8	0.7	6.4	7.1	0.4

Table A2.33: Innovative enterprises that received financial support for innovation activities from government sources, 2002–2004

	Total				Industry				Services			
Size classes	1	2	3	4	1	2	3	4	1	2	3	4
Number of innovative enterprises												
Metros and municipalities	6	0	0	0	0	0	0	0	6	0	0	0
Provincial government	7	23	0	0	1	23	0	0	6	0	0	0
National government	64	53	299	0	44	51	286	0	19	2	13	0
National funding agencies	46	5	339	198	27	5	302	157	19	0	38	41
Foreign government/public sources	8	2	0	0	6	2	0	0	2	0	0	0
Percentage of innovative enterprises												
Metros and municipalities	0.0	0.0	0.0	0.0	0.0	0.0	0.0	0.0	0.1	0.0	0.0	0.0
Provincial government	0.0	0.1	0.0	0.0	0.0	0.3	0.0	0.0	0.1	0.0	0.0	0.0
National government	0.4	0.3	1.8	0.0	0.6	0.7	3.7	0.0	0.2	0.0	0.1	0.0
National funding agencies	0.3	0.0	2.1	1.2	0.3	0.1	3.9	2.1	0.2	0.0	0.4	0.5
Foreign government/public sources	0.1	0.0	0.0	0.0	0.1	0.0	0.0	0.0	0.0	0.0	0.0	0.0

Table A2.34: Number and percentage of staff with a degree or diploma, 2004

Size classes	Total				Industry				Services			
	1	2	3	4	1	2	3	4	1	2	3	4
Total number of staff												
Enterprises with innovation activity	832,194	183,930	203,060	70,973	462,727	123,607	116,254	66,642	369,466	60,323	86,807	4,330
Enterprises without innovation activity	114,020	126,497	95,123	29,415	55,132	88,239	55,416	18,252	58,888	38,258	39,707	11,163
Number of staff with a degree or diploma												
Enterprises with innovation activity	133,769	13,980	19,969	11,354	84,026	8,446	8,529	10,267	49,744	5,534	11,440	1,087
Enterprises without innovation activity	10,089	4,077	8,271	8,535	3,963	2,586	1,168	2,639	6,127	1,491	7,103	5,896
Percentage of staff with a degree or diploma												
Enterprises with innovation activity	16.1	7.6	9.8	16.0	18.2	6.8	7.3	15.4	13.5	9.2	13.2	25.1
Enterprises without innovation activity	8.8	3.2	8.7	29.0	7.2	2.9	2.1	14.5	10.4	3.9	17.9	52.8

Table A2.35: Enterprises with organisational and/or marketing innovations, 2002–2004

	Total				Industry				Services			
Size classes	1	2	3	4	1	2	3	4	1	2	3	4
Number of enterprises with organisational and/or marketing innovations												
Enterprises with organisational innovation	1,039	3,217	7,409	2,653	435	1,776	1,549	1,729	604	1,441	5,860	924
Enterprises with marketing innovation	620	2,488	2,849	2,813	254	1,505	820	1,406	365	982	2,029	1,407
Innovative enterprises with organisational and/or marketing innovation	825	2,885	6,412	3,312	360	1,554	1,678	1,906	466	1,331	4,734	1,406
Product only innovative enterprises with organisational and/or marketing innovation	129	359	756	1,221	50	312	326	0	79	46	430	1,221
Process only innovative enterprises with organisational and/or marketing innovation	119	476	935	78	49	212	161	14	70	264	774	64
Product and process innovative enterprises with organisational and/or marketing innovation	563	2,045	3,607	1,801	255	1,025	1,163	1,680	308	1,020	2,444	121
Non-innovative enterprises with organisational innovation	246	623	1,412	980	88	469	286	247	158	155	1,126	733
Non-innovative enterprises with marketing innovation	110	430	444	606	44	351	0	493	66	79	444	113
Non-innovative enterprises with organisational **or** marketing innovation	274	682	1,422	1,235	104	527	286	493	170	155	1,136	742
Non-innovative enterprises with organisational **and** marketing innovation	82	372	435	351	27	293	0	247	54	79	435	104

Size classes	Total				Industry				Services			
	1	2	3	4	1	2	3	4	1	2	3	4
Percentage enterprises with organisational and/or marketing innovations												
Enterprises with organisational innovation	63.7	60.0	48.9	28.5	66.3	51.9	33.9	32.7	61.9	74.4	55.4	22.9
Enterprises with marketing innovation	38.0	46.4	18.8	30.2	38.8	44.0	17.9	26.6	37.5	50.7	19.2	34.9
Innovative enterprises with organisational and/or marketing innovation	84.2	84.3	79.5	87.1	83.8	74.4	59.0	83.8	84.6	100.0	90.7	91.9
Product only innovative enterprises with organisational and/or marketing innovation	13.1	10.5	9.4	32.1	11.5	14.9	11.4	0.0	14.4	3.5	8.2	79.8
Process only innovative enterprises with organisational and/or marketing innovation	12.2	13.9	11.6	2.1	11.5	10.1	5.7	0.6	12.7	19.8	14.8	4.2
Product and process innovative enterprises with organisational and/or marketing innovation	57.5	59.8	44.8	47.3	59.4	49.0	40.9	73.9	55.9	76.7	46.9	7.9
Non-innovative enterprises with organisational innovation	37.7	32.1	19.9	17.8	38.6	35.1	16.5	8.2	37.3	25.5	21.0	29.4
Non-innovative enterprises with marketing innovation	16.8	22.2	6.3	11.0	19.2	26.4	0.0	16.4	15.5	13.0	8.3	4.5
Non-innovative enterprises with organisational **or** marketing innovation	42.0	35.1	20.0	22.4	45.9	39.5	16.5	16.4	40.0	25.5	21.2	29.7
Non-innovative enterprises with organisational **and** marketing innovation	12.5	19.2	6.1	6.4	11.9	22.0	0.0	8.2	12.8	13.0	8.1	4.2

Table A2.36: Collaborative partnerships for innovation activities by type of partner and their location (number), 2002–2004

	Total				Industry				Services			
Size classes	1	2	3	4	1	2	3	4	1	2	3	4
Other enterprises within your enterprise group												
South Africa	135	37	474	0	72	20	47	0	63	18	427	0
Rest of Africa	29	1	4	0	12	1	0	0	17	0	4	0
Europe	125	113	371	0	75	111	0	0	50	2	371	0
USA	59	81	416	41	44	81	0	0	15	0	416	0
Asia	21	56	4	0	11	10	0	0	10	46	4	0
Other countries	27	5	0	0	15	5	0	0	12	0	0	0
Suppliers of equipment, materials, components or software												
South Africa	291	1,012	1,912	1,608	141	319	323	1,491	150	694	1,590	117
Rest of Africa	7	100	0	0	4	6	0	0	4	94	0	0
Europe	193	745	191	266	123	216	163	211	71	529	27	55
USA	59	128	113	240	36	71	21	211	23	57	92	29
Asia	49	10	5	0	30	10	3	0	19	0	2	0
Other countries	53	10	383	0	29	10	0	0	24	0	383	0
Clients or customers												
South Africa	303	1,000	2,902	1,788	156	347	555	1,648	147	653	2,346	140
Rest of Africa	71	195	390	21	28	25	3	0	43	170	388	21
Europe	101	147	46	29	63	90	0	0	38	57	46	29
USA					34	47	0	0	20	46	21	9
Asia	23	89	13	21	9	43	0	0	13	46	13	21
Other countries	53	86	27	0	24	31	0	0	29	55	27	0
Competitors or other enterprises in your sector												
South Africa	222	716	2,078	1,718	103	160	191	1,648	119	556	1,887	70
Rest of Africa	26	62	4	0	9	5	0	0	16	57	4	0
Europe	56	74	38	240	32	26	0	211	24	48	38	29
USA	36	54	24	240	19	6	3	211	18	48	21	29
Asia	23	72	383	0	13	26	3	0	10	46	379	0
Other countries	31	7	4	0	20	5	0	0	12	2	4	0

	Total				Industry				Services			
Size classes	1	2	3	4	1	2	3	4	1	2	3	4
Consultants, commercial labs or private R&D institutes												
South Africa					124	146	53	1,491	123	76	798	99
Rest of Africa	6	5	0	0	0	5	0	0	6	0	0	0
Europe	62	68	8	21	38	12	0	0	24	57	8	21
USA	21	63	0	0	13	17	0	0	8	46	0	0
Asia	6	5	0	21	4	5	0	0	2	0	0	21
Other countries	20	20	5	0	15	20	0	0	4	0	5	0
Universities or technikons												
South Africa	185	215	503	1,602	99	143	53	1,491	86	73	450	111
Rest of Africa	2	0	0	0	2	0	0	0	0	0	0	0
Europe	20	48	5	21	12	1	0	0	7	46	5	21
USA	5	48	5	0	2	1	0	0	2	46	5	0
Asia					0	0	0	0	2	0	0	0
Other countries	8	15	5	0	6	15	0	0	2	0	5	0
Government or public research institutes												
South Africa	153	126	508	1,362	73	52	56	1,280	80	74	451	82
Rest of Africa	4	9	0	0	0	0	0	0	4	9	0	0
Europe	9	46	0	9	4	0	0	0	4	46	0	9
USA	5	46	0	0	0	0	0	0	5	46	0	0
Asia	2	0	0	0	0	0	0	0	2	0	0	0
Other countries	10	16	0	0	6	16	0	0	4	0	0	0

Table A2.37: Collaborative partnerships for innovation activities by type of partner and their location (%), 2002–2004

	Total				Industry				Services			
Size classes	1	2	3	4	1	2	3	4	1	2	3	4
Other enterprises within your enterprise group												
South Africa	13.8	1.1	5.9	0.0	16.8	0.9	1.7	0.0	11.5	1.3	8.2	0.0
Rest of Africa	3.0	0.0	0.1	0.0	2.7	0.1	0.0	0.0	3.2	0.0	0.1	0.0
Europe	12.8	3.3	4.6	0.0	17.4	5.3	0.0	0.0	9.2	0.1	7.1	0.0
USA	6.0	2.4	5.2	0.0	10.3	3.9	0.0	0.0	2.7	0.0	8.0	0.0
Asia	2.1	1.6	0.1	0.0	2.5	0.5	0.0	0.0	1.8	3.5	0.1	0.0
Other countries	2.8	0.1	0.0	0.0	3.4	0.2	0.0	0.0	2.3	0.0	0.0	0.0
Suppliers of equipment, materials, components or software												
South Africa	29.7	29.6	23.7	42.3	33.0	15.2	11.3	65.6	27.2	52.1	30.5	7.6
Rest of Africa	0.7	2.9	0.0	0.0	0.8	0.3	0.0	0.0	0.7	7.0	0.0	0.0
Europe	19.8	21.8	2.4	7.0	28.6	10.3	5.7	9.3	12.9	39.8	0.5	3.6
USA	6.0	3.7	1.4	6.3	8.3	3.4	0.7	9.3	4.2	4.3	1.8	1.9
Asia	5.0	0.3	0.1	0.0	7.0	0.5	0.1	0.0	3.4	0.0	0.0	0.0
Other countries	5.4	0.3	4.8	0.0	6.8	0.5	0.0	0.0	4.4	0.0	7.4	0.0
Clients or customers												
South Africa	31.0	29.2	36.0	47.0	36.4	16.6	19.5	72.5	26.8	49.1	45.0	9.2
Rest of Africa	7.2	5.7	4.8	0.5	6.5	1.2	0.1	0.0	7.7	12.8	7.4	1.3
Europe	10.3	4.3	0.6	0.8	14.6	4.3	0.0	0.0	6.9	4.3	0.9	1.9
USA	0.0	0.0	0.0	0.0	7.8	2.2	0.0	0.0	3.7	3.5	0.4	0.6
Asia	2.3	2.6	0.2	0.5	2.2	2.0	0.0	0.0	2.4	3.5	0.2	1.3
Other countries	5.4	2.5	0.3	0.0	5.6	1.5	0.0	0.0	5.3	4.1	0.5	0.0

Size classes	Total				Industry				Services			
	1	2	3	4	1	2	3	4	1	2	3	4
Competitors or other enterprises in your sector												
South Africa	22.7	20.9	25.8	45.2	24.0	7.7	6.7	72.5	21.7	41.8	36.2	4.6
Rest of Africa	2.6	1.8	0.1	0.0	2.2	0.2	0.0	0.0	3.0	4.3	0.1	0.0
Europe	5.7	2.2	0.5	6.3	7.4	1.3	0.0	9.3	4.4	3.6	0.7	1.9
USA	3.7	1.6	0.3	6.3	4.3	0.3	0.1	9.3	3.2	3.6	0.4	1.9
Asia	2.3	2.1	4.7	0.0	3.0	1.3	0.1	0.0	1.8	3.5	7.3	0.0
Other countries	3.2	0.2	0.1	0.0	4.6	0.2	0.0	0.0	2.1	0.1	0.1	0.0
Consultants, commercial labs or private R&D institutes												
South Africa	0.0	0.0	0.0	0.0	29.0	7.0	1.9	65.6	22.4	5.7	15.3	6.5
Rest of Africa	0.6	0.1	0.0	0.0	0.0	0.2	0.0	0.0	1.1	0.0	0.0	0.0
Europe	6.3	2.0	0.1	0.5	8.9	0.6	0.0	0.0	4.3	4.3	0.2	1.3
USA	2.2	1.8	0.0	0.0	3.0	0.8	0.0	0.0	1.5	3.5	0.0	0.0
Asia	0.6	0.1	0.0	0.5	0.8	0.2	0.0	0.0	0.4	0.0	0.0	1.3
Other countries	2.0	0.6	0.1	0.0	3.6	0.9	0.0	0.0	0.8	0.0	0.1	0.0
Universities or technikons												
South Africa	18.9	6.3	6.2	42.1	23.2	6.8	1.9	65.6	15.6	5.5	8.6	7.3
Rest of Africa	0.2	0.0	0.0	0.0	0.5	0.0	0.0	0.0	0.0	0.0	0.0	0.0
Europe	2.0	1.4	0.1	0.5	2.8	0.1	0.0	0.0	1.3	3.5	0.1	1.3
USA	0.5	1.4	0.1	0.0	0.5	0.1	0.0	0.0	0.4	3.5	0.1	0.0
Asia	0.0	0.0	0.0	0.0	0.0	0.0	0.0	0.0	0.4	0.0	0.0	0.0
Other countries	0.8	0.4	0.1	0.0	1.3	0.7	0.0	0.0	0.4	0.0	0.1	0.0
Government or public research institutes												
South Africa	15.6	3.7	6.3	35.8	17.0	2.5	2.0	56.3	14.5	5.6	8.7	5.4
Rest of Africa	0.4	0.3	0.0	0.0	0.0	0.0	0.0	0.0	0.8	0.7	0.0	0.0
Europe	0.9	1.3	0.0	0.2	1.0	0.0	0.0	0.0	0.8	3.5	0.0	0.6
USA	0.5	1.3	0.0	0.0	0.0	0.0	0.0	0.0	0.9	3.5	0.0	0.0
Asia	0.3	0.0	0.0	0.0	0.0	0.0	0.0	0.0	0.4	0.0	0.0	0.0
Other countries	1.1	0.5	0.0	0.0	1.4	0.8	0.0	0.0	0.8	0.0	0.0	0.0

Table A2.38: Innovative enterprises performing process innovations, 2002–2004

	Total				Industry				Services			
Size classes	1	2	3	4	1	2	3	4	1	2	3	4
Number of process innovators	756	2,969	5,215	2,193	341	1,685	1,912	1,905	414	1,284	3,303	289
Percentage of process innovators	46.3	55.4	34.4	23.6	52.0	49.2	41.8	36.0	42.5	66.3	31.2	7.2

Table A2.39: Innovative enterprises performing specific process innovations, 2002–2004

	Total				Industry				Services			
Size classes	1	2	3	4	1	2	3	4	1	2	3	4
Number of specific process innovators												
Methods of manufacturing or production	470	2,261	4,024	1,049	280	1,263	1,233	897	190	998	2,791	152
Delivery or distribution methods	420	1,854	2,919	1,496	157	912	1,116	1,363	263	942	1,803	133
Supporting activities	562	2,564	2,912	942	227	1,375	779	715	335	1,189	2,134	227
Percentage of specific process innovators												
Methods of manufacturing or production	6.0	29.0	51.6	13.4	7.6	34.4	33.6	24.4	4.6	24.2	67.6	3.7
Delivery or distribution methods	6.3	27.7	43.6	22.4	4.4	25.7	31.5	38.4	8.4	30.0	57.4	4.2
Supporting activities	8.1	36.7	41.7	13.5	7.3	44.4	25.2	23.1	8.6	30.6	54.9	5.9

Table A2.40: Responsibility for process innovations, 2002–2004

	Total				Industry				Services			
Size classes	1	2	3	4	1	2	3	4	1	2	3	4
Number of process innovators												
Mainly own	358	1,603	2,180	2,007	175	1,220	1,281	1,875	183	383	899	132
Own together with others	320	926	2,314	166	121	284	121	29	198	642	2,193	137
Mainly others	82	460	626	21	48	200	419	0	33	260	207	21
Percentage of process innovators												
Mainly own	5.8	26.1	35.5	32.6	3.9	26.8	28.1	41.2	11.4	24.0	56.3	8.3
Own together with others	8.6	24.9	62.1	4.4	21.9	51.1	21.8	5.2	6.3	20.3	69.2	4.3
Mainly others	6.9	38.7	52.7	1.7	7.3	30.0	62.8	0.0	6.4	50.0	39.7	3.9

Table A2.41: Origin of process innovation, 2002–2004

	Total				Industry				Services			
Size classes	1	2	3	4	1	2	3	4	1	2	3	4
Number of process innovators												
South Africa	575	2,675	3,512	1,848	230	1,397	1,368	1,588	345	1,277	2,143	260
Abroad	183	240	1,609	346	114	231	453	317	70	9	1,156	29
Non-process innovators	874	2,445	10,033	7,118	313	1,794	2,754	3,380	561	651	7,278	3,738
Percentage of process innovators												
South Africa	35.2	49.9	23.2	19.8	35.0	40.8	29.9	30.0	35.3	65.9	20.3	6.4
Abroad	11.2	4.5	10.6	3.7	17.3	6.8	9.9	6.0	7.1	0.5	10.9	0.7
Non-process innovators	53.6	45.6	66.2	76.4	47.7	52.4	60.2	64.0	57.5	33.6	68.8	92.8

Table A2.42: Enterprises which introduced new or improved products to the market as a percentage of enterprises engaged in innovation activity by sector, 2004

	Total				Industry				Services			
Size classes	1	2	3	4	1	2	3	4	1	2	3	4
Number of enterprises	802	2,842	5,986	3,451	350	1,775	2,655	2,048	452	1,067	3,331	1,403
Percentage enterprises	49.1	53.0	39.5	37.1	53.3	51.9	58.0	38.7	46.3	55.1	31.5	34.8

Table A2.43: Enterprises stating they were part of a larger group

	Total				Innovative				Non-innovative			
Size classes	1	2	3	4	1	2	3	4	1	2	3	4
Number of enterprises												
Part of a larger group	790	1,512	1,465	523	569	1,259	1,322	264	221	253	143	259
Not part of a larger group	836	3,848	13,055	8,789	404	2,162	6,730	3,540	431	1,686	6,324	5,249
No response	6	0	634	0	6	0	8	0	0	0	625	0
Percentage of enterprises												
Part of a larger group	2.5	4.8	4.7	1.7	3.5	7.7	8.1	1.6	1.5	1.7	0.9	1.7
Not part of a larger group	2.7	12.2	41.5	27.9	2.5	13.3	41.4	21.8	2.8	11.1	41.6	34.6
No response	0.0	0.0	2.0	0.0	0.0	0.0	0.1	0.0	0.0	0.0	4.1	0.0

Table A2.44: Innovative enterprises involved in intramural R&D continuously or occasionally, 2002–2004

Size classes	1	2	3	4	Total
Number of enterprises					
Continuously	381	894	1,450	573	3,298
Occasionally	248	1,356	1,042	1,593	4,239
Percentage of enterprises					
Continuously	38.8	26.1	18.0	15.1	20.3
Occasionally	25.3	39.6	12.9	41.9	26.1

Appendix 3

Open letter from the European Commission, Eurostat to non-EU member states

ANNEX 3

EUROPEAN COMMISSION
EUROSTAT

Directorate A: Statistical information systems; research and data analysis; technical cooperation with Phare and Tacis countries
Unit A-4: Research and development, methods and data analysis

Luxembourg, 5 March 2001
ESTAT/A-4/FF/INNO

To
Non-EU Member States

Subject: Third Community Innovation Survey – core questionnaire and survey methodology

Please find the final version of the core questionnaire for the third Community Innovation Survey. In addition you will find the survey methodology that will be used.

This survey will be launched in the EEA Member States in 2001. In case you plan to launch an innovation survey in your country we would appreciate that you used the core questionnaire and the survey methodology as basis for your national survey. This would improve the comparability of innovation indicators between regions and economies worldwide.

Harald Sonnberger
Head of Unit A4

Person to contact: Frank Foyn (+352 4301 33037/ frank.foyn@cec.eu.int)

Appendix 4

The Fourth Community Innovation Survey (CIS 4): Methodological recommendations and Core Questionnaire

The Fourth Community Innovation Survey (CIS 4) Methodological recommendations

(In accordance with section 7 of the annex to the Commission Regulation on innovation statistics No 1450/2004)

Final version 9 November 2004

Introduction

The Commission Regulation No 1450/2004, implementing Decision No 1608/2003/EC of the European Parliament and of the Council concerning the production and development of Community statistics on innovation (= Commission Regulation on innovation statistics), puts innovation statistics on a statutory basis and makes compulsory the delivery of certain variables. This document, which outlines the harmonized methodology to be used for CIS 4, is related to section 7, paragraph 2 of the annex of this Commission Regulation on innovation.

1. Target population

The target population of the CIS 4 shall be the total population of enterprises related to market activities (NACE activities C to K).

1.1. NACE

Core coverage

In accordance with section 2 of the annex of the Commission Regulation on innovation statistics, the following industries shall be included in the core target population of the CIS 4:

- mining and quarrying (NACE 10-14)
- manufacturing (NACE 15-37)
- electricity, gas and water supply (NACE 40-41)
- wholesale trade (NACE 51)
- transport, storage and communication (NACE 60-64)
- financial intermediation (NACE 65-67)
- computer and related activities (NACE 72)
- architectural and engineering activities (NACE 74.2)
- technical testing and analysis (NACE 74.3)

Additional coverage, in order of descending priority (to be done on a voluntary basis):

- research and development (NACE 73)
- construction (NACE 45)
- motor trade (NACE 50)
- retail trade (NACE 52)

- legal, accounting, market research, consultancy and management services (NACE 74.1)
- advertising (NACE 74.4)
- labour recruitment and provision of personnel (NACE 74.5)
- investigation and security activities (NACE 74.6)
- industrial cleaning services (NACE 74.7)
- miscellaneous business activities n.e.c. (NACE 74.8)
- real estate activities (NACE 70)
- hotels and restaurants (NACE 55)
- renting of machinery and equipment without an operator (NACE 71)

These economic activities should be regarded as "non-core" and do not necessarily have to meet the same quality requirements as for the core coverage e.g. for item and unit non-response (i.e. a non-response survey does not have to be carried out in respect of these NACE industries) or the required level of precision.

1.2 Size-classes

It is recommended that **all** enterprises be included in the target population. However, the minimum coverage shall be all enterprises with **10 employees or more**.

1.3. Statistical units

The main statistical unit for CIS 4 shall be the enterprise, as defined in the Council Regulation 696/1993 on statistical units or as defined in the national statistical business register. EU Regulation 2186/1993 requires that Member States set up and maintain a register of enterprises, as well as associated legal units and local units.

In the Council Regulation 696/1993[1], the enterprise is defined as "the smallest combination of legal units that is an organisational unit producing goods or services, which benefits from a certain degree of autonomy in decision making, especially for the allocation of its current resources. It may carry out one or more activities at one or more locations and it may be a combination of legal units, one legal unit or part of a legal unit."

In general, innovation activities and decisions usually take place at the enterprise level, which leads to the enterprise being used as the statistical unit. If the use of the enterprise as a statistical unit is not feasible, other units such as the division of the enterprise group, the kind of activity unit (KAU), the local kind of activity unit (LKAU) or the enterprise group may be used instead.

1.4 The observation period

The observation period to be covered by the survey shall be 2002-2004 inclusive i.e. the three-year period from the beginning of 2002 to the end of 2004. The reference period of the CIS 4 shall be the year 2004.

[1] Council Regulation (EEC) N° 696/1993 of 15 March 1993, OJ N° L76 of the 3 March on the statistical units for the observation and analysis of the production system in the Community.

2. Survey methodology

2.1. Sampling frame

The **official, up-to-date, statistical business register**[2] **of the country** should be used.

2.2 Census or sample survey

Data should be collected through a census, sample survey or a combination of both.

2.3 Stratification

The target population shall be broken down into similar structured subgroups or strata (which should be as homogeneous as possible and form mutually exclusive groups). Appropriate stratification will normally give results with smaller sampling errors than a non-stratified sample of the same size and will make it possible to ensure that there are enough units in the respective domains[3] to produce results of acceptable quality.

The stratification variables to be used for the CIS 4, i.e. the characteristics used to break down the sample into similarly structured groups, should be:

– The economic activities (in accordance with NACE)[4].

  In accordance with the requirements of section 5, paragraph 2 of the annex of the Commission Regulation on innovation statistics, stratification by NACE should be done at least at two-digit (division) level, except for NACE 74. Here the three digit sections NACE 74.2 and 74.3 should be treated as separate NACE categories while NACE 74.1 and 74.4 to 74.8 should be treated as a single NACE category.

– Enterprise size according to the number of employees[5].

  The size-classes used should at least be the following:
  - 0-9 employees
  - 10-49 employees
  - 50-249 employees
  - 250+ employees.

  More detailed breakdown by size classes may also be used, but, whatever size-classes are chosen, they should fit into the above size groups.

– Regional aspects:
  In accordance with section 7, paragraph 2 of the annex of the Commission Regulation on innovation statistics, the methodology will include regional aspects. Therefore, the regional allocation of the sample shall be taken into consideration when sampling.

---

[2] Council Regulation (EEC) N° 2186/1993 of 22 July 1993.

[3] Domains are defined as strata or combinations or strata, for which results will be published.

[4] The NACE code to use for stratification should be that of the enterprise at the end of the reference period 2004.

[5] The enterprise size to use for stratification should be the number of employees at the end of the reference period 2004.

2.4. Sample size

There is no minimum sample size needed, as long as the sample size chosen will meet the precision levels required (see section 4.6). However, if a particular stratum has less than 6 enterprises, then all the enterprises in this stratum should be selected for the survey.

The expected response rate should be borne in mind i.e. the sample size should take into account the non-response rates experienced in CIS 3 and compensate accordingly. Finally, there should be no replacement of deleted or not-relevant units. The sample size should be large enough to compensate for any of these types of units.

2.5 Sample selection and allocation

The selection of the sample should be based on random sampling techniques, with known selection probabilities, applied to strata. It is recommended to use simple random sampling without replacement within each stratum.

Different allocation schemes can be used, depending on the structure of the population. It is recommended to use optimum allocation, taking into account the need to "compromise" the allocation, in order to obtain the required levels of precision for all indicators and domains.

The variance in each stratum to be used for sample selection can be based on previous CIS 3 results, if there is reliable information available. If not, one can either use the CIS 3 national average or assume that a problem stratum will be close to a stratum for which reliable results are available. If new sectors of the economy are added for the CIS 4, one can either use the national average for the CIS 3 or assume that the new sector will be close to a sector that has been sampled previously.

Member States are free to use whatever sampling methods they prefer, as long as the quality thresholds for the results are achieved. However, in accordance with section 7, paragraph 4 of the annex of the Commission Regulation on innovation statistics, Eurostat should be informed in advance of the method of sampling and allocation scheme being used.

3. Collecting and processing of data

3.1 SAS programs for processing the data

The SAS programs which were used for CIS 3 will be updated for use for the CIS 4 and provided free (along with good user documentation) to those Member States that want them[6]. There will be some user support for these programs once the CIS 4 starts. The program rules will also be provided.

[6] There are also now procedures available in SAS such as PROC SURVEYSELECT, PROC SURVEYMEANS and PROC SURVEYREG that can perform statistical procedures for complex sample surveys.

3.2 Survey questionnaire

In accordance with section 7, paragraph 1 of the annex of the Commission Regulation on innovation statistics, the CIS 4 will be based on a harmonised survey questionnaire for all NACE sectors. The questionnaire shall cover the main themes listed in the Oslo Manual. This harmonised questionnaire shall be used in all national innovation surveys.

3.3 Data collection

The CIS 4, like the previous innovation surveys, shall be mainly based on mail surveys. These provide a relatively inexpensive means of gathering information from a widely dispersed sample. Other data collection methods, such as internet surveying or personal interviews may also be used, as long as data quality is assured.

Member States may combine the CIS 4 questionnaire with other surveys, **as long as this does not negatively affect the quality of the output of the CIS 4**.

3.4. Data editing

Throughout the processing cycle, there should be a systematic and sustained follow up with the responding enterprises to make sure that the data provided is of good quality and passes all edit checks. Data quality checks have to be done at micro- and macro-level by Member States before the results are finally processed and sent to Eurostat. The checking routines of the SAS programs will be delivered to the Member States.

Of course, the SAS edits can be adapted for other computer systems and Member States can also develop their own checks and edits, i.e. the CIS 4 data could be linked with other national data or be compared with R&D survey data.

4. Data quality

4.1. Response rates

The units that do not respond to the CIS 4 survey questionnaire may have different characteristics than those that do respond. Therefore, all efforts shall be made to minimise unit (and item) non-response.

The recommended technique to elicit response is to send at least two reminder letters to the sampled enterprise. These should be sent out within an acceptable period after the sending of the original questionnaire. In some cases, timely telephone reminders may also prove useful.

4.2 Unit non-response and non-response survey

If non-respondents, as an unweighted percentage of all relevant enterprises in the sampling frame, exceed 30%, then a simple random sample of **at least** 10% of the non-respondents (excluding non-relevant enterprises) should be selected. The form to be used for this non-response survey is to be specified. It shall include some of the questions of the standard CIS 4 questionnaire, in order to determine if the non-respondent is an innovator or not. If non-response is not equally distributed across strata, Member States may use a stratified non-response sample.

The non-response survey should have a very high response rate. This non-response survey should be carried out for at least the core target NACE population.

If the results from the non-response analysis indicate that there is a difference between respondents and non-respondents for a certain type of enterprise, this information should be used when calculating the weighting factors (see section 4.5). Member States shall describe how the information from the non-response survey has been used to reduce eventual bias in the estimates.

4.3 Item non response

Item non-response should be kept at a minimum by asking the enterprises for the additional information needed. Item non-response for general variables on the enterprises should not exist, as this information should be available in the business register or from other sources. Some respondents may return questionnaires that have some items filled in, but these cases should only be counted as respondents if they are usable in the processing stage.

Before carrying out automatic imputation, Member States should, as far as possible, make use of administrative, historical (e.g. the CIS 3 survey) or other available data sources such as R&D surveys.

4.4 Imputation

To correct for item non-response (after every attempt is made to get the information from the enterprises concerned) imputations shall be done. Imputed values should be flagged as this enables proper non-response analysis to be done.

The SAS software package (see section 3.1) will impute metric (or measurement) variables separately from ordinal (or ranking) variables, as was done for the CIS 3.

(1) Metric variables
A weighted mean of each metric variable, by NACE and size class, is calculated and applied as a ratio to the enterprises with the missing values, within the stratum concerned.

(2) Ordinal, nominal and percentage variables
This imputation shall be done after the metric estimation. The technique used is nearest-neighbour hot decking using entropy[7]. This technique will use data from clean records (a donor with a record not violating any error check), in order to copy the missing data. The donors are chosen in such a way that the distance between the donor and recipient be minimised[8].

---

[7] Cold deck imputation, on the other hand, makes use of a fixed set of values, which covers all of the data items. These values can be constructed with the use of historical data, subject-matter expertise, etc. A 'perfect' questionnaire is created in order to answer complete or partial imputation requirements.

[8] Nearest neighbour imputation: In this case a criteria is developed to determine which responding unit is 'most like' the unit with the missing value in accordance with the predetermined characteristics. The closest unit to the missing value is then used as the donor.

Member States may also use other reliable methods of imputation, as long as the quality of results is at least identical.

4.5 Weighting and calibration

The survey results should be weighted in order to adjust for the sampling design and for unit non-response to produce valid results for the target population. Additional auxiliary information should also be incorporated, if it is considered that this will enhance the accuracy of the estimates.

The basic method for adjusting for different probabilities of selection used in the sampling process is to use the inverse of the sampling fraction i.e. using the number of enterprises or employees. This would be based on the figure N_h/n_h where N_h is the total number of enterprises/employees in stratum h of the population and n_h is the number of enterprises/employees in the **realised** sample in stratum h of the population, assuming that each unit in the stratum had the same inclusion probability. This will automatically adjust the sample weights of the respondents to compensate for unit non-response.

However, if a non-response analysis is carried out (and the results indicate that there is a difference between respondents and non-respondents), then the results of the non-response analysis should also be used when calculating the final weighting factors. One approach is to divide each stratum into a number of response homogeneity groups with (assumed) equal response probabilities within groups. A second approach could be to use auxiliary information at the estimation stage for reducing the non-response bias.

If the frame contains auxiliary information about the sampling units i.e. variables that are correlated with at least some of the measurement variables of interest, this information should be used to improve the estimation further[9]. In general, the variables to use for calibration are turnover and the number of enterprises, both by NACE and size classes but others can also be used.

Various software packages are available to do the calculations needed to derive calibrated weights. These include:

- CLAN. This was developed by Statistics Sweden and it is a suite of SAS-macro commands.
- CALMAR (Calibration on Margins). This is another SAS macro developed by INSEE in France.
- CALJACK. This is also a SAS macro developed by Statistics Canada.

Several different sets of weights may be produced, depending on the variables of interest. In practice however, there will probably be only up to three different weights produced.

Member States are free to use whatever calibration technique they prefer but, in accordance with section 7, paragraph 4 of the annex to the Commission Regulation on innovation statistics, they should provide information about the calibration methods used.

[9] It can be done for balancing purposes (in the sense that after calibration, "the sample looks like the population") or for improved consistency of estimates (in production systems, each sampled unit is given a unique final weight as part of the calibration process; as a result, estimates are consistent in the sense that the parts add up to the totals).

4.6 Precision of results

The CIS 4 should be carried out in order to achieve a certain level of precision for the total population concerning the following indicators:

1. Percentage of innovation active enterprises.
2. Percentage of innovators that introduced new or improved products to the market.
3. New or improved products, as a percentage of total turnover.
4. Percentage of innovation active enterprises involved in innovation cooperation.

These variables are listed in section 1 of the annex of the Commission Regulation on innovation statistics. In addition, the CIS 4 should also achieve a certain level of precision for the total population with regard to the following indicator:

5. Total turnover per employee.

Article 6 of the Commission Regulation on innovation statistics states that quality evaluation shall be carried out by Member States. Therefore, after processing the data, the 95% confidence intervals[10] for the first three indicators should be $\hat{\theta} \pm 0.05$, for indicator 4 the 95% confidence interval should be $\hat{\theta} \pm 0.10$, and for indicator 5 the confidence interval should be ± 10% of the estimate $\hat{\theta}$.

In accordance with section 7, paragraph 4 of the annex of the Regulation on innovation statistics, Member States shall transmit these quality results to Eurostat.

5. Transmission of data

5.1 Data to be transmitted

Article 5 of the Commission Regulation on innovation statistics lays down two types of data to be transmitted to Eurostat. The first set refers to aggregated statistics that will be transmitted on a compulsory basis while the second refers to individual data records that will be transmitted on a voluntary basis.

The annex to the Regulation says that, beyond the statistics listed in section 1 of the annex, additional tabulated statistics will be decided in close cooperation with Member States. Eurostat will provide the tabulation scheme as well as the transmission format to be used for both data sets (the micro-data set and the tabulated dataset) to Member States.

Aggregated statistics shall be treated in accordance with the standard confidentiality rules at national level (including secondary confidentiality), before transmission to Eurostat.

[10] The confidence interval for the parameter, $\hat{\theta}$, with approximate confidence level of 95%, is given by:

$$\hat{\theta} \pm 1.96 \cdot \sqrt{Variance(\hat{\theta})}$$

Confidential tabulated data may also however be transmitted, in accordance with Council Regulation 1588/1990[11], article 3.

In accordance with section 7, paragraph 4 of the annex of the Commission Regulation on innovation statistics, metadata (which Eurostat will specify) should also be sent. This will include key quality indicators such as non-response rates, coefficient of variation, etc.

The individual data records will be submitted to quality checks. This data will also be used for the compilation of an anonymised micro data set and be made available for further scientific research, according to the procedures laid down in Commission Regulation 831/2002. [12]

5.2 Output tabulation

In accordance with section 5, paragraphs 1 and 2 of the annex of the Commission Regulation on innovation statistics, results will be broken down by economic activity and employment size classes. The output tabulation scheme (which will be produced in accordance with annex 1 of the Commission Regulation on innovation statistics) will be orientated towards the NewCronos CIS3 dissemination structure.

However, with regard to regional data, the tabulation scheme will also contain results broken down by:

- NUTS 2 level by industry (NACE C to E) and services (NACE G to K).
- NUTS 2 level by size classes (as listed in section 2.3).

5.3 Transmission tools

CIS 4 data shall be transmitted to Eurostat via STADIUM. This safe, secure procedure guarantees a method of tracking transmission. All necessary steps should be taken to ensure that the STADIUM system is working at national level.

5.4 Deadlines

The deadlines for data transmission listed in the annex of the Commission Regulation on innovation statistics should be respected. These deadlines are:

- Transmission of tabulated data – at the latest by 30th June 2006. This will be the main source for data dissemination.
- Transmission of micro data - at the latest by 30th June 2006.

This deadline should also be respected with regard to the transmission of the information related to section 7, paragraph 4 of the annex of the Commission Regulation on innovation statistics i.e. information concerning the methodology used in the national innovation survey.

[11] Council Regulation 1588/1990 on the transmission of data subject to statistical confidentiality to the Statistical Office of the European Communities.

[12] Commission Regulation 831/2002 mentions the Community Innovation Survey as one of the surveys where anonymised micro data may be made available to researchers under specific conditions (controlled access).

Annex 1: Target population changes

The following are situations where the target population may change or cause difficulty during the survey:

- Subsidiaries of multinationals requesting contact with the parent organization. While the subsidiaries may get the information from abroad, the information should only relate to the particular national subsidiary. There is a general difficulty with getting multi-national organizations to report information at national level but they will have to make every effort to delineate their data for national units at least. Only domestic units of multi-national corporations should be included in the survey.

- Companies under liquidation or that were liquidated during the observation period (2002-2004 inclusive). Companies that were liquidated before the period should not be considered as part of the target population. Companies that were liquidated during the period should also be deleted from the sample and target population, unless it is decided that their liquidation was so late in the survey period that they should be included in the target population.

- New companies created during the observation period. These should be added to the population.

  Enterprises changing NACE section. These should be recoded accordingly and considered as part of the new NACE section rather than the old one.

- Two or more enterprises combine to form one enterprise. If this happened before or at the beginning of the survey period (and one or more of the units is in the sample) then the new unit should respond with a single form for both (or more) enterprises. Additionally the population should be changed to delete the two (or more) individual units and to include the new unit only. If neither unit was in the sample then the population should simply be amended to reflect the changes.

- If the merger happened late in the survey period, then the original units can be treated as they are, i.e. separately, and ignore the merger. Care will have to be taken however that neither unit returns information for more than its' original elements and they do not send in responses covering the other merged elements as well.

- Enterprises that split to form new units. If this happened early in the survey period then the target population should be amended to reflect the new units. Any such enterprise that is part of the sample should return forms for each new unit separately. If the split happens late in the survey period or if the enterprise cannot supply information on each new element separately, keep the unit as it was before the split.

- Enterprises that are outside the target population, i.e. in NACE sections not covered by CIS4. These should be excluded from all processing if they are in the sample. In addition, the target population should be adjusted before the calculation of weights, in order to exclude these and other types of non-relevant enterprises.

Annex 2: Sample size calculation and allocation[13]

Generally, the factors that affect precision of the results are:

- Size of the population
- Variability of characteristics in the population
- Sample plan and estimators
- Non- response
- Cost and time
- Operational constraints (like training of staff etc.)

I. Estimation of parameters

Consider a set of variables $y_1,\ldots,y_a,\ldots,y_A$ and let $y_a(k)$ be the value of variable y_a for unit k in the finite population U. Also, consider a partitioning of U into D possibly overlapping domains $U_1\ldots U_2\ldots U_D$. For each one of the A^xD possible combinations of variables and domains, a number of parameters θ of interest can be defined for the whole population or for different domains.

II. Sample design

The sample is drawn as stratified sample with simple random sampling without replacement within strata. The stratification is according to section 2.3, taking into account the study-domains for the output tabulation in section 5.2.

III. Sample size in domains of study

Each domain is considered as a population, which is divided into one or more strata. The sample size, n_D , in domain D is calculated as:

$$n_D = \frac{\left(\sum_{h=1}^{H} W_h \cdot S_h\right)^2}{V(\hat{\theta}_D) + \frac{1}{N_D}\sum_{h=1}^{H} W_h \cdot S_h^2} \tag{2.1}$$

where $V(\hat{\theta}_D)$ is the variance for the estimated parameter; H is number of strata in domain D; $W_h = N_h / N_D$, where N_h is the number of enterprises in stratum h; N_D is the number of enterprises in domain D; and S_h^2 is the stratum variance for the variable, y_a.

$$S_h^2 = \frac{1}{N_h - 1}\sum_{k\in a_h}\left(y_a(k) - \frac{1}{N_h}\sum_{k\in a_h} y_a(k)\right)^2 \tag{2.2}$$

[13] For general information on sampling, see Cochran W. G. (1977) Sampling Techniques, third edition, John Wiley.

The expression in (2.1) is obtained by considering the cost to be equal for all strata, e.g. $c_h = c$ for all h, as in formulae (5.25) in section 5.5 in Cochran[14].

IV. Precision

The confidence interval for the parameter, θ, with approximate confidence level of 95%, is given by:

$$\hat{\theta}_D \pm 1.96 \cdot \sqrt{V(\hat{\theta}_D)} \tag{2.3}$$

The precision, α_D, in terms of the length of the confidence interval:

$$\alpha_D = 1.96 \cdot \sqrt{V(\hat{\theta}_D)} \tag{2.4}$$

From (2.4) the variance, $V(\hat{\theta}_D)$, can be expressed as:

$$V(\hat{\theta}_D) = \left(\frac{\alpha_D}{1.96}\right)^2 \tag{2.5}$$

By combining (2.1) and (2.5), the sample size in domain D is given by:

$$n_D = \frac{\left(\sum_{h=1}^{H} W_h \cdot S_h\right)^2}{\left(\frac{\alpha_D}{1.96}\right)^2 + \frac{1}{N_D}\sum_{h=1}^{H} W_h \cdot S_h^2} \tag{2.6}$$

Note

1. To calculate n_D, the true variances in each stratum, S_h^2, is needed and the precision, α_D.
2. In practice, the standard deviations for each stratum, S_h, are not known. Therefore, the CIS 3, CIS Light or other sources might have to be used, but these estimates might be rather unreliable.
3. The above-described sample size calculation will ensure that the sampling error of a specific variable does not exceed the predetermined value. However, in section 4.6 there are 5 indicators for which a certain level of precision should be attained. The sample size thus needs to be calculated for each indicator and the largest sample size should be used.

---

[14] Cochran W. G. (1977), Sampling Techniques, third edition, John Wiley; section 5.5 (Optimum Allocation)

II. Allocation

If the cost per unit is the same in all strata, then the *Neymann allocation* can be used. The total sample size in the domain, *D*, is distributed among strata, e.g. the sample size in stratum *h*, n_h, is given by:

$$n_h = n_D \cdot \frac{N_h \cdot S_h}{\sum_{h=1}^{H} N_h \cdot S_h} \cdot \qquad (2.7)$$

<u>Note</u>

1. The determination of an optimum allocation is often an iterative process. The first step may yield, in some strata, a sample size larger than the number of enterprises in the population. The usual procedure is to take all enterprises in those strata as part of the sample and subsequently reduce the total sample size and recalculate n_h again for the remaining strata.

2. The above-described allocation is optimal for a specific variable. It might not be the case when allocating the sample for other variables and "compromise" allocation schemes are needed. For the CIS4 the sample has to be allocated in order to meet the precision criteria for the 5 indicators for which a certain level of precision of results is required (see section 4.6).

3. Several different such schemes can be used. A simple procedure for multivariate allocation is to compute the average sample sizes for each stratum but methods that are more sophisticated may also be used.

Annex 3: Data editing

The types of checks being done in the SAS programmes are:

- Completeness checks. This is where the questionnaire is not fully completed. Contact should be made with the reporting unit to get the information as soon as possible after receipt of the incomplete form.

- Out of scope units. These are units which do not belong to the target population i.e. wrong NACE, wrong size etc. If this is the case, i.e. if the units are not part of the target population, then they will be dropped from further data processing.

- Data validation checks. This tests whether answers are permissible i.e. the answer is within the range of answers allowed. If a validation error occurs then the answer must be amended (by getting further information from the enterprise for example) to bring it into line with the range allowed.

- Relational checks. This checks that the relationship between two variables is within specific bounds i.e. innovation expenditure should equal the total given. These errors may be "hard" (a violation of the rule indicates that something is incorrect) or "soft" (just a warning that something might be wrong). The hard errors will have to be corrected while the soft errors should be confirmed with the enterprise (and corrected if the information is actually wrong).

- Routing errors. This tests whether all questions that should have been answered have been answered, i.e. innovators answered questions on effects of innovation. An error here indicates that the respondent did not understand the sequencing of questions. They should be contacted to correct the information.

A more complete description of the data editing (and also imputation, estimation etc.) procedure will be provided with the updated SAS programs.

Annex 4: Total Design Method

The Total Design Method (Dillman, D. (1978): The Total Design Method, Wiley) consists of a combination of actions (or moments) that have proven effective in reducing non-response when using mail questionnaires.

The theory underlying the TDM is social exchange, which suggests that the likelihood that individuals will respondent to a survey questionnaire is a function of how much effort is required to respond, and what they feel they are likely to get in exchange for completing the questionnaire.

The TDM was originally developed for individual and household surveys. An adaptation for the business environment is described in Tailored Design Method (Dillman, 2000) and Moore & Baxter (Moore, D. and Baxter, R. 1993) in "Increasing Mail Questionnaire Completion for Business Populations: The Effects of Personalization and a Telephone Follow-up Procedure as Elements of the Total Design Method".

Five main actions that can be used to improve response rates in business surveys are:

Have a respondent-friendly questionnaire. This should be easy and clear to understand, have a relevant question order and a comprehensible, "user-friendly" layout.

There should be up to five contacts with the potential respondent. A pre-notice letter (sent to respondents a few days prior to the questionnaire), the questionnaire (sent a few days to a week after the pre-notice letter, a thank you/reminder postcard (sent about one week after the questionnaire). If necessary, there should also be a replacement questionnaire (sent to non-respondents between 2-4 weeks after questionnaire was mailed) and a final contact (made a week after the replacement questionnaire was sent out.

In all cases where mail response is requested, the use of a real stamp on return envelopes can increase the response rates (It represents something of value and is something the respondent is less likely to throw away).

Personalised correspondence could be used by using real stationery, real names and real signatures.

Finally, a small token or financial incentive can significantly improve response rates. However, incentives can have modest and, in some cases, no effect at all.

Other references that can be consulted for more information are:

Paxson, M.C.; Dillman, D.A.; Tarnai, J.: Improving Response to Business Mail surveys.
Dillman, D.A.: Mail & Internet Surveys: The Tailored Design Method. Wiley, 2000

Annex 5: Testing the non-response survey

The aim of this analysis is to sample a selection of non-respondents and find out if they have a different behaviour than that of the original respondents.

If a non-response survey has been carried out (as it should be if the non-response rate is above 30%, i.e. 30% or more of relevant enterprises did not respond to the survey), a statistical test has to be carried out to check whether the population of non-respondents is significantly different from the populations of respondents.

Test for the equality of two proportions:

H_0: $P_R = P_{NR}$ or $P_R - P_{NR} = 0$ where $\mathbf{P_R}$ is the weighted percentage of innovators in the respondent population and $\mathbf{P_{NR}}$ is the weighted percentage of innovators in the non-respondent population.

H_1: $P_R \neq P_{NR}$

Test statistic:

$$Z = \frac{\left(\hat{P}_R - \hat{P}_{NR}\right)}{\sqrt{S^2\left(\hat{P}_R\right) + S^2\left(\hat{P}_{NR}\right)}}$$

$S^2(\hat{P}_R)$ is the estimated variance of the proportion of innovators in the original, realised sample, calculated after weighting for sampling fractions while $S^2(\hat{P}_{NR})$ is the estimated variance of the proportion of innovators in the non-response sample.

If a simple random sample or a stratified sample of the non-respondents is drawn then the variance , $S^2(\hat{P}_{NR})$, would be calculated as:

$$S^2\left(\hat{P}_{NR}\right) = \Sigma\left(\frac{N_h(1-r_h)}{N(1-r)}\right)^2\left(\frac{\hat{P}_{NRh}\left(1-\hat{P}_{NRh}\right)}{n_{NRh}}\right)\left(1-\frac{n_{NRh}}{N_h(1-r_h)}\right)$$

Where $\left(\frac{N_h(1-r_h)}{N(1-r)}\right)$ is the weight of stratum *h*.

$\hat{P}_{NRh}$ is the percentage of innovators in the non-response sample in stratum *h*
N_h is the total number of units in the frame population in stratum *h*
n_{NRh} is the number of units in the non-response sample in stratum *h*
r_h is the response rate of the original sample in stratum *h*

With large enough sample sizes, the Z-statistics will be approximately normally distributed. Therefore, if the test statistic is in the critical region (usually defined as greater than 1.96 or less than -1.96, for a 95% confidence interval) then H_0 can be rejected i.e. there is a statistically significant difference between the two proportions[15].

---

[15]For further information, see Wonnacott, H., and Wonnacott, J. R., Introductory Statistics, 5th Edition, John Wiley, 1990, chapter 9.

Annex 6: Imputation procedures

The SAS program documentation for CIS 4 describes the process of imputation in more detail. However, a brief description is given here.

Metric imputation

Metric imputation shall take the "clean" data set, estimate the missing items and create a complete metric data set.

The steps involved are:

- Detect and exclude outliers from calculations of the mean.
- Impute the weighted ratio mean, taking into account the amount of missing values within each stratum.

The key factors affecting metric imputation are:

- Values of the three parameters (factor1, factor2 and remout) which control the process
- Amount of item non-response

Factor1 is the outlier value used to remove extreme values from the dataset (of responses for that variable) before imputation. By default, this is 1.5 (or 1.5 times of the inter-quartile range). In a skewed distribution, this might lead to too many records being rejected. This criterion is checked by the value of the Remout variable. By default this is 30, i.e. do not use factor1 where its use leads to the rejection of 30% or more of the records. If the remout value is exceeded, then the imputation procedure moves onto factor2. By default this is set at 3.0 i.e. use all records within 3.0 times of the inter-quartile range.

The three variables controlling the imputation procedure can be amended within the SAS program but, for comparability purposes, it is important that the values used should be as close to the default values as possible. Therefore, the first step to improve item non-response should be to improve response rates. It is very important that item non-response should be kept to a minimum.

After this has been done, if the variables controlling imputation have to be changed (because records are still not being imputed), start off by increasing the remout value little by little until the imputation procedure improves (for example reduce from 30% to 25% to 20%). If this does not work increase factor2 and remout (from its original value) until the imputation procedure produces acceptable results.

If item non-response within a stratum is higher than 50% then the stratum is merged with a neighbouring size class in the same NACE class. If the proportion of non-missing values is still lower than 50% for all size groups within the NACE class the imputation is implemented within subsections of NACE or ultimately by using the whole population. Where strata have non-response rates higher than 50%, every effort should be made to improve the results for these critical strata.

Ordinal and nominal imputation

After the metric estimation comes the Ordinal estimation. The objective of this process step is to estimate nominal and ordinal variables (and in some cases metric variables). As for the metric estimation, it is the amount and structure of the item non-response that is the main factor influencing the outcome of the imputation process.

The basic method is:

- Metric variables are broken down into classes. Respondents are partitioned into classes such that the elements in the same class are considered similar. The variables used here are NACE and size class.
- Metric and ordinal variables are used to estimate nominal variables.

The key factors affecting the ordinal imputation are:

- Values of one parameter (classl) which controls the process
- Amount of item non-response

ClassL determines how much data to include for each variable in the imputation process. If ClassL=2 then only one class is created around the median, excluding large proportions of the data (outliers). ClassL=5 includes more data and creates 4 classes etc.

If there is still item non-response after ordinal estimation, there might be several reasons for this:

- Item response is very low, too low for some strata. This should be addressed by trying to improve response rates in these critical strata at least.
- The setting of ClassL is too strict, reducing the critical mass of data for the estimation procedure. Therefore, increase ClassL to include more data.

However, as for metric estimation, it is important that the final setting is as close to the benchmark (set for each variable in the SAS programs) as possible, in order to maintain comparability of data.

Annex:

The Fourth Community Innovation Survey
(CIS IV)

THE HARMONISED SURVEY QUESTIONNAIRE

The Fourth Community Innovation Survey (Variable names: October 20 2004)

This survey collects information about product and process innovation as well as organisational and marketing innovation during the three-year period 2002 to 2004 inclusive. Most questions cover new or significantly improved goods or services or the implementation of new or significantly improved processes, logistics or distribution methods. Organisational and marketing innovations are only covered in section 10. In order to be able to compare enterprises with and without innovation activities, we request all enterprises to respond to **all** questions, unless otherwise instructed.

Person we should contact if there are any queries regarding the form:

Name: ______________________
Job title: ______________________
Organisation: ______________________
Phone: ______________________
Fax: ______________________
E-mail: ______________________

General information about the enterprise

Name of enterprise ______________________________ *ID*
Address[1] ______________________________ *NUTS*
Postal code __________ **Main activity**[2] ______________________________ *NACE*

1.1 Is your enterprise part of an enterprise group?
GP
(A group consists of two or more legally defined enterprises under common ownership. Each enterprise in the group may serve different markets, as with national or regional subsidiaries, or serve different product markets. The head office is also part of an enterprise group.)

Yes ☐ In which country is the head office of your group located? [3] __________
HO
No ☐

If your enterprise is part of an enterprise group, please answer all further questions <u>only</u> for your enterprise in [your country]. Do not include results for subsidiaries or parent enterprises outside of [your country].

1.2 In which geographic markets did your enterprise sell goods or services during the three years 2002 to 2004?

	Yes	No	
Local / regional within [your country]	☐	☐	*MARLOC*
National	☐	☐	*MARNAT*
Other European Union (EU) countries, EFTA, or EU candidate countries*	☐	☐	*MAREUR*
All other countries	☐	☐	*MAROTH*

*: Include the following countries: Austria, Belgium, Bulgaria, Croatia, Cyprus, Czech Republic, Denmark, Estonia, Finland, France, Germany, Greece, Hungary, Iceland, Italy, Ireland, Latvia, Liechtenstein, Lithuania, Luxembourg, Malta, Netherlands, Norway, Poland, Portugal, Romania, Slovenia, Slovakia, Switzerland, Turkey, Spain, Sweden and the United Kingdom.

2. Product (good or service) innovation

A product innovation is the market introduction of a **new** good or service or a **significantly** improved good or service with respect to its capabilities, such as improved software, friendliness, components or sub-systems. The innovation (new or improved) must be new to your enterprise, but it does not need to be new to your sector or market. It does not matter if the innovation was originally developed by your enterprise or by other enterprises.

[1] NUTS 2 code
[2] NACE 4 digit code
[3] Country code according to ISO standard

2.1 During the three years 2002 to 2004, did your enterprise introduce:

	Yes	No	
New or significantly improved goods? (Exclude the simple re-sale of new goods purchased from other enterprises and changes of a solely aesthetic nature.)	☐	☐	*INPDGD*
New or significantly improved services?	☐	☐	*INPDSV*

If no to both options, go to question 3.1.

2.2 Who developed these product innovations? *INPDTW*

	Select the most appropriate option only
Mainly your enterprise or enterprise group	☐
Your enterprise together with other enterprises or institutions	☐
Mainly other enterprises or institutions	☐

2.3 Were any of your goods and service innovations during the three years 2002 to 2004:

		Yes	No	
New to your market?	Your enterprise introduced a new or significantly improved good or service onto your market before your competitors (it may have already been available in other markets)	☐	☐	*NEWMKT*
Only new to your firm?	Your enterprise introduced a new or significantly improved good or service that was already available from your competitors in your market	☐	☐	*NEWFRM*

Using the definitions above, please give the percentage of your total turnover[4] in 2004 from:

Goods and service innovations introduced during 2002 to 2004 that were **new to your market**	☐☐☐ %	*TURNMAR*
Goods and service innovations introduced during 2002 to 2004 that were **only new to your firm**	☐☐☐ %	*TURNIN*
Goods and services that were **unchanged or only marginally modified** during 2002 to 2004 (include the re-sale of new goods or services purchased from other enterprises)	☐☐☐ %	*TURNUNG*
Total turnover in 2004	1 0 0 %	

[4] For Credit institutions: Interests receivable and similar income, for insurance services: Gross premiums written

3. Process innovation

A process innovation is the implementation of a **new** or **significantly** improved production process, distribution method, or support activity for your goods or services. The innovation (new or improved) must be new to your enterprise, but it does not need to be new to your sector or market. It does not matter if the innovation was originally developed by your enterprise or by other enterprises. Exclude purely organisational innovations.

3.1 During the three years 2002 to 2004, did your enterprise introduce:

	Yes	No	
New or significantly improved methods of manufacturing or producing goods or services?	☐	☐	*INPSPD*
New or significantly improved logistics, delivery or distribution methods for your inputs, goods or services?	☐	☐	*INPSLG*
New or significantly improved supporting activities for your processes, such as maintenance systems or operations for purchasing, accounting or computing?	☐	☐	*INPSSU*

If no to all options, go to section 4.

3.2 Who developed these process innovations? *INPCSW*

Select the most appropriate option only

Mainly your enterprise or enterprise group	☐
Your enterprise together with other enterprises or institutions	☐
Mainly other enterprises or institutions	☐

4. Ongoing or abandoned innovation activities

Innovation activities include the acquisition of machinery, equipment, software, and licenses; engineering and development work, training, marketing and R&D[5] when they are *specifically* undertaken to develop and/or implement a product or process innovation.

4.1 Did your enterprise have any innovation activities to develop product or process innovations that were abandoned during 2002 to 2004 or still ongoing by the end of 2004?

Yes ☐

No ☐

INONAB

If your enterprise had no product or process innovations or innovation activity during 2002 to 2004 (no to all options in questions 2.1, 3.1, and 4.1), go to question 8.2.

Otherwise, go to question 5.1

[5] Include basic R&D as an innovation activity even if not specifically related to a product and/or process innovation.

5. Innovation activities and expenditures

5.1 During the three years 2002 to 2004, did your enterprise engage in the following innovation activities:

		Yes	No	
Intramural (in-house) R&D?	Creative work undertaken within your enterprise to increase the stock of knowledge and its use to devise new and improved products and processes (including software development)	☐	☐	*RRDIN*
	If yes, did your firm perform R&D during 2002 to 2004: Continuously? ☐ Occasionally? ☐			*RDENG*
Extramural R&D?	Same activities as above, but performed by other companies (including other enterprises within your group) or by public or private research organisations and purchased by your enterprise	☐	☐	*RRDEX*
Acquisition of machinery, equipment and software?	Acquisition of advanced machinery, equipment and computer hardware or software to produce new or significantly improved products and processes	☐	☐	*RMAC*
Acquisition of other external knowledge?	Purchase or licensing of patents and non-patented inventions, know-how, and other types of knowledge from other enterprises or organisations	☐	☐	*ROEK*
Training?	Internal or external training for your personnel specifically for the development and/or introduction of new or significantly improved products and processes	☐	☐	*RTR*
Market introduction of innovations?	Activities for the market introduction of your new or significantly improved goods and services, including market research and launch advertising	☐	☐	*RMAR*
Other preparations?	Procedures and technical preparations to implement new or significantly improved products and processes that are not covered elsewhere.	☐	☐	*RPRE*

5.2 Please estimate the amount of expenditure for each of the following four innovation activities in 2004 only (personnel and related costs)[6]:

Tick 'nil' if your enterprise had no expenditures in 2004		**Nil**	
Intramural (in-house) R&D (Include capital expenditures on buildings and equipment specifically for R&D)	☐	☐	*RRDINX*
Acquisition of R&D (extramural R&D)	☐	☐	*RRDEXX*
Acquisition of machinery, equipment and software (Exclude expenditures on equipment for R&D)	☐	☐	*RMACX*

[6] Give expenditure data in national currency units to eight digits.

Acquisition of other external knowledge	[ ]	☐	*ROEKX*
Total of these four innovation expenditure categories	[ ]	☐	*RTOT*

5.3 During the three years 2002 to 2004, did your enterprise receive any public financial support for innovation activities from the following levels of government? Include financial support via tax credits or deductions, grants, subsidised loans, and loan guarantees. Exclude research and other innovation activities conducted entirely for the public sector under contract.

	Yes	No	
Local or regional authorities	☐	☐	*FUNLOC*
Central government (including central government agencies or ministries)	☐	☐	*FUNGMT*
The European Union (EU)	☐	☐	*FUNEU*
If yes, did your firm participate in the EU's 5th (1998-2002) or 6th (2003-2006) Framework Programme for Research and Technical Development?	☐	☐	*FUNRTD*

6. Sources of information and co-operation for innovation activities

6.1 During the three years 2002 to 2004, how important to your enterprise's innovation activities were each of the following information sources? Please identify information sources that provided information for new innovation projects or contributed to the completion of existing innovation projects.

		Degree of importance				
		Tick 'not used' if no information was obtained from a source.				
	Information source	**High**	**Medium**	**Low**	**Not used**	
Internal	Within your enterprise or enterprise group	☐	☐	☐	☐	*SENTG*
Market sources	Suppliers of equipment, materials, components, or software	☐	☐	☐	☐	*SSUP*
	Clients or customers	☐	☐	☐	☐	*SCLI*
	Competitors or other enterprises in your sector	☐	☐	☐	☐	*SCOM*
	Consultants, commercial labs, or private R&D institutes	☐	☐	☐	☐	*SINS*
Institution -al sources	Universities or other higher education institutions	☐	☐	☐	☐	*SUNI*
	Government or public research institutes	☐	☐	☐	☐	*SGMT*
Other sources	Conferences, trade fairs, exhibitions	☐	☐	☐	☐	*SCON*
	Scientific journals and trade/technical publications	☐	☐	☐	☐	*SJOU*
	Professional and industry associations	☐	☐	☐	☐	*SPRO*

6.2 During the three years 2002 to 2004, did your enterprise co-operate on any of your innovation activities with other enterprises or institutions? Innovation co-operation is active participation with other enterprises or non-commercial institutions on innovation activities. Both partners do not need to commercially benefit. Exclude pure contracting out of work with no active co-operation.

Yes ☐
No ☐ **(Please go to question 7.1)**
CO

6.3 Please indicate the type of co-operation partner and location. *(Tick all that apply.)*

Type of co-operation partner	[Your country]	Other Europe*	United States	All other countries
A. Other enterprises within your enterprise group	*Co11*	*Co12*	*Co13*	*Co14*
B. Suppliers of equipment, materials, components, or software	*Co21*	*Co22*	*Co23*	*Co24*
C. Clients or customers	*Co31*	*Co32*	*Co33*	*Co34*
D. Competitors or other enterprises in your sector	*Co41*	*Co42*	*Co43*	*Co44*
E. Consultants, commercial labs, or private R&D institutes	*Co51*	*Co52*	*Co53*	*Co54*
F. Universities or other higher education institutions	*Co61*	*Co62*	*Co63*	*Co64*
G. Government or public research institutes	*Co71*	*Co72*	*Co73*	*Co74*

*: Include the following European Union (EU) countries, EFTA, or EU candidate countries: Austria, Belgium, Bulgaria, Croatia, Cyprus, Czech Republic, Denmark, Estonia, Finland, France, Germany, Greece, Hungary, Iceland, Italy, Ireland, Latvia, Liechtenstein, Lithuania, Luxembourg, Malta, Netherlands, Norway, Poland, Portugal, Romania, Slovenia, Slovakia, Switzerland, Turkey, Spain, Sweden and the United Kingdom.

6.4 Which type of co-operation partner did you find the most valuable for your enterprise's innovation activities? (Give corresponding letter.) _______ *PMOS*

7. Effects of innovation during 2002-2004

7.1 How important were each of the following effects of your product (good or service) and process innovations introduced during the three years 2002 to 2004?

		Degree of observed effect				
		High	**Mediu m**	**Low**	**Not relevant**	
Product-oriented effects	Increased range of goods or services	☐	☐	☐	☐	*ERANGE*
	Entered new markets or increased market share	☐	☐	☐	☐	*EMAR*
	Improved quality of goods or services	☐	☐	☐	☐	*EQUA*
	Improved flexibility of production or service provision	☐	☐	☐	☐	*EFLEX*

Process-oriented effects	Increased capacity of production or service provision	☐	☐	☐	☐	*ECAP*
	Reduced labour costs per unit output	☐	☐	☐	☐	*ELBR*
	Reduced materials and energy per unit output	☐	☐	☐	☐	*EMAT*
Other effects	Reduced environmental impacts or improved health and safety	☐	☐	☐	☐	*EENV*
	Met regulatory requirements	☐	☐	☐	☐	*ESTD*

8. Factors hampering innovation activities

8.1 During the three years 2002 to 2004, were any of your innovation activities or projects:

	Yes	No	
Abandoned in the concept stage?	☐	☐	*HCON*
Abandoned after the activity or project was begun?	☐	☐	*HBEG*
Seriously delayed?	☐	☐	*HDLAY*

TO BE ANSWERED BY ALL ENTERPRISES:

8.2 During the three years 2002 to 2004, how important were the following factors for hampering your innovation activities or projects or influencing a decision not to innovate?

		Degree of importance				
		High	**Medium**	**Low**	**Factor not experienced**	
Cost factors	Lack of funds within your enterprise or group	☐	☐	☐	☐	*HFENT*
	Lack of finance from sources outside your enterprise	☐	☐	☐	☐	*HFOUT*
	Innovation costs too high	☐	☐	☐	☐	*HCOS*
Knowledge factors	Lack of qualified personnel	☐	☐	☐	☐	*HPER*
	Lack of information on technology	☐	☐	☐	☐	*HTEC*
	Lack of information on markets	☐	☐	☐	☐	*HINF*
	Difficulty in finding cooperation partners for innovation	☐	☐	☐	☐	*HPAR*
Market factors	Market dominated by established enterprises	☐	☐	☐	☐	*HDOM*
	Uncertain demand for innovative goods or services	☐	☐	☐	☐	*HDEM*
Reasons not to innovate	No need due to prior innovations	☐	☐	☐	☐	*HPRIOR*
	No need because of no demand for innovations	☐	☐	☐	☐	*HMAR*

8

9. Intellectual property rights

9.1 During the three years 2002 to 2004, did your enterprise:

	Yes	No	
Apply for a patent?	☐	☐	*PROPAT*
Register an industrial design?	☐	☐	*PRODSG*
Register a trademark?	☐	☐	*PROTM*
Claim copyright?	☐	☐	*PROCP*

10. Organisational and marketing innovations

An organisational innovation is the implementation of new or significant changes in firm structure or management methods that are intended to improve your firm's use of knowledge, the quality of your goods and services, or the efficiency of work flows. A marketing innovation is the implementation of new or significantly improved designs or sales methods to increase the appeal of your goods and services or to enter new markets.

10.1 During the three years 2002 to 2004, did your enterprise introduce:

		Yes	No	
Organisational innovations?	New or significantly improved knowledge management systems to better use or exchange information, knowledge and skills within your enterprise	☐	☐	*ORGSYS*
	A major change to the organisation of work within your enterprise, such as changes in the management structure or integrating different departments or activities	☐	☐	*ORGSTR*
	New or significant changes in your relations with other firms or public institutions, such as through alliances, partnerships, outsourcing or sub-contracting	☐	☐	*ORGREL*
Marketing innovations?	Significant changes to the design or packaging of a good or service (Exclude routine/ seasonal changes such as clothing fashions)	☐	☐	*MKTDES*
	New or significantly changed sales or distribution methods, such as internet sales, franchising, direct sales or distribution licenses	☐	☐	*MKTMET*

10.2 If your enterprise introduced an organisational innovation during the three years 2002 to 2004, how important were each of the following effects?

	Degree of observed effect				
	High	Medium	Low	Not relevant	
Reduced time to respond to customer or supplier needs	☐	☐	☐	☐	*EFORED*
Improved quality of your goods or services	☐	☐	☐	☐	*EFORQU*
Reduced costs per unit output	☐	☐	☐	☐	*EFORCO*
Improved employee satisfaction and/or reduced rates of employee turnover	☐	☐	☐	☐	*EFORSA*

11. Basic economic information on your enterprise

11.1 What was your enterprise's total turnover for 2002 and 2004?[7] Turnover is defined as the market sales of goods and services (include all taxes except VAT[8]).

2002	2004
☐☐☐☐☐☐☐☐	☐☐☐☐☐☐☐☐
TURN02	*TURN04*

11.2 What was your enterprise's total number of employees in 2002 and 2004?[9]

2002	2004
☐☐☐☐☐☐☐☐	☐☐☐☐☐☐☐☐
EMP02	*EMP04*

[7] Give turnover in '000 of national currency units to nine digits.

[8] For Credit institutions: Interests receivable and similar income; for Insurance services: Gross premiums written.

[9] Annual average. If not available, give the number of employees at the end of each year. Give figures to six digits.

10

Appendix 5

South African Innovation Survey 2005 Questionnaire

Copy of the 2005 Innovation Survey Questionnaire that was sent to enterprises and the accompanying letter from the Minister of Science and Technology

DEPARTMENT: SCIENCE AND TECHNOLOGY
REPUBLIC OF SOUTH AFRICA

Private Bag X894, Pretoria, 0001, South Africa. Tel: (+27 21) 317 4300 Fax: (+27 21) 317 4636
www.dst.gov.za

Dear Sir/Madam

The South African Innovation Survey 2005

The Centre for Science Technology and Innovation Indicators (CeSTII) has been commissioned to undertake a National Innovation Survey on behalf of the Department of Science and Technology (DST).

The South African survey will be internationally comparable and will assist South African companies and industrial and service sectors to benchmark their innovation activities. The results of the survey will also provide information for the DST to develop policies and incentives to further foster innovation in the country.

We herewith request your participation in the South African Innovation Survey 2005. Your enterprise has been drawn in a random stratified sample from the official business register as provided by Statistics South Africa (Stats SA). Ultimately, the survey is aimed at producing official statistics as defined in the South African Statistical Act (Act No. 6 of 1999) and as agreed between DST and Stats SA.

The numbers of businesses sampled and questions asked are kept to the minimum required to produce reliable results. As a selected business your participation is thus essential to the success of the survey. The responses of firms that do not regard themselves as innovators are equally important as we need to understand the barriers to innovation, particularly in small firms. A particularly high response rate is required in an internationally comparable survey of this nature and your enterprise's cooperation will be greatly appreciated.

Yours sincerely

Mr M Mangena
Minister of Science and Technology

Department van Wetenskap en Tegnologie
Umnyango Wezesayensi Nobuchwepheshe
Lapha laSasense leTekenoloji
Ndzawulo ya Sayense ni Thekinoli

Survey ID number

South African National Innovation Survey 2005

Mining, Manufacturing and Services

In line with the European Union (EU) Fourth Community Innovation Survey (CIS IV), this survey is being undertaken in all EU and numerous other countries in 2005.

PLEASE NOTE
In order to be able to compare enterprises with and without innovation activities, we request ALL enterprises to respond to ALL questions, unless otherwise instructed.

Please change address label if necessary

Department of Science and Technology

In association with Statistics South Africa

Statistics South Africa

HSRC
HUMAN SCIENCES RESEARCH COUNCIL

South African National Innovation Survey 2005

page 2 of 12

About this survey: This survey collects information about product and process innovation as well as organisational and marketing innovation during the three-year period 2002 to 2004 inclusive.

Scope: The statistical unit for the survey is the **enterprise** as defined by Statistics South Africa. An enterprise refers to a business, company or firm and can range from a very small concern with only one or two employees to a much larger and more formal business or firm.

Authority: The Department of Science and Technology (DST), as a component of the National Statistics System, commissions the HSRC to perform this survey.

Confidentiality: All information gathered by this survey will be held in strictest confidence. Under no circumstances will the HSRC, DST or Statistics South Africa publish, release or disclose any information on, or identifiable with, individual firms or business units.

If you have any problems in completing this form and/or meeting the due date, please do not hesitate to contact the Survey Call Centre Operators listed below for assistance:

Name of Operator	Sector of responsibility	Telephone	E-mail
Monique Ritter	CeSTII Survey Manager	021 466 7808	mritter@hsrc.ac.za
Karen Heath	Wholesale and Retail Trade	021 466 7830	kheath@hsrc.ac.za
Ikageng Moduka	Mining & Quarrying, Transport, Storage and Communication	021 466 7813	imoduka@hsrc.ac.za
Cheryl Moses	Manufacturing (Food, Beverages, Textiles and Wood Products)	021 466 7843	cmoses@hsrc.ac.za
Mtembukazi Sibindlana	Wholesale Trade	021 466 7815	msibindlana@hsrc.ac.za
Prudence Sotashe	Manufacturing (Metal Products, Electrical Machinery, Radio and Transport Equipment)	021 466 7811	psotashe@hsrc.ac.za
Maalikah van der Schyff	Electricity, Gas & Water, Financial Intermediation and Engineering	021 466 7800	mvanderschyff@hsrc.ac.za

For any general enquiries by e-mail: innovation@hsrc.ac.za

Person completing this questionnaire:

Name:

Job title:

Phone:

E-mail:

South African National Innovation Survey 2005

page 3 of 12

1. General information about the enterprise, business, company or firm

1. Short description of your main business activity:

1.1 **Is your enterprise part of a larger group?**
A group consists of two or more legally defined enterprises under common ownership. Each enterprise in the group may serve different markets, as with national or regional subsidiaries, or serve different product markets. The head office is also part of an enterprise group.

Yes ☐ No ☐

In which country is the head office of your group located?

If your enterprise is part of an enterprise group, please answer all further questions only for your enterprise in South Africa. Do not include results for subsidiaries or parent enterprises outside of South Africa.

1.2 In which geographic markets did your enterprise sell goods or services during the three years 2002 to 2004?

- South Africa (only some provinces) ☐
- South Africa (national) ☐
- Rest of Africa ☐
- Europe ☐
- United States ☐
- Asia ☐
- Other countries ☐

1.3 What was your enterprise's total number of employees in 2002 and 2004?
Annual average number of employees, both full-time and part-time. If not available, give the number of employees at the end of each year.

2002 ☐☐☐☐☐☐
2004 ☐☐☐☐☐☐

1.3.1 Approximately what percentage of your total employees had a university or technikon degree or diploma in 2004?

☐☐☐ %

1.4 What was your enterprise's approximate total turnover for 2002 and 2004?
Turnover is defined as the market sales of goods and services (Include all taxes except VAT).
Please give turnover in Thousands ('000s) of Rand e.g. One million Rand or R1 000 000 should be entered as 1 000: ☐ 1 0 0 0 000 = R1m.

2002 ☐☐☐☐☐☐☐☐☐ 000
2004 ☐☐☐☐☐☐☐☐☐ 000

South African National Innovation Survey 2005

2. Product (goods or services) innovation

A product innovation is the introduction to market of a new good or service or a significantly improved good or service with respect to its capabilities, such as improved user-friendliness, components, software or sub-systems. The innovation (new or improved) must be new to your enterprise, but it does not need to be new to your industry sector or market. It does not matter if the innovation was originally developed by your enterprise or by other enterprises.

Please note: The latest terminology classifies "products" as consisting of both "goods" and "services". For example a firm in the financial services sector may talk of a "new financial product". The provision of innovative services is of increasing importance in competitive economies and the survey aims to cover both manufacturing and services orientated firms.

2.1 During the three years 2002 to 2004, did your enterprise introduce:

→ New or significantly improved goods. Yes ☐ No ☐
Exclude the simple resale of new goods purchased from other enterprises and minor changes that only alter the appearance of the product.

→ New or significantly improved services. Yes ☐ No ☐

↳ If no to **both** questions, please go to question **3.1**

2.2 By whom were these product (goods and services) innovations developed?

→ Mainly your enterprise or enterprise group ☐

→ Your enterprise together with other enterprises or institutions ☐

→ Mainly other enterprises or institutions ☐

Select the single most appropriate option only

2.2.1 Did these innovations originate mainly in South Africa or abroad? South Africa ☐ Abroad ☐

2.3 Were any of your goods and service innovations during the three years 2002 to 2004 new to your market or new to your firm?:

→ New to your market? Yes ☐ No ☐
Your enterprise introduced a new or significantly improved good or service onto your market before your competitors (it may have already been available in other markets).

→ Only new to your firm? Yes ☐ No ☐
Your enterprise introduced a new or significantly improved good or service that was already available from your competitors in your market.

2.4 Using the definitions above, please estimate the percentage of your total turnover in 2004:

2004 TURNOVER DISTRIBUTION

→ Goods and service innovations introduced during 2002 to 2004 that were **new to your market** ☐☐☐ %

→ Goods and service innovations introduced during 2002 to 2004 that were only **new to your firm** ☐☐☐ %

→ Goods and services that were unchanged or only marginally modified during 2002 to 2004 ☐☐☐ %
Include the resale of new goods or services purchased from other enterprises.

Total turnover in 2004 = 100% 1 0 0 %

page 4 of 12

South African National Innovation Survey 2005

3. Process innovation

Process innovation is the use of new or significantly improved methods for the production or supply of goods and services. The innovation (new or improved) must be new to your enterprise, but it does not need to be new to your industry sector or market. It does not matter if the innovation was originally developed by your enterprise or by other enterprises. Exclude purely organisational innovations such as changes in firm structure or management practice – these are covered in question 10.

3.1 During the three years 2002 to 2004, did your enterprise introduce any:

	Yes	No
→ New or significantly improved methods of manufacturing or producing goods or services?	☐	☐
→ New or significantly improved logistics, delivery or distribution methods for your inputs, goods or service?	☐	☐
→ New or significantly improved supporting activities for your processes, such as maintenance and operating systems for purchasing, accounting or computing?	☐	☐

↳ If no to **all** questions, please go to section **4**

3.2 By whom were these process innovations developed?

- → Mainly your enterprise or enterprise group ☐
- → Your enterprise together with other enterprises or institutions ☐
- → Mainly other enterprises or institutions ☐

Select the single most appropriate option only

	South Africa	Abroad
3.2.1 Did these innovations originate mainly in South Africa or abroad?	☐	☐

4. Ongoing or abandoned innovation activities

Innovation activities include the acquisition of machinery, equipment, software, licenses, engineering and development work, training, marketing and research and experimental development (R&D) when they are specifically undertaken to develop and/or implement a product or process innovation.

4.1 Did your enterprise have any innovation activities to develop product or process innovations that were abandoned during 2002 to 2004 or still ongoing by the end of 2004?

	Yes	No
Abandoned	☐	☐
Still ongoing	☐	☐

↳ If your enterprise also had no product or process innovations or innovation activity during 2002 to 2004 (no to **ALL** options in questions 2.1, 3.1, and 4.1), please go to question 8.2. Otherwise, please proceed to question **5.1**.

5. Innovation activities and expenditures

5.1 During the three years 2002 to 2004, did your enterprise engage in the following innovation activities?

A. **Intramural (in-house) Research and Experimental Development (R&D)** — Yes ☐ No ☐
Creative work undertaken on a systematic basis within your enterprise to increase the stock of knowledge and its use to devise new and improved products and processes (including software development).

If yes, did your firm perform R&D during 2002 to 2004: Continuously ☐ Occasionally ☐

B. **Extramural or outsourced R&D** — Yes ☐ No ☐
Same activities as above, but purchased by your enterprise and performed by other companies (including other enterprises within your group) or by public or private research organisations.

C. **Acquisition of machinery, equipment and software** — Yes ☐ No ☐
Acquisition of advanced machinery, equipment and computer hardware or software to produce new or significantly improved products and processes.

D. **Acquisition of other external knowledge** — Yes ☐ No ☐
Purchase or licensing of patents and non-patented inventions, know-how, and other types of knowledge from other enterprises or organisations.

E. **Training** — Yes ☐ No ☐
Internal or external training for your personnel specifically for the development and/or introduction of new or significantly improved products and processes.

F. **Market introduction of innovations** — Yes ☐ No ☐
Activities for the market introduction of your new or significantly improved goods and services, including market research and launch advertising.

G. **Other activities (including design)** — Yes ☐ No ☐
Procedures and technical preparations, including design, to implement new or significantly improved products and processes that are not covered elsewhere.

5.2 Please estimate the amount of expenditure <u>in 2004 only</u> for the first four innovation activities mentioned in 5.1 (A to D).

Include personnel and related costs.

Please provide expenditure in thousands of Rands e.g. Five hundred thousand Rand or R500 000 should be entered as 500 in the box provided: 5 0 0 000 = R500 000.

Please enter 0 in the category box if your enterprise had no expenditures in 2004.

STRICTLY CONFIDENTIAL

Please report for 2004 only

A. Intramural (in-house) R&D in 2004. *Include labour costs, capital expenditures on buildings and equipment specifically for R&D.*	000
B. Acquisition of R&D. *Extramural or outsourced R&D.*	000
C. Acquisition of machinery, equipment and software. *Exclude expenditures on equipment for R&D.*	000
D. Acquisition of other external knowledge.	000
Total of these four innovation expenditure categories (A+B+C+D)	000

5.3 During the three years 2002 to 2004, did your enterprise receive any public financial support for innovation activities from the following levels of government?

Include financial support via tax credits or deductions, grants, subsidised loans, and loan guarantees.

Exclude research and other innovation activities conducted entirely for the public sector under contract.

	Yes	No
→ Metros and municipalities		
→ Provincial government		
→ National government		
→ National funding agencies (such as NRF, MRC, IDC)		
→ Foreign government/ public sources (e.g. European Commission)		

6. Sources of information and co-operation for innovation activities

6.1 During the three years 2002 to 2004, how important to your enterprise's innovation activities were each of the following information sources?
Please identify information sources that provided information for new innovation projects or contributed to the completion of existing innovation projects.

INFORMATION SOURCE		DEGREE OF IMPORTANCE *Tick 'not used' if no information was obtained from a source.*			
		High	Medium	Low	Not used
Internal sources	Sources within your enterprise or enterprise group	☐	☐	☐	☐
External sources					
		High	Medium	Low	Not used
Market resources	Suppliers of equipment, materials, components or software	☐	☐	☐	☐
	Clients or customers	☐	☐	☐	☐
	Competitors or other enterprises in your sector	☐	☐	☐	☐
	Consultants, commercial labs or private R&D institutes	☐	☐	☐	☐
Institutional sources	Universities and Technikons	☐	☐	☐	☐
	Government or public research institutes	☐	☐	☐	☐
Other sources	Conferences, trade fairs, exhibitions	☐	☐	☐	☐
	Scientific journals and trade/technical publications	☐	☐	☐	☐
	Professional and industry associations	☐	☐	☐	☐

6.2 **During the three years 2002 to 2004, did your enterprise co-operate on any of your innovation activities with other enterprises or institutions?**
Innovation co-operation is active participation with other enterprises or non-commercial institutions on innovation activities. Both partners do not need to benefit commercially.
Exclude pure contracting out of work with no active co-operation.

Yes ☐ No ☐

↳ If no, please go to question 7.1

6.3 Please indicate the type of co-operation partner and their location. *Tick all that apply.*

TYPE OF CO-OPERATION PARTNER	South Africa	Rest of Africa	Europe	USA	Asia	Other countries
A. Other enterprises within your enterprise group	☐	☐	☐	☐	☐	☐
B. Suppliers of equipment, materials, components or software	☐	☐	☐	☐	☐	☐
C. Clients or customers	☐	☐	☐	☐	☐	☐
D. Competitors or other enterprises in your sector	☐	☐	☐	☐	☐	☐
E. Consultants, commercial labs or private R&D institutes	☐	☐	☐	☐	☐	☐
F. Universities or technikons	☐	☐	☐	☐	☐	☐
G. Government or public research institutes (e.g. CSIR)	☐	☐	☐	☐	☐	☐

6.4 Which type of co-operation partner was the most valuable for your enterprise's innovation activities? ☐
Give corresponding letter from 6.3. For example, customers = C

7. Effects of innovation during 2002–2004

7.1 How successful were each of the following types of outcomes for your products (goods or services) and process innovations introduced during the three years 2002 to 2004? *Tick "Not relevant" if there were no innovation outcomes.*

		LEVEL OF SUCCESS OF OUTCOMES			
		High	Medium	Low	Not relevant
Product outcomes	Increased range of goods or services	☐	☐	☐	☐
	Entered new markets or increased market share	☐	☐	☐	☐
	Improved quality of goods or services	☐	☐	☐	☐
Process outcomes	Improved flexibity of production or service provision	☐	☐	☐	☐
	Increased capacity of production or service provision	☐	☐	☐	☐
	Reduced labour costs per unit output	☐	☐	☐	☐
	Reduced materials and energy per unit output	☐	☐	☐	☐
Other outcomes	Reduced environmental impacts or improved health and safety	☐	☐	☐	☐
	Met governmental regulatory requirements	☐	☐	☐	☐

South African National Innovation Survey 2005

8. Factors hampering innovation activities

8.1 During the three years 2002 to 2004, were any of your innovation activities or projects:

	Yes	No
→ Abandoned in the concept stage	☐	☐
→ Abandoned after the activity or project was begun	☐	☐
→ Seriously delayed	☐	☐

QUESTIONS 8.2, 9 and 10 TO BE ANSWERED BY ALL ENTERPRISES:

8.2 During the three years 2002 to 2004, how significant were the following factors in hampering your innovation activities or projects or influencing a decision not to innovate? *Please also indicate particular factors that were not experienced.*

DEGREE OF SUCCESS

		High	Medium	Low	Factor not experienced
Cost factors	Lack of funds within your enterprise or group	☐	☐	☐	☐
	Lack of finance from sources outside your enterprise	☐	☐	☐	☐
	Innovation costs too high	☐	☐	☐	☐
Knowledge factors	Lack of qualified personnel	☐	☐	☐	☐
	Lack of information on technology	☐	☐	☐	☐
	Lack of information on markets	☐	☐	☐	☐
	Difficulty in finding co-operation partners for innovation	☐	☐	☐	☐
Market factors	Market dominated by established enterprises	☐	☐	☐	☐
	Uncertain demand for innovative goods or services	☐	☐	☐	☐
Reasons not to innovate	No need due to prior innovations	☐	☐	☐	☐
	No need because of no demand for innovations	☐	☐	☐	☐

page 10 of 12

9. Intellectual property rights

9.1 During the three years 2002 to 2004, did your enterprise:

	Yes	No
→ Secure a patent in South Africa?		
→ Apply for a patent outside of South Africa?		
→ Register an industrial design?		
→ Register a trademark?		
→ Claim copyright?		
→ Grant a licence on any intellectual property rights resulting from innovation?		

10. Organisational and marketing innovations

An organisational innovation is the implementation of new or significant changes in firm structure or management methods that are intended to improve your firm's use of knowledge, the quality of your goods and services, or the efficiency of work flows.

A marketing innovation is the implementation of new or significantly improved designs or sales methods to increase the appeal of your goods and services or to enter new markets.

10.1 During the three years 2002 to 2004, did your enterprise introduce:

	Yes	No
Organisational innovations		
→ New or significantly improved knowledge management systems to better use or exchange information, knowledge and skills within your enterprise *Exclude routine upgrades.*		
→ Major changes to the organisation of work within your enterprise, such as changes in the management structure or integrating different departments or activities		
→ New or significant changes in your external relations with other firms or public institutions, such as through alliances, partnerships, outsourcing or sub-contracting		
Marketing innovations		
→ Significant changes to the design or packaging of a good or service *Exclude routine/seasonal changes such as clothing fashions.*		
→ New or significantly changed sales or distribution methods, such as internet sales, franchising, direct sales or distribution licenses.		

South African National Innovation Survey 2005

10.2 If your enterprise introduced an organisational innovation during the three years 2002 to 2004, how important were each of the following results?

	IMPORTANCE OF RESULTS			
	High	Medium	Low	Not relevant
→ Improved market share	☐	☐	☐	☐
→ Reduced time to respond to customer or supplier needs	☐	☐	☐	☐
→ Improved quality of your goods or services	☐	☐	☐	☐
→ Reduced costs per unit output	☐	☐	☐	☐
→ Improved employee satisfaction and/or reduced rates of employee turnover	☐	☐	☐	☐

- Thank you for your participation. It is sincerely appreciated.
- Please make a copy of this questionnaire for your records and internal use which may also be referenced if we need to follow-up with any specific issues.
- Please return the completed questionnaire to the HSRC in the enclosed stamped, addressed envelope.
- Our Postal Address: Centre for Science, Technology and Innovation Indicators (CeSTII)
  Knowledge Management Group
  Human Sciences Research Council
  Private Bag X2
  Vlaeberg
  8018

E-mail: innovation@hsrc.ac.za
Website: www.hsrc.ac.za

page 12 of 12

Appendix 6

South African Innovation Survey 2005: Frequently asked questions

GENERAL QUESTIONS ABOUT THE SURVEY

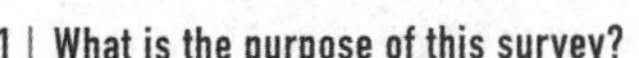

1 | What is the purpose of this survey?

The Innovation Survey will provide an internationally comparable report on innovation activities in the mining, manufacturing and services (including wholesale and retail trade) sectors of South Africa. The Department of Science and Technology has commissioned the survey and will use the results to improve policy and support measures for innovation in the economy.

2 | What will my business gain from completing the survey?

The published results of the Innovation Survey will offer your enterprise the opportunity to benchmark your activities against those of other enterprises in your sector or industry, both nationally and internationally. Such benchmarking is a valuable measure of the overall position of your company. The added benefit of completing the survey is the opportunity for an internal evaluation of potential development areas that might otherwise not have been explored. The collective benefit is thus twofold. In short, the survey highlights internal development needs that could secure a stronger relative position for your business in its sector.

3 | Why has my company been selected?

For the survey on innovation, Statistics South Africa has drawn a random sample of firms from the official business register in accordance with the Memorandum of Agreement on official national statistics with the Department of Science and Technology. This sample consists of a variety of businesses, ranging from very small to very large firms, that operate in the services, mining and manufacturing sectors.

4 | What will my company information be used for?

The Innovation Survey collects data from the individual firms that have been randomly selected. The data provided by each firm will become part of the overall aggregated result for the sector. Only these aggregated results will be published, and no data on individual firms will be made public or disclosed to a third party in any way.

Your firm is one of the firms included in this random sample.

5 | What if I need someone who speaks my mother tongue to assist me in answering the questions?

A survey call centre has been established to support this survey. Survey call centre staff are in place to deal with the questions and concerns of respondents.

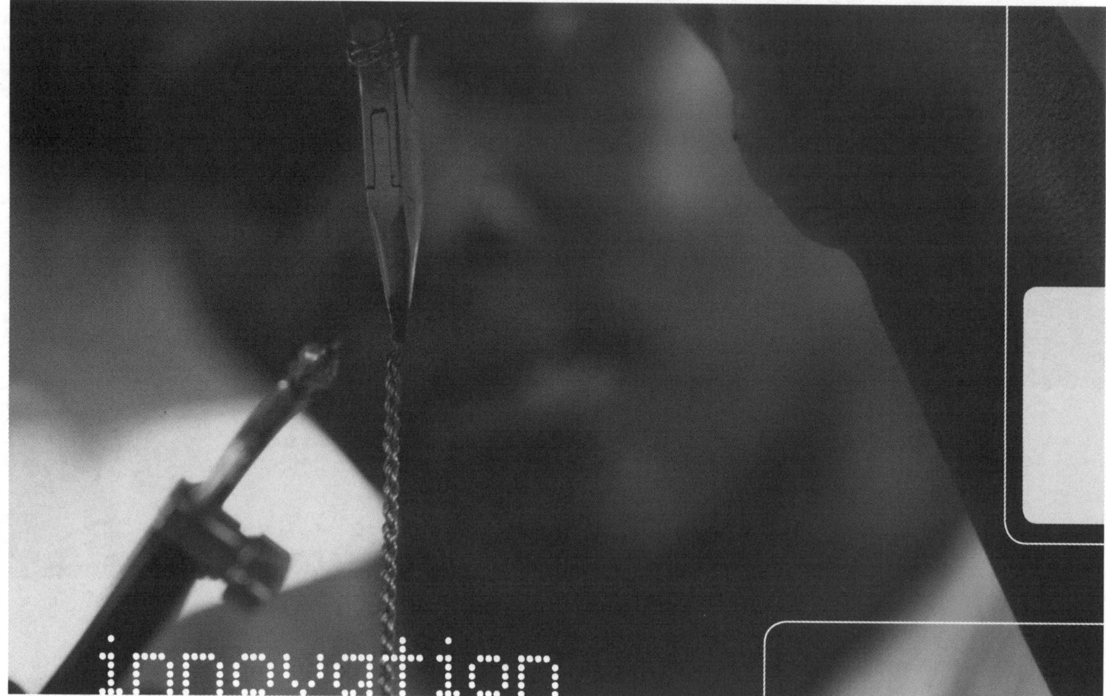

Should you need to speak to one of the call centre staff in your mother tongue regarding the survey, they will gladly assist you in any of the following languages: English, Afrikaans, IsiXhosa, Sesotho, IsiZulu, Northern Sotho or Setswana.

6 | What if I do not wish to participate?

The Innovation Survey falls within the scope of the Memorandum of Agreement between Statistics South Africa and the Department of Science and Technology and is therefore an official survey. The Innovation Survey is being undertaken in such a way that the results will be comparable with those of European Union and other countries. In order for South Africa to achieve such comparability, the response rate for the survey must be at least 71%. It is extremely important that we are able to compare our economic status with those of other countries, and we are doing our utmost to ensure that we achieve the 71% response rate. The main function of the survey call centre is to boost the response rate by following up each targeted respondent and ensuring that each survey questionnaire is returned, complete with all the data requested.

7 | What are the criteria for deciding whether a change is an innovation?

In deciding whether an activity should be considered an innovation, two central criteria must be considered:

- Does the product or activity represent significant change or improvement?

AND/OR

- Is the activity or product new to the firm?

If the change meets either of these criteria, it can be considered an innovation.

8 | I own a very small business. Is this survey intended for me?

Yes, the Innovation Survey aims to cover the

GENERAL QUESTIONS REGARDING INNOVATION

innovation activities of small, medium and large enterprises in each of the sectors. It is very important for the outcome of the survey that small businesses complete the questionnaire.

9 | What do these criteria mean?

With the above two criteria in mind, it is clear that a given change could be an innovation for one firm, while the same change may not be an innovation for another firm. Each firm thus has to decide for itself whether any particular change is new to the firm and/or whether the product, process or service has been significantly changed.

10 | How many types of innovation are there, and what are they?

- The Innovation Survey recognises four types of innovation in firms:
- Product innovation (comprising both goods and services)
- Process innovation
- Organisational innovation
- Marketing innovation.

11 | When does an innovation belong to my firm?

An enterprise can consider an innovation to be its own under the following circumstances:

- When the enterprise has implemented a new or significantly improved change, which may have originated elsewhere, such as your head office or a subsidiary company, another company, sector or country
- When your enterprise has internally developed and implemented its own significant changes
- When your enterprise has significantly improved or modified existing products, processes, services, methods or delivery processes, either by internal development or by introducing a new idea from external sources.

In short, an innovation belongs to your enterprise when the change is new or significantly improved.

INNOVATION EXPENDITURE

12 | How do I report expenditure data?

We request that you provide financial data for the financial year 2007/08. However, if financial data are not available for 2007, please provide estimates of the financial data for the latest financial year.

All financial data that you provide must be based on only one financial year.

We also remind you that all data provided in this section are kept strictly confidential and not made public in any way. All survey staff have signed strict agreements on the confidentiality of the data.

FOUR TYPES OF INNOVATION

1 PRODUCT INNOVATION

13 | What is a 'product innovation'?

Product innovation relates to both goods and services. When a good or service is introduced to the firm and:

- Is new to that firm

OR

- Shows significant improvement with respect to the capabilities or planned uses, then the change represents a product innovation. This may include significant changes in technical specifications, components and materials, incorporated software, user friendliness or other functional characteristics of the good or service.

14 | What are some examples of product innovations that relate to goods and services in my sector?

MINING:

Goods:

- Improved purity of final mining product

Services:

- New information technology applications in serving mine clients

MANUFACTURING:

Goods:

- Change of materials in goods, e.g. breathable textiles
- New type of paper for specific printers

Services:

- Introduction of lifelong guarantees on new or used products
- Remote maintenance

SERVICES:

Goods:

- Introduction of central cards that enable direct clearance with hospitals
- Anti-fraud software that profiles and tracks individual transactions

FOUR TYPES OF INNOVATION >

1 PRODUCT INNOVATION

Services:
- New or significantly improved insurance services
- Introduction of modular life insurance concepts
- Ticket automation for cash or pay cards
- Remote software maintenance

WHOLESALE AND RETAIL TRADE:

Goods:
- Including eco-friendly products in the products range
- Introduction of client or loyalty cards

Services:
- New kinds of certification services
- Combining solutions, e.g. technical and consulting services in one
- Introducing client card systems
- Sales via the Internet or direct sales to end-user

15 | What, for example, would not be considered a product innovation?

- Design changes that do not alter the function or technical characteristics of a good or service
- Routine upgrades
- Minor changes or improvements
- Customisation for a single client that does not include significantly different attributes compared to products made for other clients

2 PROCESS INNOVATION

16 | What is a 'process innovation'?

For the purpose of this survey, a process innovation relates to improvements in production methods, delivery methods or distribution methods. For these improvements to be considered innovations, they must be:
- New to the firm

OR
- Significantly improved.

These significant changes include those that relate to:
- Specific techniques
- Equipment and/or software
- Changes that are intended to improve the quality, efficiency or flexibility of a production or supply activity or logistics
- Changes that reduce environmental or safety hazards

17 | What are some examples of process innovations for my sector?

MINING:
- Introducing clean technology applications in ore extraction
- New methods that significantly reduce hazardous environmental waste

MANUFACTURING:
- Printing process made digital
- Automated packaging
- Computerised equipment for quality control of production

SERVICES:
- Online banking
- Introduction of new rating or scoring methods
- Improved premium clearing systems
- Electronic data interchange
- Case tools for customer-specific hardware

WHOLESALE AND RETAIL TRADE:
- Introduction of software to identify optimal delivery routes
- New or improved software or routines for purchasing, accounting or maintenance systems
- Scanner cash box

18 | What, for example, would not be considered a process innovation?

- An increase in production or service capabilities through the addition of manufacturing or logistical systems that are similar to those already in use

3 ORGANISATIONAL INNOVATION

19 | What is an 'organisational innovation'?

Significant changes in workplace organisation, business practices and external relations implemented in the firm can be classified as organisational innovations if they are intended to significantly improve the firm's innovative capacity or performance characteristics.

20 | What would some examples of organisational innovations include?

- A reduction in the number of management levels to create greater flexibility in decision-making
- Integrated monitoring system for firm activities (production, finance, strategy, marketing)

21 | What is not considered an organisational innovation?

- Changes in management strategy, not linked to significant organisational change
- Introduction of new technology that has limited benefits, restricted to a small division of the firm

4 MARKETING INNOVATION

22 | What is a 'marketing innovation'?

The implementation of a significant change in sales and marketing methods would qualify as marketing innovation. Significant changes in this regard would include product appearance and packaging that is intended to increase product appeal or consumer awareness.

23 | What are some examples of marketing innovations?

- Bundling existing goods or services in new ways to appeal to market segments
- Design of new consumer products e.g. appliances designed for very small apartments

24 | What is not considered a marketing innovation?

- Routine or seasonal changes
- Minor updates in the appearance of packaging
- Advertising, unless based on the use of new media or a new advertising technique

OTHER EXAMPLES OF INNOVATION

25 | I own a business that operates in the services sector. What would examples of innovations in the services sector include?

PRODUCT (GOODS OR SERVICES) ORIENTATED
- Ticket automation for cash or pay card
- Remote maintenance of software and remote consulting
- New methods of statistical analysis
- Development of flexible customer software
- Supply of new multi media applications
- New logistics services
- Dial in services

PROCESS ORIENTATED:
- Electronic data interchange
- Electronic banking
- Computational document creation
- Network monitoring systems
- Call management systems
- Internet based runtime tracking

CONTACT DETAILS OF THE SURVEY STAFF

STAFF MEMBER	SECTOR OF RESPONSIBILITY	TELEPHONE	E-MAIL
Karen Heath	Wholesale and Retail Trade	021 466 7830	kheath@hsrc.ac.za
Nombongo Mongo	Mining & Quarrying, Transport, Storage and Communication	021 466 7813	nmongo@hsrc.ac.za
Mtembukazi Sibindlana	Wholesale Trade	021 466 7815	msibindlana@hsrc.ac.za
Prudence Sotashe	Manufacturing (Metal Products, etc)	021 466 7811	psotashe@hsrc.ac.za
Michelle Reddy	Electricity, Gas & Water, Financial Intermediation and Engineering	021 466 7840	mreddy@hsrc.ac.za
Aeysha Semaar	Manufacturing (Food, etc)	021 466 7800	asemaar@hsrc.ac.za
For general or specific enquiries please call			
Cheryl Moses	Researcher	021 466 7843	cmoses@hsrc.ac.za
Weziwe Sikaka	Researcher	021 466 7839	wsikaka@hsrc.ac.za
William Blankley	Director	021 466 7806	wblankley@hsrc.ac.za